EVERYONE SAID
I SHOULD
WRITE A THIRD BOOK

Jonathan White

Front cover photo: The Cap'n relaxing at anchor aboard 'JoJo',
Catfisher 32 catamaran. Tenacatita Bay, Mexico. 2000.

DEDICATION

To my aunt and uncle, Josephine and Lewis Simmons of London.

Always there for me...

BOOKS BY JONATHAN WHITE

Everyone Said I Should Write A Book
The Travels And Adventures Of A Sailor And Explorer

Everyone Said I Should Write Another Book
More Travels And Adventures Of A Sailor And Explorer

Everyone Said I Should Write A Third Book
Blimey! Even More Travels And Adventures Of A Sailor And Explorer

Success Through Appreciation
Proven Methods To Grow Any Business Through Recognition And Appreciation

All books are published by JoJo Publishing and are available on Amazon.com and Kindle

'Everyone Said I Should Write A Book' is also available on Audible.com and iTunes, narrated by the author.

CONTENTS

"Life is what happens to you while you're busy making other plans."

John Lennon

ACKNOWLEDGEMENT

As *you* are reading this, I want to acknowledge and thank <u>you</u> for taking the time to vicariously adventure with me and Joell...

PREFACE

It was gratifying to read the great reviews on Amazon and to receive emails asking me to write more stories, after my first book was published. The second book received equally positive comments and I was asked by many readers for a third! So I traveled back in my memory, found notes from various periods of my sometimes colourful life and enjoyed reliving them as I wrote.

It is also very satisfying to know that more people all over the world, most of whom I'll never meet, may be inspired or entertained by my tales. So here it is, the final book in the 'Everyone Said I Should Write A Book' trilogy. There are sailing stories and tales of adventuring in Asia. Fast cars, slow trucks, whales and hyenas, rascals and villains...

I recently 'pitched' my books to several Hollywood executives – there is some interest in a TV mini series! But it's a long, strange trip navigating the obstacles of that industry. We'll see...

Between books two and three, I wrote a short, concise volume about the power of gratitude and appreciation in the business world. It's a bit daunting, committing to writing one book, let alone penning four in two and a half years! Sometimes the words flowed smoothly, easily. Sometimes I had to battle procrastination, writers block, lack of confidence, inability to get traction – similar to what many face daily, as we meet life's challenges.

Several people have told me after seeing the title of my books, that everyone said *they* should write a book. My usual response is: "Why don't you?" And others have told me they've dreamed of getting a sailboat and heading for the islands. Well, if you *really* want to do that, do it! Or they'd love to buy an RV and explore

North America. Or own a beach house. Or travel the world, go tocooking school, open a bed & breakfast...

Everyone has dreams, few have goals. Many have big 'buts'... To live your dream, make it a goal, give it a timeline, stop saying 'but' – then devote yourself to it. Committing and following through are what make dreams come true.

Sometimes you have no control over the timeline. I can look back over the tapestry of my life and see that I've managed to reach most of my goals. Rarely did I go directly from point A to point B – usually it was via points C, D, E and F!

And if you do write a book, let me know the title and I'll buy a copy, I promise...

Stay adventurous, my friend...

Cap'n Jon
Half Moon Bay, CA.
August, 2014
My web site, www.EveryoneSaid.com has a link to my Facebook page. Please like me! Also, you can contact me there.

Photos relating to some of the stories in this book are available on my Facebook page:

www.facebook.com/EveryoneSaidIShouldWriteABook

and Pinterest:

www.pinterest.com/captainjon44/

A review on Amazon is truly appreciated – it helps others decide if this is a book they'd be interested in...

THE PRINCE OF WHALES

As we sailed down the coast of Baja Mexico and across the wide entrance to the Sea of Cortez in January of 2000, we saw at least two dozen whales each day. One spectacular sunset, about ten miles offshore, as we watched the sun sink in glorious shades of red and pink, two grey whales shot up from the depths. They hurtled out of the water side-by-side, hovered for a moment with just their flukes under the surface and joyfully crashed sideways onto the water! Each made a loud 'thwumph' as their thirty tons splashed back, glistening water cascading around them.

"Oh my God, did you see that?" I whispered to Joell, sitting next to me in the cockpit of JoJo, our 32' catamaran.

I turned my head and her open-mouthed stare answered my question. As the awesome display was only a couple of hundred yards off our starboard side, it was a redundant question!

"Wow – magnificent!" was her subdued reply. "There must be hundreds of whales around us each day migrating south."

"Yes, indeed – look there's a pod about half a mile away," pointing behind us. "We'll need to keep a vigilant lookout – we don't want to hit one or have one breach next to us."

We had left San Diego in late December, 1999 and arrived in the broad Magdalena Bay in Mexico two days before the celebrations for the new century. There were half a dozen southbound cruisers anchored off the small town and we were told there was to be a huge party on New Year's eve and hundreds of people would be there – everyone was invited, from miles around. Joell and I showed up outside a large, rectangular cinder block building around 9:00 pm, where a line of locals were waiting patiently to pay their admission fee. We edged up to a small window and a pretty lady took our few pesos and smiled.

Walking through a narrow doorway we were confronted by hundreds of tables, lined with chairs, filled with Mexicans in their finest clothes. Along one wall was a raised stage with about two dozen musicians, dressed in their brightest costumes, playing lively, traditional music. A pungent odour of too much cheap perfume enveloped us! As we continued, feeling a little out of place, we were welcomed with warm smiles and boisterous greetings.

"Ay, amigos! Como estan? Bienvenidos!"

The walls were quite high, probably thirty feet and as I looked up I was amazed to see a rectangle of black sky and glistening stars-the building had no roof!

The wooden dance floor was filling with gyrating couples and we could see that we were the only gringos there amidst hundreds of people. Looking around for an empty table, a young man came up to us, bowed dramatically and in broken English, with a big smile, asked if we would like to join his family. They were gracious and charming and told us they had driven fifty miles in their two pick-up trucks to be there. And so we spent the night with a spirited, lively extended family of about twenty-five men and women, young and old, drinking massive quantities of tequila and cerveza and dancing with everyone.

A group of ten yachties wandered in later, but rather than mix with the locals, they chose to sit at a table by themselves. They didn't participate, didn't even seem to be enjoying themselves, but what a great way for us to bring in the new century, laughing, drinking and dancing with these warm, welcoming people, under the stars. It was a terrific start to our cruising adventure and a wonderful introduction to Mexico, a country and people we came to know and love.

We relaxed for two days and then sailed down the coast for Cabo

San Lucas, a marked difference with its economy now based on catering to American tourists, mostly young, loud and obnoxious.

Our time in Cabo was not particularly enjoyable. We were caught in a strong storm about a hundred miles north and had experienced a very bumpy, uncomfortable overnight passage before reaching the calm anchorage the following morning. There was another boat just behind us and the captain and his wife were new to sailing. This was the worst weather they had ever been in and they were scared. I spent most of the night on the VHF radio, offering encouragement and advice.

Joell got very sick in Cabo San Lucas and we spent the few days at anchor while she recovered. She had last been to the town several years earlier, when her ex brother-in-law, the rock star Sammy Hagar, had built his bar, Cabo Wabo. Prior to opening this establishment, which had helped set off a chain of construction and growth in the town, she remembered it as a quiet, sleepy fishing village. Sadly, it had become trashy and raucous, filled with American kids getting drunk and stupid into the early hours of the morning. It wasn't a pleasant place for us to be. After five days there, we gladly headed south and our next planned stop was at Manzanillo, almost four hundred miles away.

Now, with less than a hundred miles to go, we prepared for our fourth consecutive night at sea, the weather warm and breezy. Millions of stars twinkled above and the loom of Puerta Vallarta could be seen behind us. We kept a vigilant eye out for whales and occasionally we could hear them, as they blew and breached – luckily none were too close. As the sun came up to welcome another beautiful day, we were both quite tired.

Joell was on watch with the engine running and the auto-pilot steering. I was asleep on the cockpit bench when suddenly I heard her call out and the throttle was pulled back. I immediately woke and jumped up, as Joell disengaged the auto-pilot and spun the wheel to port.

"What – what's going on?" I asked, a bit groggily.

"Phew, we just missed running into a huge whale, right in front of us!" replied an obviously startled Joell.

I ran up to the bow in time to see the giant flukes of a massive grey whale disappear under the surface ten yards ahead! It was awe-inspiring and scary.

"I was motoring along and saw some large bubbles on the surface about thirty yards ahead," she said, when I came back into the cockpit, shaking slightly. "I didn't know what they were and then realized they were probably from a whale and maybe he was coming up. And then he appeared suddenly right in front of us and that's when I throttled back and woke you!"

"Wow- that was really close. If you hadn't stopped the boat, he could have come up directly under us and that would have been the end. Well done, love. Quick thinking..."

These gigantic mammals can grow up to fifty feet long and weigh thirty tons. Considering JoJo was thirty-two feet long and weighed around seven tons, our boat would likely have suffered severe damage, or possibly sunk.

Now wide awake, I put her back on course and as the morning wind was settling in, raised the sails. Off to our right, was another large pod of whales heading in our direction and occasionally one would leap out of the water, roll and splash back in, making a muffled crash and sending rainbow-coloured spray dancing around it. The rest of that day was filled with whale sightings, some close, some on the horizon. We must have seen a hundred!

In mid-afternoon, we closed with the land and decided to drop anchor in a small bay just north and west of Manzanillo, to get a good night's sleep before clearing into the main town. I lowered the sails and followed the chart around a rocky promontory, with low hills and green, stunted growth. There were few trees and no signs of human habitation. As we rounded the point, Joell called out to me from her lookout position on the bow.

"STOP, Jon. Stop the boat NOW!"

Fearing there was an uncharted rock or shoal directly ahead, I jammed the throttle in reverse and stopped the boat, about two hundred feet parallel to the shore on our left.

"There's a huge whale, slowly swimming across the entrance to the bay!" she called back to me.

I stood on the seat and could see its back as it swam across the entrance which was about fifteen hundred feet wide. Then it would slowly turn around and swim back to the other side. It was about three hundred feet in front of us. We watched it do this several times, then, when we were sure it was not deviating from its path, I gently put JoJo in gear and timing it just right, moved up into the bay, which was less than half a mile long.

The anchor was dropped in twenty feet of water and held firmly. We sat on the bow for a while, watching this huge grey leviathan slowly swim in one direction for about three minutes, turn and go back. It kept repeating this and did not come any further into the bay.

"Perhaps it's sick?" suggested Joell.

"Yes, could be. This is pretty unusual behaviour, I would think. Look, I'm exhausted and I'm sure you are. Let's set up the salon to sleep in and I'll get up every couple of hours and shine the search light on it, make sure it's not coming further into the bay."

We relaxed on the foredeck having a drink as twilight arrived and the sun sank over the low hills to our left, mesmerised as the lone

whale continued its slow, endless journey back and forth across the bay, just a few hundred yards in front of us. There was no one else there that night, just the whale and us.

I got up several times and shone my powerful searchlight toward it. About three in the morning I couldn't find it and swept the entrance with the beam. I thought I saw a hump in the water near some rocks on the right of the entrance, but couldn't be sure. It wasn't swimming any more, that I was certain of. As I crawled back into bed, I heard a distant sound and some far-off splashing, but was so tired, I went back to sleep for the rest of the night.

When we woke, I told Joell that I thought the whale had gone, but I wasn't sure. We lay in bed for a while, happy to be in a protected, comfortable anchorage after four days and nights at sea. I slipped on some shorts and went through the companionway door into the cockpit. The first thing I did was check the three reference points on shore that I had noted after we had anchored. JoJo hadn't moved during the night, the anchor had held firm.

Then I walked along the short side deck to the bow, coffee mug in hand. I gazed ahead toward the entrance between the rocky headlands and couldn't believe what I saw!

"Joie, come up here, you won't believe this. Bring the binoculars. Bloody amazing!"

She made her way up to the foredeck where I was standing open-mouthed. I pointed ahead to where the whale was swimming across the entrance again. But it wasn't alone any longer...

Swimming alongside and next to it was a smaller version, a baby!

Our whale wasn't an 'it' – it was a 'she' and she had calved during the night...

"Oh, wow! Oh, this is amazing! She wasn't sick, she was getting ready to have a baby, right here in this little bay!" said an ecstatic Joell. Many years earlier, Joell had been a zookeeper in Rochester, New York and she has always had a strong affinity for animals.

I looked through the binoculars and was astonished at the size of her progeny. It must have been about fifteen feet long and was following its mother very closely. Through the binoculars I could see the skin of the mother covered in barnacles, creating different patterns. But the baby's back was smooth, fresh, newborn...

And then our jaws dropped even further. The mother turned on her side and waved a flipper in the air – the baby copied her exactly. Then mother whale made a shallow dive and the baby followed, like synchronized swimming. They surfaced in front of us a few hundred yards off and both 'blew' at the same time. Then the mother slapped her giant flukes three times on the surface, making a sound that reverberated around the little bay. And her baby did the same thing, slapped its flukes three times, although the noise wasn't quite so loud!

We sat on the foredeck spellbound, sharing the binoculars, the only humans for miles around, witnessing this unforgettable event.

"I'm going to get in the dinghy and row closer," I said.

"That might not be a good idea, Jon" replied Joell, concerned for them and for me.

"I won't get too close and I definitely won't get between the calf and its mother."

So I lowered our rubber dinghy over the side and put in the oars –

I wasn't going to disturb them with the raucous noise of the outboard. With Joell admonishing me to be careful, I quietly rowed away from JoJo toward the two whales, languidly swimming across the bay, side-by-side. As I got closer, I could smell them, a distinctly fishy smell from the blow.

I rowed to within a hundred yards, which I felt wouldn't disturb them and would allow me a close up of both. As they swam by me, I bobbed gently in the dinghy. The mother looked at me, looked at me directly through one dark eye and it seemed we had a momentary 'connection'. She seemed to acknowledge my presence with pleasure and reached out to her calf and touched him with her flipper. He too cast a look in my direction, peering at me, then they both made a shallow dive together. When they came up they were fifty yards away and slowly heading toward the ocean.

As they grew parallel with the two headlands, the mother whale slapped her flukes on the water and the baby followed suit – it was already imprinting, the genetics of thousands of generations being passed down to him. I stood precariously in the dinghy and turned to see Joell looking through the binoculars and waving at me.

I looked back in time to see them both exhale though their blow holes, and could hear them gulp in fresh air. Then they sank under the surface and we never saw them again.

I rowed back slowly to JoJo and climbed aboard, feeling honoured and privileged to have had a moments 'communication' with them.

"Whoa, that was incredible. They looked me in the eye, Joie – both of them. It was like they were saying hello and goodbye at the same time. I'll never forget that."

"Yes, I saw it all through the binocs. Utterly amazing! I wonder if it was a male or female?"

"We'll never know, but I'm going to assume it was a male. We'll name him the Prince of Whales!"

THE BBC AND THE PIRATES

In early 1995, after I had sold my parasailing business and my two catamarans, I rented a ranch house in the small, bucolic town of Bluffton, S.C., close to the tourist resort of Hilton Head Island. Back then the area was undeveloped, there were no strip malls and car dealerships lining Highway 278, the only way onto the island. I had been living in Hilton Head since I returned from my extended cruise through the Caribbean to South America aboard my trimaran 'Imagine...'

My girlfriend at the time, a petite, feisty blonde named Tamela, was the daughter of an eccentric, established family who lived on a large, rambling estate next to a back river in a sleepy, oak-covered outskirt of town. It probably hadn't changed in a hundred years, the Spanish moss hanging from the trees, the herons and egrets going about their hunting on the banks of the winding streams, the dolphins herding fish onto the creek banks for a feeding frenzy.

Tamela had a part-time job as an anchor woman for the BBC and one day she asked me if I would be her co-anchor and help host the daily round-up of news and events in the community. I thought it would be fun and early one Monday evening we drove to the small television studio, where I nervously sat next to her, waiting for Vern, the producer to give us our scripts for the evening show.

"Three, two, one... you're on," he whispered, dramatically pointing his finger at us.

"Good evenin', y'all," announced Tamela. "Welcome to the Bluffton Broadcasting Company's seven o'clock news and events. With me tonight as co-anchor is Jonathan White, who many of you know as the English guy who dashes around the area in his funny blue Boo-gatti sports car."

10

"Hello everyone," I said, smiling into the wrong camera. Vern was flapping his hand around pointing to camera two. As I turned my face in that direction, the little red light went out and lit up on camera one! I turned my head back that way and continued reading the notes in front of me.

"The top story tonight is that Andy Pinckney's small boat somehow untied itself from his dock and is drifting somewhere in the area. If anyone spots a fifteen foot green skiff floating around, please give Andy a call..."

"Next Saturday is the annual Bluffton Picnic and Parade an' Mizz Carter is in need of some help with her float," chimed in Tamela. "So go on down to her house an' give her a hand, 'specially if you've got a hammer. Ahz tea will be provided."

"Jimmy Smith's dog just had a litter of puppies and they're available for free to good homes. They're really cute and come from a long line of hunting dogs, so be the first to claim one. You all know where Jimmy lives, just down from the Squat and Gobble Cafe," I announced seriously.

As you can probably tell, the news was not particularly earth-shattering and the BBC was not the venerable British Broadcasting Company. But to the locals in this small town, it provided entertainment and an effective means of communication and gossip!

After the weather and local high school sports report, the phone lines were open and calls started to come in. This was an opportunity for those who had little else to do but watch T.V. instead of enjoying the beauty of the area, to have their five minutes of local fame. Practically everyone in this rustic community of about two thousand people (it has since exploded to over twelve thousand!) knew everyone else, most families tracing their roots back many generations. Tamela hit one of the

11

red flashing buttons on the phone.

"BBC, this is Tamela. How can ah help y'all this evenin'?"

A stentorian female voice, elderly with a distinct southern belle accent boomed over the speaker phone,

"TAMELA! Tamela, this is Mizz Julie Taylor. Ah do declare that bearded man next to you is NOT from the South! Now let me tawk to him, if y'all doan mind..."

"Well of course, Miss Julie. Ah'm sure he'll be delighted to talk to you..."

I looked into the camera and put on my most charming smile and in my strongest English accent said,

"Hello Miss Julie. I understand you're concerned that I'm not from the South, is that correct?"

"Whah, yes, young man. You weren't raised in the South now, were you?

"Ectually, I was, ma'am. Born and raised in South London, definitely a southerner. Have a nice evening. Pip, Pip!" and I looked over to Tamela who was trying to hold back her laughter off camera.

The next couple of months as a news anchor were fun, as three times a week Tamela and I would do our half hour broadcast, mostly local news but occasionally commenting on the outside world. In August I made mention of the passing of Jerry Garcia of The Grateful Dead, a band I had followed avidly and once met back in the seventies. Apparently no one in the area, at least those watching our show, had heard of him or cared about his death. The only caller wanted to know why I was announcing the death of a Mexican guy who no one around these parts knew anyway!

Although the town was fairly small, the local schools drew from a large rural area and served a mixed variety of children. There were kids from wealthy families who lived in gated communities just off Hilton Head Island – the sons and daughters of attorneys, doctors, restauranteurs, business people who got rich off the influx of tourists. But the majority of local children who attended the Bluffton schools were from poor, rural families, most of them black. Probably their ancestors had been owned by the ancestors of the rich, established white families who still clung to the faded glory of their plantation past.

In the mid-1950's, Charles Fraser, who owned most of the island, had a grand plan to develop it into a luxurious tourist destination, which he ultimately succeeded in doing. In 1983, the town of Hilton Head was incorporated and has thrived ever since. Besides its natural beauty, which the township has tried to preserve, it is only a one day drive from the giant population areas of the Northeast, so it appeals to those who don't want to drive another full day to the jaded tourist towns in Florida. When I lived there in the early nineties it was already getting overcrowded and the dense pine trees lining Highway 278 were being cut down to make way for tacky shops and fast food outlets and the ugly, neon sprawl that is Anytown, USA.

As with most schools across the country, each year Bluffton put on a play to which families and other children were invited. One day a good friend of mine, an attorney from a wealthy Charleston family who lived in a gated community near Bluffton, asked me if I would be interested in helping him with a play his sixth-grade daughter would be starring in.

"Well, I've never done anything like that, John. What play is it and how could I help?"

"It's right up your alley, my sailing friend," he replied. "The school's putting on Gilbert & Sullivan's 'The Pirates of Penzance'

13

and we want you to coach the kids to talk with appropriate English accents."

"Wow, that sounds like fun and I love that play! When's it going to be and how much time will you need from me? Remember, I'm working for The Moorings doing boat deliveries, so I'll be gone sometimes for a couple of weeks at a time."

"We have three months to rehearse and as much time as you can spend with the kids after school would be great," he replied enthusiastically. "It's a real mixture of kids. My daughter Elizabeth is playing Mabel and there are a whole bunch of black kids who've never heard of this play and we're going to turn them into pirates and policemen and the Major-General's daughters! It's a wonderful way to introduce these rural kids to a different era and have fun doing it. Will you help us?"

"Of course. I'm just trying to visualize southern kids with British accents! When do I start?"

"Today, if you can, Jon. Come to the school at 3:00 and we're meeting in the gym. See you then."

And off he went back to his office to wrestle with someone else's problems. I went to the deserted seven mile beach for a long, chilly and pleasant walk...

I drove the Bugatti up to the school and found my way to the gym building. Pushing open the double doors, I was confronted by quite an amazing sight. There were about forty kids trying on bits of costumes and some were waving swords around, engaging in mock battles, running around, yelling and laughing. A minute after I walked in, John called for quiet and everyone sat down on the floor.

"OK, everyone," he called out. "Settle down, we have a lot of rehearsing to do. Now, I know y'all are from the south and we all

14

talk properly, but for this play, y'all need to sound like you're from England. Who knows where England is?"

Every hand shot up. This was encouraging, at least they knew where the play took place! But I wondered if they had any idea that this play, besides being a fun and unlikely story was sprinkled with political satire. Probably not and who cared – they just wanted to play pirate!

"Well y'all, we're really lucky because we have a genu-ine Englishman here and not only that, he's a real life sailor!" He pointed to me standing in the back and every head turned. "He's goin' to help y'all with learnin' a real English accent so you can sound like actual pirates and policemen and daughters. His name is Cap'n Jon."

"Hey, he's dah guy on dah TV nooze who tawks funny!"

"Ah know him, he drav dat ol' blue race cah!"

"Ah wen' up in dah air las' year on his boat in a para-shoot – it was cool!"

All of a sudden a whole bunch of kids came running over, each one wanting to shake my hand. They were mostly poor black girls and boys, but there were a few obviously middle-class white kids as well.

"Kin ah go fer a ride in yer race car, Cap'n Jon?"

"Ah wanna flah in de air!"

"Will yah teach me to tawk lak a py-rate, Cap'n?"

"Hi everyone!" I responded with a huge grin on my face. "Yes, you can all go for a ride in my car and those of you who get your parents permission can fly in the air on my friends parasail boat if you want. And I'll do my best to have you all talking like English

15

pirates of old. But only if you study hard, listen to me and the other teachers and put on a terrific show that everyone will be proud of. Deal?"

A chorus of "Yeah, yay, sure thing, OK, Cap'n!" put smiles on all the kids faces.

And so started an amazing twelve-week journey transforming forty youngsters from mostly impoverished, country-bred, southern backgrounds to pirates and policemen and dancing sisters in Victorian England. They diligently learned their lines and had countless questions about the meaning of many words and phrases which, even in the glorious English phraseology of those more pedantic times, were obscure and contrived.

A couple of days after we had begun rehearsing, one of the Major-General's daughters, a pretty black girl, shyly walked up to me and asked, quietly, with a look of fierce concentration on her face,

"Cap'n Jon, what do 'con-ju-gal-lee matree-mohnee-fahd' mean?"

If you are familiar with the play, then you'll understand – the band of pirates are going to carry off all the Major-Generals daughters (there are many!) and marry them. They will be married ('matrimonified') and have conjugal ('conjugally') rights. But how do you explain that to a twelve-year old, who comes from a different world?

"Hmm!" I muttered, stalling for time to get my thoughts together. Now there were half a dozen kids around me, seriously looking up, wanting to know as well. "Well, hmm!" I spluttered, "Ah, let's just say the pirates want to take the daughters and marry them. The word 'matrimony' is an old-fashioned word for marriage."

"Yeah OK, but what's conji – gally?" asked another.

"Well, um, ah. I think you should ask your parents about that word. Now, let's get back to properly pronouncing the words of 'Climbing Over Rocky Mountain'. Ladies, pay attention..." quickly steering everyone away from that potential landmine!

This happened many times over the weeks of rehearsal as they wrestled with unfamiliar words and phrases. All the kids were enthusiastic, dedicated and enthralled by the concept of this timeless play. No one missed a rehearsal and apart from an occasional spontaneous sword fight by over-excited young pirates, they were all very well-behaved. There were never any indications of racism or superiority between the few rich white kids and the three dozen black girls and boys – everyone acted and conducted themselves like brothers and sisters – it was a joy to behold.

A week after I started with them, I was called to make another boat delivery down to the Caribbean. When I announced to everyone the next day that I would be gone for two weeks, there were cries of dismay.

"Where yah goin', Cap'n?"

"Iz yah comin' back?

"Doan go, Cap'n. Dere could be py-rates out on dah oshun!"

I was touched and gratified that they cared for my safety and I assured them that I could outrun any pirates that approached! When I returned from that delivery, during which I was confronted by a knife-wielding crew member, I faced a monumental task which had concerned me from the beginning. I had to instruct the boy playing Major-General Stanley (and his understudy) not only how to sing his famous, fast-paced, song, but to do it with an upper-class English accent! It is difficult enough just to read the almost nonsensical words, but to memorize them and sing them without forgetting a word or phrase was a daunting task indeed...

Major-General Stanley was being played by an overweight, very intelligent black kid named Rodney. His mother was making his uniform, as were most of the other parents – the play had become a community affair, with most of the families supporting and helping their children.

But there was one little girl who came in distraught that afternoon. She tearfully told me that her Daddy had said she "couldn't be in de play no longer – she had too many chores aroun' de house."

I promised to see what I could do and asked my friend John if I should intervene – he had been raised in the South and could trace his family back to the 1700's. He understood the relationship between blacks and whites and the cultural differences much better than I did. He was also an attorney and did a lot of pro bono work for the black folks in the area.

"Well, you've gotta be real careful in this situation, Jon. These folks live very differently than we do and sometimes they don't take kindly to our interfering in their lives. You can ask Emily where she lives and when her Daddy gets home, but be prepared for a hostile reception..."

Later that day after the rehearsal without Emily was over, I drove my conspicuous car down several sleepy, oak-lined country roads outside of Bluffton into an area that I had never been before. It was like sepia photos of the deep South generations ago. Ramshackle houses and shacks surrounded by clucking chickens and the occasional pig. Lines of laundry hanging heavy and wet in the sultry heat. Half-naked little boys and girls running around playing with sticks in the dirt. They stopped running and stood awkwardly and stared as I drove past with a wave, my vintage

Bugatti replica looking to them like an alien spaceship. The adults sitting on broken and rusted sofas on their porches regarded me with hooded eyes and an occasional reluctant raised hand. It was not a comfortable feeling and several times I almost turned back.

But then I remembered Emily's tears and how she had enjoyed learning the songs as one of the Major-General's daughters. I checked her address on a piece of paper, pulled up outside her tumbledown house and got out of my car. I saw Emily on the right with a makeshift broom, sweeping the yard – she stopped what she was doing, looked at her Daddy, then looked back at me, her eyes very big; she looked startled and scared.

On an ancient and sprung sofa on the porch in front of a house in dire need of paint, sat an immobile man, maybe in his late forties. His hair and beard sprouted some grey, in his hand he held a can of beer and his eyes stared at me menacingly, never wavering. He wore a patched checkered shirt, faded blue bib overalls and boots with a hole in one sole.

I reached into my car, withdrew a six-pack of Bud, turned and walked purposefully through the yard, hens and chickens scattering, never taking my eyes off the man who stared right into mine, no expression on his tired and etched face. I stopped before I reached the two crooked front steps. We locked eyes for a full thirty seconds. Just to his left I caught a swish of faded curtains as a scared looking woman peeked out through a cracked and dirty window, then swiftly disappeared.

I wondered how many white men had come to this house over the generations and if any had come in a spirit of reconciliation, not hatred? Probably no bearded Englishman driving a 1927 Bugatti!

"Mr. Jones, my name is Jonathan White and I'm helping your daughter rehearse for the school play," I said in a quiet, yet forceful tone.

He looked at me for fifteen seconds, a very long fifteen seconds...Without taking his eyes off mine, he responded slowly, carefully picking his words,

"Ah know whoo you iz, Mistah Whaht, an' ah knows whah you he-yah. Took a lotta guts drivin' into dah nigger part of town, speshlly in dat crazy cah you got. You bring dat beer up he-yah an' sit yoself on dat dere rockin' chair an' mebbe we drink an' tawk a little."

I didn't know whether he had a gun next to him and suddenly realized I was taking a huge risk. But a wave of relief flooded through me as I climbed the rickety steps, bent down and offered my hand. He reached out and shook it firmly, still keeping his eyes fixed on mine. I pulled up the rocking chair and gingerly sat down, hoping it wouldn't collapse! But it was strong and although scarred and old, looked like it had been lovingly made a hundred years ago; through the smooth, worn seat of the chair, rocking gently back and forth, I felt connected to generations of this family who had lived, like so many of them, on the outer edges of society; a situation not of their choosing but one that a cruel history had destined.

I removed two beers from the rings and handed one to Mr. Jones, opening mine and taking a sip.

"Then I don't need to tell you that your daughter is very important to the success of this play, Mr. Jones. Without her we'll have to find a replacement and she's so good at singing and dancing. And she loves being a part of this production, learning her lines and all the time with a big smile on her face. And besides Emily being important to us, we're also important to her."

He shifted his stare from mine to some point over my shoulder and took a long swig of his beer. Then he looked back at me, not saying a word. Emily had edged closer and was staring at us, leaning on her broom, listening to every word. The woman in the window, probably her mother, was now quietly standing in the doorway, looking at me, not moving – she seemed scared of her husband and how he would react to what I was saying.

"Look, Mr. Jones, she's not my daughter and I know I've no right to tell you what you should or shouldn't do. But what's happening with these kids, with her friends and with Emily as they learn this old play and question us about what the words mean and what life was like a hundred years ago, what's happening is their curiosity is aroused, they learn things they never knew, they grow. And even though it's just a silly play, perhaps it will ignite a spark within some of them, maybe it will encourage them to expand their world view, perhaps even enable them to reach for a star that's been out of reach for so many of your forefathers..."

He still said nothing, but looked at me piercingly, took another long swig of his beer. He waited a full minute, then said softly in a voice barely audible,

"Whah you care 'bout dese nigger kids, Mistah Whaht? Dey never gonna be moh dan dey iz now. Mah gal prob'ly be a maid in some rich whaht woman's house, same as all de girls befoh her. Her playactin' ain't gonna change nuttin'."

I thought about what he had said and understood the despair and quiet rage in his voice. What chance was there for a poor black girl from rural South Carolina to break out of the confinement and restriction that had been handed down from the days of slavery?

"Mr. Jones, I grew up in England and didn't see a black person until I was ten years old. I asked my grandfather, himself from a persecuted background, about the man I had seen earlier that day when I was with my mother shopping in London. I have never

21

forgotten his words, Mr. Jones and have always lived by them. 'You cannot judge a man by virtue of the colour of his skin or the shape of his eyes.'

"Although the words were confusing to a ten-year old, I eventually understood what he meant. I have been in Buckingham Palace and I have sat and talked with beggars in the streets of New Delhi in India, and I have learned that there are good and bad people of every race, colour and creed. And I have also learned that people are capable of incredible things and can rise above any situation life has thrown at them, if they really want to..."

He stared into space, said nothing, didn't move. I kept going...

"Look what Ghandi accomplished, look at how that bastard Wallace eventually had to integrate schools in his state, look how Dr. King inspired all of us to live harmoniously. It doesn't happen overnight, but it *does* happen. And what if by being a part of our play, by widening Emily's view of the world, what if that ignited the spark that changed her life and got her out of the repetitive treadmill that the past keeps visiting on her and other poor black girls here in Bluffton, South Carolina? What if she goes to college and gets a good-paying job and raises a family of her own and has kids who go to college and better themselves and do wonderful things and break the cycle? What if that happened, Mr. Jones, what if...?"

He sat immobile, perhaps not believing that a white man who talked with a funny accent should even care what happened to his daughter and others like her. The lady in the door smiled at me and faded like a ghost back into her home. Emily hadn't moved, was holding her breath, mesmerized.

There wasn't any more I could say, so leaving the rest of the six pack on his porch I got up, turned around and left, with a slight nod to Emily. I climbed into my car and slowly drove off, never once looking back at Mr. Jones. I didn't know what type of man he was, but judging by the looks on the faces of his wife and daughter, probably one to be feared. I just hoped I hadn't provided him grist for his mill, hoped I wouldn't be the cause of outrage or violence. I didn't mention to anyone what I had done.

The next afternoon, I sat on the floor in the gym by myself, going over the words of Major-General Stanley's song, preparing to inculcate them into the mind of a black youngster from the South! The school bell rang and within a minute groups of cast members ran into the gym, some of them singing snatches of the songs they were learning so well and enthusiastically. And there in the middle of one group of girls, singing heartily about the weather was a beaming, smiling, happy Emily... My impassioned words had apparently resonated with her father. I wonder today what has become of her; is she a maid in some Hilton Head mansion, or is she following her own star, stretching out for her special dream?

I was more surprised when I led Rodney and James (his understudy) off to one side of the large gym, where I could start to teach them the verses of the fantastic song the Major-General sings with its convoluted and complex phrases and rhymes.

"OK gentlemen, now this is not an easy song and I'm sure you've got lots of questions about the difficult words, but let's start off by Rodney singing the first verse. Don't worry if you forget some of it, we've only been at this a couple of weeks..."

Rodney immediately stood at attention and with a big grin on his face, little beads of sweat running down his forehead, he belted out with gusto:

"Ah am dee very model uv a modern Major-General, ah've infoh-mation vegee-table, aminal and mineral.

reekal; from Marathon tah Water-loo in order categorkical!"

I was about to congratulate him for memorizing the first two lines (in his own inimical way!), when he took a deep breath and looking at me expectantly, heartily sang the next two long verses all the way to "...dat infernal non-sense Pinafore!" I was dumbfounded. In the two weeks I'd been off sailing down to the Caribbean, young Rodney had studied and learned and memorized what for an adult is a challenging song. I was beaming and about to congratulate him when he asked,

"Hey Cap'n, what's it mean, 'dat infernal non-sense Pinafore'? Ah doan get it!"

"Well you know that Gilbert and Sullivan wrote many musical operettas and the one before The Pirates of Penzance was about the English Navy and was called 'H.M.S. Pinafore', the unlikely name of a navy ship. So the Major-General (you!) is making a satirical comment about another play that the public was familiar with and really loved. Does that make sense to you?"

"Yeah, OK, I get it. They were making fun of themselves, right?"

"Absolutely. You know something, Rodney – you're speaking better English, but we've got to really work on your pronunciation! I cannot believe that you've learned so much of this difficult and crazy song, my friend. How did you do it?"

"Well, before y'all left to go sailin', yah tol' me an' James it was gonna be *real* difficult and yah said it would take me a long time to learn dah words and they wouldn't make no sense to me. Well, you was raht about dem not making no sense, but ah wahn-nett to show yah ah could do it, so after ah finished mah homework and mah chores, mah mammy an' me sat down at dah kitchin table and she learned me."

"That is really incredible, Rodney, your mammy must be so

proud of you and you of her. And it's taught, not learned..."

"Yes, Cap'n, we is – no we *are* , but she axed me to tell yah she'd really lahk to know what Babee-loniccooney-form an' the croakin' frogs is all about! And so would ah!"

"This is great – you tell your mammy that after the show, I'll take both of you and her out for a nice cold glass of iced tea and explain it all to you. But right now we're going to work on your memorizing the rest of the lyrics and we'll work on your accent. How's that?"

And then to my utter astonishment, both Rodney and James, a skinny, fidgety boy quite the opposite of the pudgy Rodney, stood side-by-side and in perfect unison, started from the beginning and recited the whole blooming song! With only a few mistakes! But with a pretty broad southern accent! When they had finished, the entire gym, staff and performers who had been listening in amazement, burst into applause and cheering! It was truly spectacular, these two boys had been helping each other, along with Rodney's mammy to learn this lengthy song in only two weeks.

The boys were suddenly surrounded by all the other kids, slapping them on the back and saying how cool that was. And begging them to do it again, which they did. John and I looked at each other and beamed...

And it also took the whole production to a higher level. The kids outdid themselves learning their parts and their songs; they all wanted to be like Rodney and James. I do believe those two boys felt a huge sense of accomplishment and pride. I hoped it would stay with them always, that they would look back on their recital that day and the praise of their peers and that it would be a strong and encouraging memory when times got tough in their already hard lives...

The weeks rolled by and the play came together far better than I could have imagined. I soon had the pirates and the policemen and the ladies talking and singing in resounding British accents, some upper class and some more 'common'. A couple of teachers told me that the more irascible members of the cast would speak in nothing but proper English accents in the classroom much to the amusement of their peers!

Two more times I disappeared on boat deliveries and each time was welcomed back with hugs and demonstrations of how they had progressed. The scenery was painted, the costumes finished and then one day came the full dress rehearsal. After school the entire cast got changed and the pirate band took their positions on stage, the music started and these beaming twelve-year old rural southern black boys transformed themselves into a band of not-quite-bloodthirsty English pirates of old!

"Pour, oh, pour the pirate sherry! Fill, oh, fill the pirate glass..."

And they were perfect. John's daughter Elizabeth was a terrific 'Mabel', the gaggle of girls were splendid in their frilly white dresses, dancing, twittering and singing. Rodney held everyone spellbound as he strutted around the stage in his white military suit with gold buttons, declaring (now in much better English!) that he was 'the very model of a modern Major-General'! The policemen were hilarious as they sang 'Tarantara, Tarantara' and rolled their eyes at the thought of doing battle with the pirates.

John, I and the other teachers who had volunteered their time over the past twelve weeks clapped and cheered. The girls and boys bowed, held hands and bowed again. There were to be a total of five shows over the next three days. Two performances for two days for the elementary, middle and high school classes, and one for the parents and families on Friday evening.

The next day I was in the gym at 8:00 a.m. along with John and the others, making sure the sets were ready, the music track was working and the chairs were set up for the audience. In came the cast, slightly subdued and somewhat nervous - this was their first performance in front of a live audience and they probably all had butterflies!

At 10:00 o'clock the outside doors were opened and a couple of hundred little kids trooped in and with guidance from their clucking teachers found their seats, fidgeting and chattering away. I wasn't sure if the play would hold the attention of young kids in first through fifth grades, or if they'd have a clue what was going on. The lights dimmed, the music started, the little kids stopped talking, the curtain went up and the pirates opened the play, waving their swords around and pouring their celebratory drinks.

I stood at the back of the gymnasium, watching the performance and the reaction of the audience. Besides the music and singing, you could have heard a pin drop. The youngsters were leaning forward on their seats, eyes wide, mouths open as song after song was directed at them. Rodney was perfect as the Major-General; the kids all clapped although they had no idea what he was singing about! When the policemen marched on to the stage, twirling their batons and singing their uproarious refrain, the whole auditorium burst into laughter. And then the pirates were pardoned and each chose the daughter the Major-General now agreed to let them marry. The curtain came down and the audience stood up and clapped and clapped! It was a success, a huge success!

The proud cast took their encores and bows and I went backstageto congratulate them. Wide grins, big smiles, lots of hugs, lots of backslapping! They were better, far better than I could have imagined three short months before. They had worked hard, helped each other, been dedicated, had c ommitted to an

27

outcome and it showed...

The next three performances were equally well received; even the high schoolers who had a cocky air of indifference when they were reluctantly brought into the gymnasium, sat transfixed and enjoyed the operetta. The understudies got their chance to perform and switched with the cast members for two of the shows.

And then it was Friday evening and the auditorium filled up with families and friends of the cast and other locals who wanted to see the show. Everyone was dressed in their Sunday finest, big black ladies with shiny dresses and fancy hats, perspiring in the stuffy heat. Old granmas with canes, being slowly guided to their seats by doting grandchildren. Well-off white families, come to see their kids perform, mixing easily and comfortably with the families of their maids and gardeners, one of the ironies of the south...

Backstage the kids were really nervous for their whole families were out there watching.

"OK everyone!" I called out. "You're the best cast I've ever seen in this play. You've performed in front of much more critical audiences than your families and friends – your school mates! Pirates, on stage, curtain call in two minutes. Break a leg, everyone!"

"Hey Cap'n!", called out Rodney, the Major-General. "What does that mean – 'break a leg'? Seems kinda cruel!"

"I have absolutely no idea, Major-General, but I wish you the best of luck. You're a terrific young man and I see great things in your future. Now get ready to sing to your mammy – create a memory she'll never forget, and neither will you..."

The evening performance was the best they had done, the songs were vibrant, the dancing full of energy, the passion obvious. For most of the people there, poor farmers and day workers, maids and cooks, it was the first time they'd even heard of The Pirates of Penzance and some of them probably couldn't follow the plot and didn't know what a paradox is. But it didn't matter – their kids were up there having the time of their lives and they clapped and cheered and laughed and were mighty proud.

After the cast took their half dozen bows to a standing, clapping, sweating and happy audience, John and I and the other teachers who had worked with the kids came on the makeshift stage and took our bows, the cast clapping the loudest. It was a very satisfactory feeling.

I wandered down into the audience and walked through the crowds, feeling slaps on my back and shaking many hands, most hard and calloused, some soft and smooth. I was heading for one group in particular.

Their daughter Emily was the beaming centre of their attention and as I approached she became quiet. Her father had his back to me, but as Emily looked over his shoulder, he slowly turned around. He was wearing an old suit, clean, but with threadbare patches. His black shoes were shined to perfection, the heels worn down. His white shirt was starched and his spotless tie was old-fashioned, but knotted perfectly.

I stood in front of him as the family became quiet. I was unaware of the noise and chatter going on around me. It was just Mr. Jones and me. As he looked into my eyes with his steady stare, his face creased into a smile and he reached his hand out to me. I clasped it and squeezed firmly. We stood like that for thirty seconds as a happy tear ran down his cheek...

FIRE DOWN BELOW!

'Ladyhawke' bobbed peacefully off Lemon Cay in a spacious anchorage, along with half a dozen cruising yachts from around the world. We had four guests aboard, family from San Francisco and Sydney. They had been with us for three days, leisurely exploring some of the remote islands of the San Blas Archipelago on the Caribbean side of Panama.

The weather was idyllic with a gentle breeze keeping the temperature perfect. The water was its usual stunning aqua blue, the sky brilliant with puffy white clouds, palm trees rustled softly on the neighbouring islands. Colourful fish swam around the boat and everyone looked forward to a relaxing day of snorkeling and exploring the empty beaches.

We had just finished a breakfast of fresh tropical fruits and strong Colombian coffee, sprawled around the large and comfortable aft 'veranda' which was one of Ladyhawkes unique features. Joell and I had been back in Panama for three months, having bought our 64' trimaran a year earlier in Florida, refitted her and sailed her down to Panama. It was January, 2005 and we were eagerly anticipating the arrival of three well-known yacht brokers who were flying down the next month to sample our charter operation for potential guests. Inviting our family was a great way to see how well we and the boat handled a group of people for a week.

Our cruising friends Alfredo and Alicia had sailed in a couple of hours before and we looked forward to introducing our family to these world voyagers. I got up to brew some more coffee and noticed the teak decking under my feet was quite warm, too warm for this time of day, especially as the veranda was protected by a large roof. I didn't think much of it and went below to the galley for a fresh pot.

When I came back five minutes later, the deck was slightly

warmer, my bare feet registering alarm. Everyone was chatting away, laughing and laid back. I sniffed a faint smell of burning and figured someone on the island was burning coconuts. Then I noticed a small wisp of smoke rising through a ventilator...

Under the veranda was the generator room, which housed the big 15KW Westerbeke generator, the autopilot motor and hydraulic pump for the two thrusters, a large amount of spare parts and various oils, grease and cleaning supplies. It was a large area about nine feet long by six feet wide and five feet high.

In a flash, my mind added it all up – the deck was warming up, there was a smell of burning and smoke was leaking out – we were on fire!

"HEY, listen up everyone! I think there's a fire in the generator room underneath us! Get up quickly and clear the area!" I said, trying to be calm, but freaking out inside!

Fire on a boat is very dangerous, especially on a boat built of wood and with two hundred gallons of fuel aboard! Everyone scrambled forward, out of the way. My mind was racing and my feet were getting noticeably warmer...

The generator room was self-contained and with the main hatch closed, a fire might burn up the oxygen inside and put itself out. But there were four ventilators to provide air for the generator, so that wasn't going to happen.

Smoke was now pouring out of the vents and it was obvious the fire was intensifying.

"Joell, sound five blasts on the air horn, let everyone in the anchorage know we've got a problem. Grant and Jeff, fill those two big buckets over the side with water. Marina and Gigi go into the main cabin and the amas and grab all the fire extinguishers, NOW!"

I had to open the hatch, had to see how bad the conflagration was. But it was a dilemma – by opening the hatch, I would let fresh air in which would fan any flames. I didn't know if it was an electrical fire, but even assuming it was, it had apparently started the wood frames or flooring below burning.

"OK, stand back, I'm going to open the hatch. Get ready with the buckets and pull the pins out of two extinguishers."

I hooked my finger around the stainless steel deck ring and winced – it was already hot! With a quick pull, the hatch was flung open and clouds of dark, acrid smoke poured out.

"My God," I thought. "Our beautiful home is burning up..."

I grabbed a full bucket of water and emptied it below. It had no effect. I thrust it back at Grant to refill and grabbed the second one from Jeff. It too had little effect. I didn't know where the fire was – at the front of the generator room, directly under the hatch where I was standing or back at the transom about eight feet further aft.

"Joell, quickly, soak a towel in water, I have to go down there." I yelled.

"No, it's too dangerous, you won't be able to breathe."

"I have to see where the fire is so we can put it out. Just chucking buckets of water won't do it. I'm going down there. Get me a flashlight, quick."

As captain, I was responsible for the safety of everyone aboard. Before I gave the dreaded order to abandon ship, I needed to see if I could put the fire out. This was not a time to panic and I was doing my best to remain calm and in control.

I wrapped the water-soaked towel around my face and grabbed

the flashlight. With everyone looking on intently, I gulped several deep breaths and quickly, before I could change my mind, lowered myself through the hatch. There was one step down and I hunched over and shone the torchlight beam around. The whole generator room was thick with smoke and I could hear flames crackling. But the torch beam couldn't penetrate the smoke, so I reached out ahead of me blindly, trying to feel for the hottest part, taking the chance of singeing my hand in the flames.

Luckily, I couldn't make out any giant, leaping yellow flames, so I hoped it was still relatively minor. After fifteen seconds, I couldn't breath anymore and pulled myself out of the hatch, gasping and panting. Grant threw a bucket of water on me...

"Look, I can't see through the smoke. Joell, get me the big searchlight. Hurry!" I coughed out to my alarmed wife.

"I don't think you should go back down there," she said, with good reason.

"NO, I have to. I can't see any flames, I think it's still small, but there's tons of smoke."

This was a rather redundant statement as smoke was now billowing twenty feet into the air and across the anchorage! While I was down below, Alfredo and Alicia had rushed over in their dinghy and I could see other cruisers heading our way at full speed.

Joell handed me the million-candlepower searchlight, Marina wrapped another wet towel around my face, I took large gulps of fresh air and dove back down into the smoke, smell, heat and darkness. Switching on the powerful light, I could make out swirls of smoke and small flames coming from the aft end of the generator room, from the small wooden work bench on the port side. I could vaguely make out that the work bench was burning, but there was also an acrid taste to the smoke, electrical wires burning and melting!

"OK, I see the fire! Start handing down the extinguishers," I coughed up through the hatch.

We had six aboard, but they weren't very big. I grabbed one, inched toward the stern of the boat, pointed it at the base of the fire and squeezed. It spewed its chemicals for about five seconds, then expired! I reached up and grabbed another one. Now it was really nasty in the enclosed space – the chemicals added another toxin to the 'air' I was breathing. I emptied this one in the direction of the flames, without much effect.

I was getting lightheaded, not thinking right and was coughing non-stop. I quickly climbed out and gulped in clean air. There was now a crowd of dinghies around the boat, everyone thrusting fire extinguishers at us. Once again the cruising community had answered the call. Without concern for themselves, every skipper had jumped in their dinghies to help another sailor. Later on, I realized what a brave and selfless thing this was – they didn't know if Ladyhawke was going to blow up, but they were determined to do everything they could to prevent that...

I must have presented quite a sight as I scrambled out of the hatch. Apparently I was black and grimy, with little rivulets running down my face from my sweat.

"The fire's contained in the very aft right now, so I'm going onto the swim-steps and open the small rear hatch. I'll shoot the extinguishers down there," I coughed and spluttered. "Someone put them in a dinghy and come around to the stern."

The teak decking was very warm now and I was afraid it would burst into flames. If that happened, our beautiful yacht would just catch fire and probably burn up in no time. I hurriedly climbed over the taffrail and got ready to open the small inspection hatch at the stern.

"Someone close the main hatch – I don't want to fan the flames with a draft," I yelled.

I grabbed a fire extinguisher from Alfredo in his dinghy next to me. I opened the hatch, smoke poured out. I pointed it in the general direction of the base of the flames and squeezed the trigger. Ten seconds later, it was used up. Alfredo pulled the pin from another one, I grabbed it and fired again. Then a third, a fourth. The smoke seemed to lessen a little, but I didn't know what else was smoldering.

"Joie", I called out, my throat rasping, "take the long hose and hook it up to the anchor wash-down pump. Then bring me the other end and turn the pump on."

She and my brother Grant ran up to the bow, sixty feet away, while I emptied another fire extinguisher into the belly of the generator room.

A minute later, someone thrust the end of the hose to me, with sea-water pouring out of it. I pointed it through the inspection hatch and pumped gallons and gallons of water into my once clean and ship-shape generator room.

"Joie," I called again. "Turn on the aft bilge pumps, hopefully they're still working. If we don't, the boat'll fill with water."

Alfredo called to me that water was coming from the bilge pump thru-hull fittings, so the wires running to the pumps hadn't burned through yet. I sat on the swim steps for a full five minutes, spraying the generator room with corrosive salt water. What a bloody awful mess this was going to be...

I looked forward to see a dozen anxious faces staring back at me.

Some I knew and some were cruisers we hadn't met yet, standing in their dinghies, holding onto our lifelines, fire extinguishers at the ready.

Slowly the smoke subsided, the fire was out. I stood up and shook the hand of my very good friend Alfredo. This competent, capable sailor had not hesitated to come to our aid and had wanted to go down the hatch with me when I first tried to see what was going on. After both of us were nearly killed months before when an errant dinghy had 'attacked' us in Roatan, he told me later that life was always exciting around Ladyhawke!

Without me telling them, Grant and Jeff had emptied bucket after bucket of sea water on the teak decks to cool them down and it had worked. I thanked everyone for coming to our aid and one by one, they headed back to their boats.

My body was black and I smelled of smoke. Over the side I went, dish soap in hand and scrubbed the grime off. Our guests were somber and subdued, but I was determined not to let this spoil their holiday.

After an hour the smoke was completely gone and Alfredo and I went below to survey the damage. The bilge pumps had sucked all the water out, but it still dripped from the sides and shelving. The only structural damage was the charred remains of my small work bench, which meant that I had saved our home and Ladyhawke would sail again...

We found the cause of the fire – a small 12-volt wire that provided power to the auto pilot had chafed through and there was no fuse in the circuit. It had grounded out, melted its wire protection and set fire to the dry, paint covered work bench. I realized how lucky I was that this hadn't happened at sea, at night, in a storm...

What I did discover the next morning, as we prepared to weigh anchor, was that I had no steering! The fire had burned a small hole in a hydraulic hose and all the fluid had leaked out. How we fixed that in this remote island chain is another story...

JOELL'S STORY

I woke up in hospital with many tubes and needles inserted into my body. It didn't hurt as I was still under the woozy influence of the anesthetics required to undergo major surgery. I was amazed-I was alive and the pain was temporarily gone. I had no idea what organs or bits and pieces they had taken out!

The doctor who had decided an hour after Jon brought me to the emergency room in Florida that he needed to operate immediately, didn't know what the infection was that had grown uncontrollably inside my belly over the past three weeks. I didn't know if it was cancer, if my intestines were still functioning, if I would need catheters for the rest of my life, or more surgeries, chemo or radiation? Still, I was happy just to be alive.

While I was being prepped for emergency surgery on that Christmas Eve in 2011, I thought that there were so many things I might never have the chance to do again... The feeling that never leaves me though, are the last thoughts that went through my mind just before I slipped into the easy state of anesthesia. My desires and dreams came to the surface. I wanted to play my violin in a string ensemble. I wanted to paint so many more pictures. I wanted to sit quietly on our sailboat at anchor with my dear husband, sipping a boat drink, watching the stars come out in the tropical night. I wanted to smell the wonderful sweetness of a horses' gentle breath. So many things I still had to do. I realized what had been outstanding in my life - what was really important.

So I was relieved when the doctors came in after surgery to find that although they'd removed some rather important body parts, including my appendix, I did not have cancer and my chances for living were pretty damn good. I was left with everything I needed to function and although they said I was "not out of the woods yet" I knew that I could depend on my body to heal well. I had had one heck of a fast-spreading infection and there would be an uncomfortable recovery period. So Jon and I braced for the time to come and we went into it without fear. I had lots of time to contemplate...

One of my earliest memories is of being a very small child in Ontario, Canada. Sandy, the teenage girl who shared the upstairs rental with her mother in my parent's house, was my babysitter. She spent most of her time teaching me to colour with crayons, how to outline and shade. I loved to colour and draw, more than anything in the world. I drew horses and the fairytale characters from storybooks for hours a day. We had a television set and in the morning when the test pattern (with the silhouette of the Indian's head) finally went away, they would play 'God Save The Queen'. I was enamoured of Queen Elizabeth - we sang 'God Save The Queen' every day at school when I entered kindergarten. She was on all of the pennies that we counted at school so I knew she must be very special!

We still had ice deliveries to our home in those days and there was also a 'junk man', a memorable character who drove a horse and wagon. People would throw their junk onto his wagon when he would come by, calling "Junkie junkie Joe!" He let me feed apples and carrots to his horse and I was in heaven.

There was a reason that we were living in Canada. My mother was born in Canada, in Winnipeg, her parents having emigrated there from Sweden in the nineteenth century. She was one of the most incredible women I have ever known. A truly kind, bright, accomplished and talented soul on this planet. She met my Dad in Chicago just before World War II. My father was a very talented photographer and after the war, they had set up a studio in La Puente, California with Mom as his assistant, developing and retouching his beautiful black and white photos, sometimes adding colour with pastels. (There was little colour photography in those days, this was back in the fifties and it was quite expensive).

Mom was a conscientious person, very active with the unions because a lot of workers had no rights or recourse in those days. She passed out lots of pro-union brochures in our neighbourhood. There was an evil man, doing awful things, in power in the States – his name was Eugene McCarthy. Neighbours reported that my mother was passing out 'communist' brochures and that she was involved in possible suspicious activity.

Mom was pregnant with my sister, Vicki and I was a baby. But the evil forces were relentless. Mom was dragged before government panels and accused of all kinds of un-American activities. Nothing could have been further from the truth. But she was found guilty and deported and my family lost everything, including the beautiful house that they had built themselves and Dad's growing photography business.

That is how I ended up in Canada at two years old. And that is how I came to love Canada as the place I delighted in making angels in the snow! I loved the winter and I loved the wide open summer fields behind our house, full of monarch and swallowtail butterflies, pheasants and blossoming apple trees. That house is where I also believed and tried to fly out of the upstairs window after having seen Peter Pan! My sister, Lois, caught me just before I left the windowsill! I was a little person without fear...

Lois was ten years older than me. On the Ed Sullivan show in September, 1956, we watched a gyrating young singer called Elvis Presley. I was impressed. Even more impressed were my sister and her friends! They were peaches and cream teenagers with bobbysox, saddleshoes, poodle skirts, sweaters and pony tails - I adored my big sister and her friends. They went to see 'Love Me Tender' at the movie theater when it first came out. My sister had to watch me that day, so I got to go with them. I will never forget the bevy of girls in the theatre, Elvis on the big screen, and the candy bar I was given to keep me quiet. A major day in my life at four years old...

We eventually moved back to Southern California when Mom received an apology from the United States government, telling us it was OK to return after six years of 'exile'. McCarthy shriveled away in shame as was appropriate. I was devastated to move to California. First, we had to leave my lovely black Cocker Spaniel in Canada with a new family-I didn't want to go, I loved my doggie. I loved my friends. Dad had suffered a heart attack at age 40 from cigarettes and the stress of the McCarthy persecution. We tiptoed around him when we got to California so he could heal, but he was never really OK after that.

There was some magic, though! My Auntie Belle lived in Los Angeles. It was the L. A. of the late 50's and early 60's. She was a real character - glamorous, a bit crazy, and the best Auntie a little girl could ask for. My other aunt, her sister Sylvia, went into a competition to see who could buy me the most and best gifts when we would come to visit! I was always happy when we would drive up to L.A. There was a huge dairy farm not far from the lovely neighbourhood where Aunt Belle lived. She would take me to see the newborn calves, pet them and let them suck on our fingers. After, we would get an ice-cream bar from the dairy's drive-through store.

Aunt Belle's daughter, my cousin Jackie Joseph, was a gorgeous up-and-coming actress. She married an actor, Ken Berry, who rose to T.V. stardom and is well-known for his role in the comedy series 'F Troop'. Jacki 's first major role was in the 1960 movie, 'Little Shop of Horrors', which was also Jack Nicholson's debut appearance on the silver screen. While I was growing up, I got to go to many Hollywood functions and performances. I saw

41

most of the major stars of those days and it was just a part of life for me. I would return home to our little town south of L.A. and it was like I was living a double life. Nobody there noticed me, or knew about my 'other life'.

I was miserable in school when we returned to California. Canada's education system was far superior to the school in our Southern California neighborhood. I was put a grade ahead and with my funny accent I didn't fit in well. By then, I was one of the best artists in school. I drew horses in class, when I was supposed to be listening to my lessons. I was told, "That's a beautiful horse, but please pay attention and quit drawing". I won contests and awards for my artwork in school, including the school science fair when I created a huge poster in colour pencils entitled 'The Anatomy of a Horse'. I created the cover for our class book, 'A Little Bit of Everything' - I also started taking violin lessons. I was that geeky kid, walking with a violin case, dropping my books and papers. The thing was, that I was good, a natural. In those pre-Reagan days, we had orchestra class in schools in California - it was a wonderful thing!

My Swedish grandfather, Nils P. Lithander had wanted to take violin lessons as a boy. His family were poor farmers. He asked his father if he could learn to play and his father told him, if he could get a violin, he could take lessons. Nils went to the violin maker in town and asked to become an apprentice. Eventually he made his own violin, learned to play, and became a 'Luthier' (violin maker) himself.

Nils was also an accomplished artist and one of the very first chiropractors by trade. It was from him that my mother and I inherited our talents for art and music. He made one very special instrument in 1901 that was handed down to me when I grew enough to play a full sized violin. I played that violin all the time and carried it with me for many years. A few years ago, when I was continually living in the tropics and on boats in a marine environment, I consulted with my Mom. I decided with her approval to send the violin back to Sweden where it will be played and appreciated for years to come by our very musical family. Now I have a student grade violin, that I feel comfortable taking on our adventures, wherever they lead us...

I can figure things out - I love to do that! I'm always working on projects that nobody else would dream of! One of the things this has led me into along with my artistic nature is that I love to do murals and faux finishing and trompe l'oeil - things that trick the eye into believing something is so, but it's not. (Joell is *incredibly* talented – Jon).

When I was in my early twenties, I studied at home (without a formal education) for the zookeeper's test at the L.A. Zoo. I scored in the top five although I didn't end up taking that job. I love animals and nature with all my heart and I had the pleasure of being a zookeeper in upstate New York for a year. Why only one year? My husband was jealous, could not tolerate my happiness and made it impossible for me to keep that position.

I married young and had a child, Benjamin, when I was only nineteen. My husband's sister, who was my best friend, was married to an unknown wannabe rock singer called Sammy Hagar; my life in San Francisco in the 1970's and 80's included hanging out with many famous rock groups, as Hagar became a better known figure. In the 1980's I went to work for him and Betsy as their nanny and personal assistant and traveled with Van Halen for a while, a fun, exhausting and grueling schedule - my husband was a roadie for them.

I also have a passion for natural healing and organic foods. Jon and I published a natural health magazine in the early 2000's. We had the pleasure of interviewing both natural healers and those who had been healed. Some of the patients had been told by western doctors that they would not live, that there was no further hope and that they should give up on life. They chose to seek further answers and in the process found the natural path to healing - many of them proved the 'traditional' western doctors wrong. My mother went to Palmer Chiropractic Institute in the 1930s and actually studied under Daniel David Palmer, the founder, in Davenport, Iowa. She believed in healthy living, keeping away from western medicine as much as possible, and having a good chiropractic adjustment now and then!

Her father, Nils, as I mentioned, was one of the very first chiropractors - pretty much self-taught. He used to save people's lives, trading services for food and necessities as the Swedish farmers were poor. My Uncle Leif was also a chiropractor and he saved the life of one of the kids I went to school with during the polio epidemic in the 1950's. I didn't know until years later when the kid, then grown up, exclaimed,

"That's your uncle? He saved my life when I had polio! My body was bent, wracked with pain and I couldn't walk. He treated me at his house with adjustments and massage and as you see I have no problem to this day!" So that is how I learned to look for the natural way of healing and it has stood me in good stead to this day.

Horses. I know there is an intelligent power for good because of flowers, butterflies, the genuine smile of little children, and horses. I was fifteen when my dad bought me my first horse, a big old gorgeous Bay named Keno – we ran wild while I had him. Where I lived in Southern California it was still sweet-smelling orange groves and fields and I remember the sun-drenched days, full of freedom and flying hooves. As I grew, my love of horses remained and I eventually became proficient at dressage riding, on my beautiful Saddlebred, 'Step To The Stars'.

44

I was riding him every day when I met Cap'n Jon in 1996 and he swept me off my feet and out to sea...

Seven years before I met Jon, my son Ben was killed in a drunk driving accident in Marin County, north of San Francisco. My world fell apart - my life abruptly changed. Mom helped me re-adjust. I left the craziness of the rock and roll world behind and got a real job as a temp. Soon I was hired by a large shipping company and rose to upper management. My job and my horse are what kept me sane and on track.

The company I worked for owned a number of rental offices in Marin County and one day in August, 1996, a bearded man drove onto our property in an antique blue boat-tail sports car, looking like something out of 'The Great Gatsby'. He and some others moved into a suite of offices above mine and over the next few weeks I would occasionally see him chatting with various pretty secretaries. He seemed like a bit of a playboy and I had no interest.

But one day we met and talked briefly and went out for lunch and got married and my life took a wonderful change to one of risk, travel and adventure...

'LOOK THROUGH ANY WINDOW'

When we made the decision to sell 'Ladyhawke' and our charter business in Panama in 2006, we were told by everyone in the cruising community there that it wasn't possible to sell a huge boat like that, especially for the price we were asking. No one would travel all the way to Panama to look at a one-off yacht, especially as there were no licensed surveyors and getting it hauled out for a survey was a big hassle. But none of them really knew us and the magic we attracted into our lives...

Prior to choosing an international yacht broker to list her with, I placed a small ad on a free boating web site, not expecting to generate any interest. Joell and I went to work getting the yacht ready for sale, varnishing, touching up the paint, making her shine. A week later I went to an internet cafe and there was an enquiry on the boat... from a Dutchman... who was in India! I responded briefly, thinking it was a waste of time, but was pleasantly surprised when ten minutes later he emailed me back that he was serious and would fly to Panama next week!

Now I paid attention and for the next hour emails flew back and forth in real time. He wanted to operate a large charter boat in Panama catering to a new sport – kite-surfing. Apparently he had put a deposit on a big catamaran somewhere in the Caribbean but the deal fell apart. He thought Ladyhawke would be the perfect boat and made me an offer subject to inspection and survey – I accepted and he wired me a deposit.

We finished preparing her to show and by the time Erik arrived, Ladyhawke looked as good as she ever had. He took a room at the American hotel close to the Balboa Yacht Club where Ladyhawke was moored and later the same day, a friend of his who would captain the boat flew in from Ft. Lauderdale. Erik and Captain Rob climbed aboard after taking a launch from the yacht club dock.

We had drinks sitting around the large table on the covered aft deck and talked about the boat and their plans. Then we let them look all over our home and inspect the equipment. It was an uncomfortable feeling, but we knew we had to sell her. Our plans to offer day sail charters in Las Perlas Islands out of the Contadora Hotel had fallen apart a few weeks earlier.

There is a TV 'reality' show called 'Survivor' that was about to film one of their not-so-real series in Las Perlas, The Pearl Islands. We had been told by locals that the year before, the producers had hired every boat in the area and that we stood a pretty good chance of them chartering Ladyhawke, perhaps as an R & R base for their crew and the participants. Joell and I had watched an episode on TV a few years earlier and were not impressed by the silly competitions they were put to nor the nasty backstabbing of the show contestants. However, if the producers were willing to pay us a couple of thousand dollars a week for our charter yacht, we decided we would overlook that, even though I felt it showed a slight lack of integrity on my part.

We had seen some of the mess they had left behind when they were there the year before - large blocks of concrete scattered around a shallow bay for them to tie their boats to. Abandoned structures near some of the beaches. But the biggest negative impact from the multi-million dollar TV show was that many of the islands were placed off-limits to tourists. The locals were told by the Panamanian government that they could not travel around the islands, couldn't fish, in fact they couldn't do anything while the film crews were there. There was a lot of resentment from the indigenous population, whose lives were seriously impacted by Survivor. It seemed the government acquiesced to whatever the producers wanted, no matter how it affected the natives; this is a country where corruption is a way of life...

We met with the heads of the various production teams and were led on for a while that they would hire Ladyhawke, but when push came to shove, they backed out. Now we had no source of revenue from hotel guests (the Survivor people took over all the rooms on the island) and no source of revenue from the TV show. This would continue for months – we were out of business...

Erik and Rob were impressed with the condition of Ladyhawke and her potential for the charters they wanted to offer. But they did want a survey of the entire boat and an inspection of the bottom of the three hulls. I had anticipated this and had found a cruising sailor who said he had experience surveying boats. I introduced him to the prospective purchasers and left them alone at the bar that evening to work out the details.

It was decided that we would leave the next day and motor to Taboga Island, eight miles away. We were there exactly an hour after high tide and to the surprise of several tourists on the beach, I steered the boat at very low speed to where the water met the sand. As we motored in, one of the guys threw an anchor over the stern and when we were positioned, Rob jumped into the water, grabbed the heavy bow anchor which I had dropped and walked it further up the beach, where he buried it in the sand.

Now Ladyhawke, a very large sailing trimaran 64' overall length, 28' wide, was held steady as the six foot tide gurgled out. Art, the 'surveyor' had his first of many beers and started his survey in the engine room. As long as he was provided with a steady stream of beers, he liked what he saw. Joell made sure he was never thirsty! Two hours later there was a slight 'thump' followed by several more as the water receded and Ladyhawke settled gracefully on the beach. Then she started to lean to the left as the last of the tide went out.

We all climbed down the swim steps and jumped onto the sand. She sat like a huge bird with her wings spread and many people came to look and take photos. Ladyhawke had been hauled out at a horrible Panamanian boatyard a few months previously and the antifouling paint was still good. With beer in hand, Art tapped my rubber mallet lightly all over the three hulls, weaving gently, looking for any soft spots. I knew there wouldn't be any as we had one bad area replaced in the yard, where their incompetent workers had punched a hole in the left ama when they hauled her out. The hulls had been thoroughly inspected by me when she was out of the water and I knew she was sound.

We sat on the beach, Sailor at my feet, waiting for the tide to come back in and float us off. Art gave Ladyhawke a glowing survey and Erik agreed to buy her. We all climbed aboard and had a snack as Ladyhawke slowly settled back into her natural element. By dusk she was afloat and we retrieved the bow anchor. I started her up and we majestically backed away, the people on the beach cheering and waving!

As we motored around the island, the lights of Panama City twinkled into view, like a shimmering Emerald City. I followed a couple of freighters on their way to a nighttime transit of the Canal. We found our mooring, tied up, hailed a launch and I took everyone out for dinner.

A week later we moved off Ladyhawke into a hotel in town. The money was transferred, Sailor went into a travel kennel, disappeared into the cargo bay and we flew out of Panama headed for northern California and an uncertain future...

Summer in Sonoma County lacked one thing – oppressive humidity! It was very welcome after years in Florida and the tropics. We rented a lovely old house near Santa Rosa and pondered our future. I bought a 1933 Frazer-Nash replica and spent a couple of satisfying months rebuilding it in the garage. We took long drives around the lovely countryside, covered with ripening grapes in the vineyards dotting the rolling hills.

Joell pulled out her paints, set up her easel in a studio in the house and painted beautiful, whimsical works of art. She is one of those very talented people to whom painting comes naturally. From childhood, she had created stunningly life-like portraits of people and animals, especially horses. Having owned and ridden them since a teenager, she had an artist's eye for their flowing form and their majesty. Not only am I in awe of her talents as a painter, she is also an accomplished musician and has a lovely singing voice. It's not surprising, her Swedish family counts internationally known artists amongst them and her cousin was the prima ballerina for the Swedish Ballet for many years.

Summer turned to fall and Sonoma County put on its glorious display of changing colours. We still hadn't decided what to do with our lives, but having sold Ladyhawke for almost twice what we had paid for her, we didn't feel pressured to do anything right away. Joell continued painting and the studio soon had several of her paintings on the walls. I thought they were as good as any in the local art galleries and suggested we see if we could place some on consignment. After several days of rejections, we thought we could do as well as any of the snooty galleries – so why not open our own?

We both felt a buzz of excitement as we sat up late into the night talking, candles burning, drinking good Sonoma wine. Where should we look? How much would the rent be? Could we attract other artists? How do galleries make money?

The next day we climbed into the Frazer-Nash, sat Sailor on Joie's lap and drove the back roads to Healdsburg, about fifteen miles north. The small town had been much gentrified since we had been there years before. There were boutiques and cafes and galleries, and a decent amount of tourists walking around - it seemed like a distinct possibility. Over the next week we drove to Sonoma, Napa, St. Helena and Calistoga; we walked around and talked to various shop owners and the Chambers of Commerce and crossed some towns off our list.

We visited the town of Sonoma a few more times and realized it was where we wanted to live and open our gallery. I had visited the pretty, historic town many times after moving to the Bay Area in 1979 and had enjoyed walking around the famous Plaza, lined with an eclectic array of shops. As we explored the alleyways and courtyards in the vicinity of the Plaza, we casually talked to gallery owners. A few were friendly and helpful, but most of them, particularly those on the high-rent Plaza were quite dismissive of our chances of succeeding as a new gallery, especially as we had no experience in the business. I told Joell they were just afraid of more competition and she agreed. She also agreed that they had no idea how we made magic happen – and what we then created was indeed magic...

There were three vacant retail shops for rent, two of them on the Plaza. One was too small and the other had the windows blanked out and a small 'For Rent' sign tacked up. I knocked on the door and a dog barked loudly – I knocked again. It opened a crack and a paint-splattered face peered out.

"What do you want?" he demanded angrily. The dog was trying to squirm his way out.

"We want to rent this store," I replied pleasantly.

"I'm in the middle of painting. Come back in an hour." And the door closed abruptly.

"Friendly chap!" I said to Joell as we headed toward a restaurant for lunch.

An hour later we knocked on the door again. This time it was promptly opened by a tall, rotund man, wiping paint off his hands. He invited us in, then swiftly closed and locked the door.

"My name's Jeff. I just bought this place. What do you want to use it for?" he asked brusquely.

"Hello Jeff, I'm Jon and this is my wife Joell," I replied, shaking his hand. "My wife's an artist and we're going to open a gallery. We'll feature her work and also promote local artists and jewelers and crafts."

Jeff looked at me piercingly.

"Well, there are a number of different people who want to rent the space, including a well-known coffee shop chain; but my wife and I would prefer an art gallery that showcases local talent, rather than these high end galleries. Let me show you the space," he said, warming up to us.

The main room was just the right size, and there was a smaller back room behind it. A bathroom, a storage room and a small, shaded yard in back, perfect for displaying statuary and hosting outside parties. We loved the place, it was old and funky, yet bright and cheerful with its newly painted walls. Jeff told us the building was over a hundred years old and he had just bought it for a million dollars! Lovely wooden floors, original stamped metal decorative ceiling, lots of wall space to hang paintings.

"What's the rent, Jeff?" I asked with some trepidation.

"Four thousand a month."

I looked at Joell and she looked at me. That was a lot of money, but it was a prime location, there were always crowds of tourists walking by, the economy was strong, the housing bubble hadn't burst yet and the future looked bright.

We had a large cushion in the bank from the sale of Ladyhawke a few months earlier. I went out into the back garden with a pen and piece of paper and started scribbling numbers. Besides selling local artwork, we had decided that we would also sell unusual gift items - statues, fairies, mobiles, chimes, all kinds of different and unique stuff. We had gone into every shop on the Plaza and none of them looked or felt like what we envisaged.

"We can do this," I told Joell. I had no doubt we could put this together, create something unusual and build a successful business.

"OK Jeff," I said walking back in. "We'd like to apply. What do we need to do?"

Over the next couple of weeks, we met his wife, all had lunch together and began a friendship. He checked our references, we provided him bank statements and showed him some of Joell's paintings. A month after we had initially met, Jeff called us and said if we wanted it, he would give us a five-year lease on the store. I asked if we could meet the next day in town so I could look at the lease agreement and he agreed.

"Hey, Joell," I called excitedly as I walked through the back door into our lovely garden in the home in Sonoma we had just moved into. "Guess what? Jeff says we can rent the store with a five-year lease!"

"That's great, Jon. But five years is a long commitment, especially for us..."

Of course, she was right. I'd never been more than two years in one place, my wanderlust always kept me searching for another adventure, another horizon...But I was caught up in the vision and the idea of settling in this lovely town, operating a fun business and living without humidity!

After reading the lease I added a clause that allowed us to transfer it to a new owner, as long as it remained an art gallery. Jeff agreed and on January 2nd 2007, we all signed the contract and I wrote him a cheque for eight thousand dollars. Joell and I had recently left our house in Santa Rosa and moved to a smaller house on the outskirts of Sonoma, next to a sprawling vineyard – it was very lovely. But we had a lot of work to do, converting an empty space into an attractive and successful art gallery - and each month, four thousand dollars was going out...

I bought a van and we scoured the area and craigslist for used display cabinets and tables – we gathered different pieces that I fitted together and painted and we created a wonderful hodgepodge of show space. I built shelves and Joell painted a magnificent mural of a fairy sitting atop a pedestal above the counter.

We went to the Gift Show and visited different wholesalers in San Francisco and ordered all manner of unusual items. Reps came knocking on our door and we would stop work and pour over their catalogues, ordering a dozen of this and two dozen of that, for delivery in March. Because we were new, it was difficult to get extended terms and everything had to be paid for COD. By mid March, the gallery was ready and the UPS guy arrived every day with boxes of merchandise. We were like kids at Christmas as we opened each box, many times discovering items that we didn't remember ordering!

Our friend Warren, who had applied the name 'JoJo' on our boat ten years before, created a magnificent hanging sign as a gift and we hung it outside. It heralded the name of our new enterprise 'Look Through Any Window', in bright, vibrant colours. We had kept the large front windows covered while we were working inside and there was a definite 'buzz' around the Plaza as to what would open there. Some shop owners were pleased to see that there was no longer a vacant space on the Plaza and were welcoming, but a lot of others were rude and we heard some disparaging comments about how a couple of sailors thought they could be successful as gallery owners in this cliquey town. Everyone was vying for the tourist dollar and we were more competition.

Through ads in local papers and by word-of-mouth in the artist communities in Sonoma, Napa and the surrounding area, we received a steady stream of colourful and creative people knocking on our door looking to sell their art and crafts on consignment. By opening day, the inside of the gallery was fully stocked and looked wonderful! Joell's paintings hung on the walls, along with those of five very talented local artists. There was unusual jewelery priced from ten dollars to a thousand, beautiful collections of fairies, statues, fountains, pottery, my wife's spectacular hand-painted furniture, mobiles hanging from the ceiling, hundreds of items!

The loveliest area was the small room in the back, which Joell had transformed into a magical kid's playroom, with a giant dragon mural, a canopy bed and shelves full of simple and clever toys for all ages. It turned out to be a huge hit with the local mums who would bring their children and let them play on the floor while they perused our merchandise. They could relax and know the kids were safe and having fun. Many friendships were formed there and it was a very special space...

A short article was printed in the Sonoma newspaper about the two adventurers whose new gallery was to open on Thursday, March 15th. At eight o'clock that morning, with my classic British Frazer-Nash parked right outside, before the shops and galleries opened, Joell and I excitedly and nervously removed the brown paper covering the gallery display windows and for the first time, the hazy morning sun shone in. All of a sudden, there were rainbows on the walls and ceiling as the sun's rays sparkled through prisms that hung in the windows. We stood outside holding hands, with our Schipperke 'Sailor' on his leash next to us and looked in – looked through any window – and it was bright, colourful and inviting. We had worked very hard over the previous ten weeks and it showed. No, those stuck-up gallery owners had no idea who we were or how we created our magic, but magic it was!

By ten o'clock there was a large gathering of people outside and with a flourish, I unlocked the door and welcomed our first customers to our 'soft' opening. Yanni played in the background on the sound system as we answered questions, greeted many curious locals and rang up sale after sale. There was a constant flow of tourists as well, and practically everyone bought something. Time flew by and it was great fun! Mothers loved the kids room and after school that day it was packed with little ones 'oohing' and 'aahing' and playing with all kinds of wooden toys on the carpet!

We recognized a few of the gallery owners from around the Plaza who had nothing to say to us, but had their noses in the air as they studiously inspected the paintings we had for sale, whispered to each other and left. But there were others who introduced themselves and wished us luck and invited us to their shops, which we did over the next few days. We were supposed to close at six o'clock, but were still open at eight, as people streamed in and out. At nine o'clock we ushered the last people out, thanked them, waved goodbye and locked the door. All day long we had received compliments and encouragement from locals and tourists alike. We hugged each other, realizing that we had created something very unique and special, which people loved.

I had no idea how much business we had done and checked the days takings on the electronic cash register. I couldn't believe the number it came up with and thought I had pressed the wrong keys. I did it again and it was confirmed – just over three thousand dollars, our first day in business, on a weekday in

March! Not a weekend and not in tourist season!

"Wow, Joell, we took in over three grand today! This is great, amazing!"

We bundled up and drove happily home in the Frazer, Sailor snuggling against Joell to keep warm. We were exhausted, drained, buzzing and collapsed into bed, gathering strength for the upcoming weekend. The next morning we went in early and re-stocked the shelves. The weekend flew by and business was terrific–everyone loved Joell's murals and we sold a lot of knick-knacks and jewelery and a couple of paintings. Some experienced retail people gave us suggestions on how to display things better and some ideas of other things to offer. Jeff and his wife Elizabeth stopped by and were delighted with our success.

Monday we were closed, but that didn't mean we could relax – we had to re-stock and re-order, thoroughly clean the gallery and answer the door to a dozen artists who wanted to consign their work. In the afternoon a reporter from the Sonoma newspaper came by and interviewed Joell about her paintings and the magical kids room she had created. Their photographer took many shots and two months later Joell was featured on the cover of the monthly magazine along with a detailed article about us.

Three weeks after we opened, on a quiet Tuesday morning, a short man dressed in western style with a cowboy hat wandered in. He started talking with Joell who was in front while I was sorting things out in the storage room. When I came out half an hour later, Joell beckoned me over and introduced me to the man, who claimed to be an art collector. He was very interested in buying several of Joells' paintings and her hand-painted furniture. We talked for a while, he was visiting from Colorado, said he had recently inherited a lot of money and wanted to decorate a large house he had just bought; he went out for lunch and I didn't expect to see him again.

But he rolled back in mid afternoon, obviously having had a liquid lunch and definitely wanting to buy art. After an hour he had picked out several of Joell's paintings, the least expensive one priced at $6,000. By the time he had finished, he had spent just under $40,000! I asked how he intended to pay for all of this and he pulled out a huge, thick wad of hundred-dollar bills! He slowly counted out the total amount on the counter and said he'd be back to pick them up the next day. After he left, I looked at Joell who also couldn't believe what had just transpired...

"Oh, I LOVE this business, darling!" I told her. But it never happened again...

We enjoyed living in Sonoma and after hiring part-time help were able to take time off and visited various vineyards, sampling wine and enjoying where we lived. I bought a small, trailerable trimaran, but didn't use it much – I preferred sailing bigger boats and having to rig it every time got tiring very quickly. I sold it for a thousand dollars more than I had paid for it two months earlier.

A few weeks later we were interviewed for a story about our being accosted by pirates off Costa Rica a few years earlier, which was published in the paper. Very quickly, we became 'characters' in the community and enjoyed our notoriety. I became a Big Brother to a local boy and he sat smiling in the passenger seat of the Frazer-Nash as we participated in the huge July 4th parade.

Our business developed a 'cult' following and we had many repeat customers. One notable, busy Saturday afternoon, a black stretch limo pulled up outside and parked in the centre strip. A uniformed chauffeur alighted and ran to the rear door, which he opened while standing at attention. A fat oriental man rolled out, followed by a richly-dressed woman and a gaggle of children. I looked out the window while ringing up one of Sophia Harrison's wonderful pieces of glass art and wondered which upscale store they were headed for?

They quickly crossed the street and made a beeline for...'Look Through Any Window'! They knew exactly what they wanted and cleaned us out of our special collection of fairy figures and politely gave me a credit card on which I rang up over two thousand dollars. The chauffeur and I loaded the cavernous trunk, the oriental gentleman and I bowed to each other in the middle of the street, the family piled aboard and the chauffeur whisked them away, leaving me and many people in the gallery gaping!

It was a marvelous spring and summer, business was very good, although it started to drop off in early fall. This was to be expected as the summer tourist season ended. But it was more than that. There were reports of a suffering economy and an unusually high number of foreclosures and people were being laid off. I noticed fewer shopping bags passing by and our sales continued to slow down...

But then came the weeks before Christmas. We had ordered wonderful, unusual ornaments and miniature electric roller coasters and town scenes, all covered in snow and Christmas cheer. Our gallery was warm and fun and cheerful and Christmas-y. People seemed to find money somewhere and sales picked up again. The holiday shopping season was marvelous! Everyone was in good spirits, although many people were paying more attention to how much they were spending and buying cautiously. Anything priced under twenty dollars flew off the shelves...

January was deadly and I started to feel uneasy. I paid more attention to the news, something I had always tried to ignore.

"Joell," I said, a few weeks into the new year. We were at home having a glass of wine, after a very slow day. "Joie, I think it's time I say what I've been dreading to for a few weeks," reaching for her hand.

"I know exactly what you're going to say, Jon. I feel the same way. You're right, there's definitely something going on with the economy and I think it's going to be a tough year ahead. What do you think we should do?"

"Well love, if I'm right, this is going to be at the least a long recession, maybe worse...Between the gallery rent and our living expenses, which I know are very reasonable, unless we can gross more each month than we have in the past two months combined, we're going to drain our reserves. This has been a wonderful experience, we've made thousands of people, especially children, happy. People love our gallery and we've put money into the pockets of a bunch of artists and creative people. We've contributed to the town and had fun doing it. But one thing my dad taught me is that it's important to know when to get into a business, but it's more important to know when to get out..."

"So you think we should sell our magical gallery, is that what you're saying?" she asked sadly.

"Yes, I think we should. I think we should sell it to someone who wants this type of business and has more financial resources than us. I think we should sell it while it's still showing a profit. If we wait six months, it may be too late. I think the economy could collapse by the end of this year..."

"Yes, I agree. The past eight years of this government have been like living under a dark cloud, and they're going to leave the country in an economic shambles, just like the president did in his home state. Let's sell it, Jon and go somewhere else."

The next day I took out a classified ad in the local paper, without naming the gallery that was for sale. Eventually I would list it with a business broker, but perhaps someone local might want to buy an existing business, especially one with a following. Even though we usually found it easy to sell anything we needed to, including a huge charter yacht in Panama, I doubted it would be so simple to sell a retail business in a nose-diving economy. Two days later a middle-aged, well-dressed woman walked briskly into the gallery, came up to me at the counter and asked peremptorily,

"Is this the gallery that is for sale?"

"Er, yes it is. Would you mind coming with me into the back garden?" I didn't want any shoppers to know that I wanted to sell.

"I'm a local attorney and judge," she said, introducing herself. "My sister and I have always wanted to own a gallery or shop on the Plaza. What is your asking price, how much is the rent and how much time is left on the lease?"

She didn't beat around the bush! I answered her questions and she said she would buy the business for my asking price, assuming her accountant was comfortable with the books. She wasn't like us, seemed very 'straight' and she didn't seem to approve of the soft music that was playing in the background. But if she was ready to buy, then whatever she wanted to do with the business was her responsibility.

Jeff and his wife, Joell and I and our prospective buyer had lunch a few days later. Her accountant had said the books were in order, we had spent a full day reconciling the inventory and she was ready to write a cheque. But Jeff had the right to refuse transfer of the lease if the purchaser was not qualified.

She was qualified, very qualified. She was well-known and respected in the community and money was not an issue. It was agreed that she would take over the remaining four years of the lease and hands were shaken and papers signed. We would turn over the business and inventory on April 1st which we did.

We had made a lot of friends and met a few celebrities. One of the Jefferson Airplane; a member of the Grateful Dead who I had smoked a joint with after a concert in 1969. Many people from all over the world, drawn to the area by its natural beauty, famous wineries and proximity to San Francisco. We enjoyed being gallery owners for a year, we had created something beautiful and unique and touched a lot of lives, but even if the economy had not been tanking, I don't think we could have lasted four more years...it was time to go sailing again...

A couple of years later we were back in the Bay Area and took a ride up to wine country to visit some friends. We walked by 'Look Through Any Window' and it was quite different. The sign was still there, but besides the fairy languidly sitting on her pedestal above the counter, everything had changed. We went in and looked around. Instead of an eclectic display of all kinds of wonderful, unusual, colourful things, it looked like any high-end shop, with average merchandise, overpriced. The clerk behind the counter was sitting on a stool, bored. There was no music playing and the couple of people inside talked in hushed tones – it felt dead, uninspired, ho-hum, unsuccessful...

Recently, a friend who had spent a weekend in Sonoma told us the gallery was no longer there, but had been turned into a coffee shop, the one thing Jeff hadn't wanted...

TORTOLA CHARTER YACHT SHOW

Aruba was a welcome respite after a week of bashing north into the wind and waves as we fought our way up the coast of Colombia. JoJo, our 32' catamaran, had pounded into the short, nasty seas, had navigated the floating islands off the River Magdalena and although we were physically and mentally beaten up, had delivered us safely to this pretty little Dutch island.

Customs and Immigration were very polite and welcoming and after clearing in, we sailed a few miles up the coast and anchored off Moomba Beach. Then we slept and slept, for hours and hours. We loved Aruba, the residents were hospitable and friendly, the beaches were pretty and Joell won several hundred dollars at a local casino! It was also a bit of a culture shock as we had spent the past year in only Spanish-speaking countries. But we had a goal and needed to move on. After a few days, we weighed anchor and headed out for the last part of this passage from Cartagena, Colombia to Tortola in the British Virgin Islands.*

We had reserved a spot in the upcoming 2001 Virgin Islands Charter Yacht Show and now had only four weeks to get to the island and prepare JoJo and ourselves for the onslaught of hundreds of charter yacht brokers. Tortola was just 600 miles away, but it was right into the teeth of the Northeast trade winds, which blew pretty constantly at twenty knots. I decided to sail to Puerto Rico, which might enable us to use the wind, although we'd be beating all the way.

As we motor sailed up the coast of Aruba and the island receded into the distance, I hoped the trades would have a little more easterly than northerly direction – and they did. I was able to keep JoJo sailing rather than motoring, although it was pretty rough with the waves slamming the starboard bow repetitively. It took us six and a half days of more relentless pounding, but our sturdy little boat kept on going and eventually we could see the highest peaks of Puerto Rico ahead. We sailed into Bahia Boqueron on the southwest corner of the island, a pretty bay I had explored on 'Imagine', my 41' Searunner trimaran, ten years before.

A relaxing week in Puerto Rico, motoring along the south coast into the wind, with stops at several little anchorages. Ponce was a vibrant town and I showed Joell the Parque de Bombas, the small Museum of Firefighters with its unusual black and red building. With only two weeks to go, we headed into the trade winds for St. Thomas, twenty four hours away. Past Vieques off to starboard, the island of Culebra appeared ahead and to our left.

I had visited this lovely island in 1990 aboard 'Imagine', a few months after Hurricane Hugo had devastated the area. There had been ample warnings of the impending storm in the Caribbean and hundreds of boats had sailed into the large harbour there. It is well-known as a 'hurricane hole', a place offering protection from large waves and known to have good holding for the multiple anchors each boat would set. But no one was prepared for the devastating 150+ mph winds of the slow moving typhoon that hovered over Culebra for several hours. The southeast facing entrance to the anchorage had allowed a storm surge of thirteen feet to roll through. Besides dozens of cruisers, various charter companies in the Virgin Islands had dispatched their boats there, about two hundred of them - two thirds were lost. A retired couple were killed when the storm hit and swept their cruising home onto the shore.

Now, little was left of the effects of the mighty storm, although eighty percent of the wooden structures on the island had been destroyed. We sailed by thinking of the dreams that had been lost there. Talking later with cruisers in the islands, we learned that the bottom of the harbour was still littered with the remains of sunken boats.

When dusk came it was easy to see our destination to the east, as lights all over the island came on. The trade winds subsided and we motored quietly toward St. Thomas and dropped our anchor the next morning. As always after an overnight passage we went straight to sleep and woke up late afternoon. I've never liked St. Thomas - there's a lot of poverty, drugs and violence and for me it's just been a place to fly into and get out of. But Joell had never been there and we spent the next day driving around the island, stopping at some of the beaches to swim and snorkel.

We needed to get to Tortola, but first I wanted to show Joell the little jewel of St. John, two miles east. We motored over and dropped the hook in Cruz Bay, a crowded anchorage on the west side of the island. Rather than spend a few days sailing around the island and stopping in its numerous gorgeous bays, we rented a jeep and took off through the Virgin Islands National Park and along North Shore Road enjoying the beautiful vistas and beaches. We drove as far east as we could, all the way to Long Bay, then back across Centerline Road – one of those magic days that will always stand out.

But we could easily see Tortola to the north and we felt it beckoning. The next day we slowly motored northeast around St. John and I promised Joell that we would come back and spend more time anchored in the spectacular bays of St. John.

We dropped the hook in Roadtown Harbour in late afternoon and the following morning dinghied ashore to clear in. It had been seven years since I had been in Tortola as a delivery captain for The Moorings and although most things hadn't changed, it was apparent when we went to check in that something very important had. The attitude of the officials who cleared us in was rude and dismissive, very different from the pleasant, cordial receptions I had received years earlier. I suppose it was understandable, as there were so many visitors to Tortola now, the officials felt justified in having a big chip on their shoulders.

Then it was off to find my old friend Mrs. Burke, who owned the 'It-Go' car rental agency. She was delighted to see me after so many years and was thrilled to meet my wife. We reminisced about old times, about the scandalous rampage two of my delivery crew went on several years earlier and how there were so many more tourists these days.**

Joell wanted to know why her rental agency had such an unusual name and in typical island style, Mrs. Burke informed her that it was because every morning when she started her fleet of aging cars, she was happy that 'it go'! All her cars were rented out because of the charter show, but she found us an old, disreputable jeep for 'de islan' rate' and off we went, happily clattering over the roads in search of the charter show venue.

Village Cay Marina was the site and as we pulled up outside the hotel the place was buzzing. Strolling down to the docks, we could see that we were one of the last boats to arrive. The show organizers had taken over two of the three docks and practically all of the spaces were filled. As we wandered down the first dock, we were intimidated by the gorgeous charter yachts, many of them twice the size of JoJo! At the end of the quay was a stunning dark blue 70' schooner, all teak and mahogany with its crew scrubbing the already gleaming yacht, so that everything shone brighter than the tropical sun!

Open-mouthed, we walked to the next dock, where there were about twenty large catamarans over 50', with expansive decks and all kinds of water-toys being cleaned and laid out. They had large dinghies with 50 h.p. motors and a collection of towable rides. They had kayaks and some even had wind surfers. Most of the boats had racks of scuba tanks and small compressors on board!

Had we made a mistake, presuming to compete with these

seasoned veterans of the highly competitive charter market? Professional crews hurried along the docks carrying supplies to entertain the brokers soon to be checking out their yachts. We heard American, British, South African and Australian accents as we slowly walked along, looking for the registration booth. At this point we thought maybe we should dinghy back to JoJo, up anchor and quietly disappear...

"Hey Jon, Joell! G'day!" a voice called loudly from behind us.

Without even turning around we easily recognized the distinctive Australian accent of our friend John 'Whitey' White, who we had last seen in Cartagena a few weeks before.

"Whitey, Max!" as we all hugged.

Even though sun-tanned and rested, it was obvious that they had both been through a lot and it showed on their faces. They had left Cartagena two days before us on the beautiful 52' catamaran 'Tamarin' that they chartered in the Caribbean and Panama. The boat had hit something at sea, which had split open a hull; they and their three young crew members had abandoned ship and were rescued by a freighter and eventually air-lifted to Tortola. It was they who had originally suggested we enter JoJo into the charter show and had reserved the last spot for us.

"Come on, mates, let's have a beer and a chat. Then we'll get you registered."

So we had lunch overlooking all the excitement and bustle and Whitey told us in detail of their harrowing experience a few weeks earlier. How they had hit something at night (Whitey was pretty sure it was a container that had fallen off a cargo ship – there are thousands of them floating around the oceans, submerged about two feet under the surface, a menace to all boats at sea), how the boat flooded quickly and they had all scrambled

67

into the life raft. How he had grabbed his sat phone and called a friend with only enough battery power for a minute or so. He just told her over and over again his coordinates and to call the Coast Guard, before the phone went dead. How the five of them were tossed about on the open ocean at night, cramped and wet. (For a detailed account of their adventure, please see the link at the end of this story).

Even though they no longer had a boat, they were still actively participating at the show, helping everyone they could. They were also there to clean out their storage unit and decide what to do with the rest of their lives. These two were legends in the charter business and their guidance and friendship were invaluable to us.

They took us to register and we were made to feel very welcome. The only slip available was on the far end of the furthest dock, a long walk past all those large, impressive catamarans. We paid the rest of our entry fee and were informed that we had five days to get ready before the preview. Five days! Not only were Joell and I tired from our long upwind passages, but JoJo looked like a well-lived in, heavily traveled cruising boat, which she was! How were we to compete with all these glorious, dedicated boats and not be laughed out of the show?

"No worries, Jon," said Whitey encouragingly. "Our three young crew are still here and we'll put them to work on JoJo. She'll look fair dinkum in no time!"

His ebullient spirit had not been dampened by the loss of his home and business-he truly fit the description in Rudyard Kipling's poem 'If'...

We brought JoJo to her slip and she was dwarfed by the big oyager catamaran docked next to us.9

"Hey mate," someone called over to us. "That slip's reserved for the charter show. You'll need to move her..."

"Actually, we are part of the show – we're a one-couple charter boat," I replied.

"You're bloody kidding, right! That thing doesn't look big enough for two people, let alone four, yuk, yuk..."

I thought this might happen and went over to introduce myself to the bronzed, blond, cocky captain.

"Look Captain. We're going to be neighbours for a week. We just sailed JoJo five thousand miles through storms and pirates and now we're going to charter her. We're no competition for you and your four luxurious staterooms. So let's be civil and have a beer, OK?"

It wasn't long before word spread of the little 'Popeye' catamaran at the end of the dock and soon many captains and crew wandered down to check us out. Some had snide remarks, some were pleasant and friendly. But we didn't have time to stand around and chat or justify our being there. JoJo showed the scars of thousands of miles of ocean sailing both inside and out and we had only a few days to get her 'ship-shape and in Bristol fashion'.

True to his word, Whitey came aboard an hour later with his three crew members, who were staying on Tortola for a while. We were thrilled to see them again and they quickly agreed to help us get ready. There was so much to do! Everything had to be taken out of every locker and be sorted and cleaned. A lot of our personal possessions were taken to Whitey's storage unit.

All the wood was sanded and varnished. Dings and scratches were repaired and touched up. The sails were removed and cleaned. The stainless rigging and fittings were polished. Thewinches were greased, fibreglass waxed, cushions cleaned, linens laundered. The dinghy was scrubbed and the outboard tuned up. When all was done, JoJo was in better condition than when she was first launched!

made up to hand out to the brokers. Joell and I went to Pusser's Pub and bought colourful shirts so that we'd have a 'uniform'. We bought food for snacks for the brokers and wine to quench their thirst. I bought an inflatable kayak, so we could claim to have a 'toy' for our potential charter guests. The days flashed by and we were told that the organizers would be previewing the yachts the next day.

The following morning there was a flurry of activity as each yacht laid out all their 'toys' and the crews dressed up in their uniforms. Each was trying to outdo the others, for they mostly had similar vessels and needed something 'special' to set them apart. There were two other 'one-couple' boats, but they were monohulls, traditional boats. We were totally unique, our jolly little JoJo defiantly gleaming in the sun, her inflatable kayak blown up and her captain and first mate resplendent in their matching coral coloured shirts and khaki shorts!

We were totally exhausted from the frantic clean up and the running around trying to find everything we'd need to be presentable. And so we sat in our cockpit and clinked our coffee cups as we waited for the organizers to inspect us before the show officially opened the next day. We watched them make their way slowly down the docks, a small group who went aboard each yacht for a few minutes, then moved to the next. The butterflies were buzzing around my stomach as they got nearer and then they were at our transom, some of them with their mouths agape! I don't think they had seen anything like our Catfisher 32 and she seemed small and out of place amongst these seasoned veterans of the Caribbean crewed charter yacht fleet.

Most of the captains and crews knew each other and many, like Whitey and Max had been doing this for years. Some of the yachts spent the summer in the Mediterranean; then they'd ride the trade winds back across the Atlantic to spend the winter entertaining high-paying guests among the pretty islands of the Caribbean chain. The only people we knew were Whitey and Max and that had only been for two days in Cartagena – we felt quite alone and out of our depth...

"Permission to come aboard, Captain."

And then three officials squeezed into JoJo's salon and looked below at our two small cabins and the toilet.

"Only one head?" we were asked.

"Yes, that's right," I responded.

"Hmmm..." with a furrowed brow.

Were we to be asked to leave before the show even started?

"Oh, that's OK," said one. "We've had a couple of boats in the past that only had one head. I'm sure that at the rate they're charging the guests won't mind."

Yes, we were definitely at the lower end of the weekly rates! We had decided, after talking with Whitey and some other captains we had become friendly with, that $3200 per week, all inclusive (except alcohol) would make us attractive to couples who wanted to experience the easy sailing of the Virgin Islands without spending too much money. The larger yachts, those with three or four cabins were commanding $12,000 per week and up and that didn't include food, booze or fuel!

And so we passed muster and could relax for the rest of the day before the show officially began. Joell and I took our old, dented jeep on a tour of the island, a magical place that I never tired of. We had lunch at Bomba's Shack, a motley and eclectic collection of rooms and hallways mostly made of driftwood and flotsam. If a storm blew through and knocked it down, Bomba and his friends would just rebuild it however it came out – it was always different! I told Joie of the famous full moon magic mushroom parties that I remembered from years before. Apparently they were still happening and we planned to go to the next one later that month (we did go and they hadn't changed - hundreds of people, live loud reggae, a distinctive aroma in the air and wild dancing on the beach all night!).

That evening, the night before the two-day show would begin, there was a large dinner party at the beautiful restaurant at Village Cay Resort, overlooking the charter yachts below decked out with flags and pennants flying in the gentle, warm breeze. All the captains and crews were there, probably three hundred sailors determined to have a good time and possibly a rum or two...

It had been announced that there would be various competitions and prizes given away. For some reason Joell had convinced me to enter the linen napkin folding competition and I managed to concoct something that resembled a bird – either I was drunk or the judges were, because I won third prize!

The next morning we woke up a little fuzzy and noticed that the normal bantering and camaraderie was subdued, either because of the serious nature of the days' upcoming proceedings or because of some serious hangovers! We had become friendly with some of the charter crews, but there were still many who sneered at our little boat and considered us upstarts without a hope of attracting any of the brokers to JoJo, especially as it was the furthest down the dock.

But we laid out our little table in the cockpit with two elegant dinner settings and had snacks and cold drinks ready, hoping that one or two brokers might wander down out of curiosity or perhaps boredom! After all, eighty percent of the boats were pretty much the same, the only difference being the captain and crew.

At the very least, we had made some new friends and JoJo had never looked so good! By late morning a couple of charter yacht brokers had come aboard and made polite sounds regarding JoJo. They had asked some perfunctory questions and then politely excused themselves...

"Hmm, this is going to be a long couple of days, Joie. And it looks like the professional captains were right – JoJo really doesn't fit into this realm..." I said morosely as the afternoon dragged on.

We could see brokers, either singly or in groups, walking down the docks and going aboard a number of boats. It seemed they knew a lot of the captains and we could hear laughter and champagne corks popping.

"Maybe we should quietly cast off and sail to Jost Van Dyke island – hang out at Foxy's and get drunk?" I suggested half-heartedly.

"Don't be silly, Jon!" my always-positive wife said. "It's not over yet. We've paid our money, let's just enjoy what's left of the show. Anyway, there's another big party tomorrow night!"

And then the captain of the catamaran next door called over.

"Hey Jon, the queen of charter brokers is heading down the docks with her entourage. Get ready, she may visit you, heh heh!"

I knew who he was referring to, but had little expectation of herdeigning to come aboard our small boat when there were so many grand yachts to see. Julie Nicholson was indeed the doyen of charter brokers. Her father, Commander Nicholson, had sailed into Antigua in 1949, had rebuilt the ruins of the once-proud English Harbour where Nelson had anchored and had pretty much single-handedly started the Caribbean yacht charter industry. Their family were legendary in the Caribbean and Julie was considered one of the most knowledgeable charter brokers in the world.

I stepped onto the dock and could see three women fluttering around a no-nonsense lady who walked determinedly down the dock, past every boat lined up there. She came closer and Joell and I expected her to disappear up the gangplank onto one of the glistening yachts tied up one after the other. My friend at the next slip told his two crew to get ready, as it looked like Miss Nicholson was heading to their boat.

He had a big, welcoming smile on his face as she marched purposefully down the docks towards his huge catamaran, but then to his amazement and certainly to ours, she marched right passed him and stopped at our transom.

"CAPTAIN WHITE. PERMISSION TO COME ABOARD, SIR!" she bellowed at me. It seemed like all her words were capitalized!

"Er, yes, of course, Miss Nicholson," I replied, standing taller and smoothing my hair down. "Yes, with pleasure, watch your step."

I caught a glimpse of several captains and crew with their mouths open as Julie settled herself on one of our cockpit cushions. She was in her fifties, had a distinctive clipped British accent, short, neat hair, tanned skin and a pleasant smile.

"Well Captain. I've heard about this jolly little catamaran and was told I should come and meet you. Where is this delightful first mate of yours – she's made quite an impression here already! Ah, there you are, m'dear."

"Right, wh-what can we get you to drink, Miss Nicholson?" I stammered.

"Nothing, nothing at all. Now, why don't you disappear for a while and I'll have a nice chat with your wife. She's the important one on a charter boat, don't you know. Off you go, then..."

And I was summarily dismissed! I went to my neighbour who was standing in his cockpit with a look of disbelief on his face. I had one as well...

"Blimey, I've been kicked off me own boat. And she isn't even a pirate! I need a beer!" I said bemusedly.

Fifteen minutes later, after giving Joell a big hug in front of everyone, Julie stepped off JoJo onto the dock. I scrambled to meet her.

"Well captain. That's a wonderful woman you have there. I think she'll do very well in this business. She told me of your adventures and your voyage from San Francisco. I have no doubt that you can handle this boat and provide a memorable experience for your guests. I like JoJo and think she is the biggest little yacht in the fleet. Cheerio!"

And she was off, striding down the dock with her assistants hovering behind, past the look-alike boats and up to the resort.

I turned to look at my wife who was standing in the cockpit, a glass of white wine in her hand and a big grin on her face. I leaped aboard and gave her a hug.

"Blimey, what were you two talking about?" I asked, pouring myself another beer.

"Oh, just girl stuff – don't you worry," she replied impishly. "We got along just fine, just fine!"

Within an hour we had dozens of curious charter brokers asking to come aboard and inspect JoJo. We found out later that word had spread quickly that Julie Nicholson had been impressed with the boat and with us and everyone wanted to see why. The most satisfying thing for me was the smug looks of the seasoned charter captains being replaced by a modicum of respect. And they all wanted to see JoJo as well...

That evening as we enjoyed dinner with Whitey and Max and some other captains and crew, we were talking about Julie's surprise visit to JoJo. Whitey leaned behind his chair, nudged me and gave me a big wink. It was pretty apparent that he had suggested to Julie, who he had known for years, that she check us out...

The following day was a constant stream of visiting charter brokers, all curious to make themselves known to us and promising bookings. And then the show was over. We stowed the flags and pennants, said goodbye to new friends and motored away from the dock, anchoring out in the harbour. Within a day most of the boats had sailed off to their various island bases throughout the Caribbean. We stayed in Tortola for a couple of reasons. Whitey and Max had decided to go back to Perth for a while to figure out what they would do with their lives, now that 'Tamarin' was gone. They had a storage unit crammed with spares for their charter cat and asked if we would hold a garage sale and get rid of it, which we eventually did.

But more interesting was the job we had been offered by a lovely South African family we had met during the show. They owned a 44' catamaran on which they took tourists from Roadtown a few miles out to Norman Island to snorkel in the caves. They were considering selling the boat and the business and wanted some free time to relax and consider their future plans.

And so, for the next few weeks, Joell and I shepherded about forty tourists from the cruise ships that were constantly docking in the harbour, on the one-hour sail across turquoise waters to the caves. There everyone would don masks and flippers that we provided and plunge into the water. We would lead them a hundred yards to the cave and they would splash around inside as I told them about the pirate treasure that had been found there a few years earlier, up on a ridge. Then they'd follow us back to the boat. It was pretty exhausting, keeping track of everyone and making sure no one drowned! With all aboard and accounted for, we'd sail to the next island where there was a funky beachside restaurant for lunch and back to Roadtown in time for them to board their giant floating resort.

Joell and I talked about buying the business and settling in Tortola for a while. We loved the island and had already made friends among the locals. It could be an idyllic life and the business was quite profitable. But as we talked to more people, we became concerned about the government and the corruption that was rife. We learned of a Swiss family who had bought a run down property four years earlier and transformed it with several million dollars into a splendid resort. Someone in the government coveted it and offered them a quarter of what they had put into it. When they refused to sell at that price, the government revoked the visas of their two young children, who were then forced to leave the island. Of course, they had to sell it at a huge loss. This story, combined with the bad attitudes of a lot of the officials gave us cause for major concern and we decided it wouldn't be a good idea...

Meanwhile we waited for bookings from the enthusiastic charter brokers who had said they could keep us booked for the next four months. Nothing happened – no phone calls, no emails, no couples eager to explore the Virgin Islands aboard JoJo. After a month we decided to leave the islands and head to South Carolina, which was our ultimate destination when we had left San Francisco three years earlier.

But it was not the end of our dreams of chartering. Four years later we sold JoJo and bought our lovely 64' trimaran

'Ladyhawke' which we successfully chartered in the San Blas Islands of Panama...

* 'Catamaran Lost At Sea'. 'Everyone Said I Should Write A Book

** 'The Longest Delivery'.'Everyone Said I Should Write A Book'

The Loss of 'Tamarin' :

http://www.deseretnews.com/article/818555/After-the-shipwreck.html?pg=all).

THE OPEN HIGHWAY

There's a mystique associated with truck drivers and the open highway, especially in America. Visions of majestic panoramas, mountains, deserts, tens of thousands of miles with adventure waiting around every curve, over the next hill. From two-lane, leafy quiet back roads in New England to frantic, buzzing ten-lane interstates pulsing with energy through Dallas and Albuquerque and Atlanta.

And the romantic figures that ride them, the last of the American cowboys, whose giant, five hundred horsepower machines conjure up images of freedom, independence and individual ruggedness. These tobacco-chewing, modern-day heroes without whom the economy would grind to a halt; if they stopped driving, supermarket shelves across the country would be empty in less than a week...

We've all seen them – towering above us as they charge down the interstate, or slowly pulling away from a stoplight in town, shifting through their multi-speed transmissions, wrapped up in their own insular world, seventy-two feet long and eight feet wide. Sometimes we are angry with them for taking up so much of the road, for driving slowly through our neighbourhoods, for holding up traffic while they back into seemingly impossible spaces to unload. They are faceless tough men and women, miles from home and their families who they may see one day a week, if they're lucky.

So how romantic is this life, how full of adventure and freedom, how unchained and independent? Joell and I found out when we spent a year as long-distance truck drivers in 2002. After four weeks in truck-driving school* and a month criss-crossing the country with our trainer Derek, we returned to Salt Lake City, home base for C.R.England, the company we would drive for.

79

Their sprawling complex included new and used trucks and repair facilities, rows of trailers and huge buildings that housed, fed and trained hundreds of drivers at a time, some in final training, some tired and haggard old-timers back for license renewals. A vast cafeteria, dormitories, administrative offices and a continuous stream of tractor-trailers, some leaving for all parts of the country and some returning 'home' for maintenance.

This is a half billion dollar-a-year business that started in 1920 and has stayed in the same family ever since. It was one of the first companies to offer refrigerated trailers and was in the forefront of getting fresh produce across the country in the 1950's. They currently provide work for over 7,500 drivers and the work force is constantly changing – there's about a 95% turnover of drivers in the trucking industry, for it is an exhausting, demanding, lonely job.

We passed a few more road tests, were given our credentials and one morning on a brisk, January day with snow on the ground, we were handed the keys to our gleaming red Freightliner truck, which we promptly named Margaret, after the intrepid ocean sailors Hal and Margaret Roth! We met John, our dispatcher, a hugely overweight, roly-poly man who was genuinely pleased to have us on his team. He was responsible for organizing and controlling two hundred drivers from a vast room with dozens of other dispatchers. Using onboard computers and cell phones, his job was to keep the trucks moving in a giant chess game across the country and into Canada. It was a daunting task with emergencies and accidents and schedules going awry every hour. We chatted for a few minutes, dozens of phones ringing and dozens of dispatchers running around working out their trucking problems with the others.

John could tell we were not 'typical truckers' and was delighted to talk for a few minutes. Then he gave us our first assignment.

There was a trailer in the yard, already loaded, that had just come in from L.A. We were to hook up to it and drive it to New Jersey. It needed to be there in three days!

"No worries, John. We'll keep the wheels turning. Talk to you later..."

Joell and I excitedly climbed aboard Margaret and drove up and down the lines of parked trailers, looking for the one with our numbers on it.

"There it is, Jon," called Joell. "I'll jump out and direct you up to it."

I backed under the front of the trailer and heard the 'clunk' as the kingpin engaged. I connected the electric cable and the air line for the trailer brakes and we eased out into the open yard. We were the only truck there at that time, which was just as well, for after pulling straight out, I turned the wheel hard right and there was an awful bang from behind. I quickly climbed down from the cab to discover the trailer king pin was not secured properly and the trailer had slid across the back of the truck and was resting on the frame! This was not a good situation, for the trailer could slide off and fall to the ground; we would have been fired instantly if anyone had seen us.

"Blimey, Joie. I guess I didn't latch it properly. OK, we've got to get it properly hooked up before someone comes along," I said in a bit of a panic. "Here's what we'll do. I'll crank down the landing gear legs and we'll raise the trailer off the truck. Then you'll back up under the trailer and we'll hook it up again. But we've got to be quick."

I grabbed my gloves and started cranking down the legs which support the trailer when it's disconnected. It was freezing cold, but I warmed up quickly. Slowly the legs went down until the

81

trailer was just resting on them. The loaded trailer weighed about thirty tons and if the legs weren't straight, they could buckle and collapse. Because Margaret was almost ninety degrees in relation to the trailer after I had made the tight right turn, I didn't know if this would work. The truck and trailer were designed to be lined up straight to disconnect. I had a vision of my cranking down the legs and the front of the trailer sliding to the left and crashing onto the concrete. That would have brought people running and ignominiously ended our short career as modern-day cowboys.

Now was the test. I slowly turned the geared handle and felt the resistance as the legs took the weight. One more turn and the trailer lifted slightly. The legs made a groaning sound and I could feel the trailer edge to the left an inch. Should I continue cranking? Would the left leg buckle and the whole trailer end up on its nose?

I could stop now and report this mishap. Then they would send a large fork lift and raise the trailer off the truck chassis and straighten everything out with no damage. And Joell and I would be on a Greyhound bus back to Florida... Or, I could continue cranking and there was an even chance I could rectify this myself and no one would know.

But I had to make the decision quickly before another trucker came looking for his trailer.

"OK, Joie, I'm going to keep cranking. Get behind the wheel and move Margaret forward as soon as I tell you."

She quickly climbed into the cab and I could hear her depress the clutch and shift into first gear. I disconnected the two umbilical cords connecting the tractor and trailer and we were ready. Less than five minutes had passed since the start of this debacle, but it felt like an hour!

I took a deep breath and turned the handle. A screeching sound, metal on metal and I thought it would bring people running. I cranked again and felt another slight shift to the left. I watched the landing gear, but it seemed to be holding. Two more turns and the nose of the heavily-laden trailer raised up an inch and the landing gear remained steady.

"Move out, Joie!" I called to my wife and co-driver.

She released the clutch and Margaret moved from under the trailer, which thankfully remained standing. Just then, another trucker drove up, searching for his assigned trailer.

"Hey, y'all need some help?' he drawled.

"No thanks, just re-hooking," I called back, with a friendly, dismissive wave.

He slowly drove off and I breathed a sigh of relief. I guided Joell as she backed the tractor under the trailer and the kingpin firmly attached itself to the fifth-wheel, the hinged round platform that the trailer rests on. I made sure it was properly locked in place, hooked up the lines, climbed behind the wheel and cleared out through the guard gate. Not the most auspicious start to our new job!

In two minutes we were headed south on I-15 and soon turned east onto I-70, through Denver toward Elizabeth, New Jersey, 2,200 miles away. The sky was bright blue, the temperature was just above freezing, the land was covered in thick snow and we started singing "On the Road Again" at the top of our lungs!

As a team, we were expected to 'keep the wheels turning' all the time, stopping only to fuel up and relieve ourselves. Margaret was self-contained, with a snug double bed, microwave, hanging closet and curtains dividing the aft area from the driving cab. In

83

theory, one of us would drive while the other slept in back, hour after hour, day after day, mile after mile. In reality, one would drive a six hour shift while the other would toss and turn in the back, feeling every bump in the road, falling asleep for an hour at a time from sheer exhaustion. Eventually we'd both be too tired to drive and would find a truck stop or rest area or Walmart parking lot and sleep for three or four hours, huddled together in the back, before finding some coffee and doing it all again.

Occasionally it *was* 'romantic', as we'd drive across the vast deserts in Arizona, watching a magnificent scarlet-pink sunset, or see snow-capped mountains in the Rockies. But the majority of over-the-road truck driving consists of thousands of miles of blacktop and white stripes, diesel-smelling truck stops and crowded rest areas where we'd try to sleep with a hundred idling diesel engines as background noise. We rarely listened to the CB radio as it was usually buzzing with southern, truck-driving drawl and was often full of hateful haranguing. On the whole, truckers didn't like blacks or gays or 'four-wheelers' or liberals. If we had the CB on while Joell was driving, there'd usually be lascivious, childish comments as other truckers went by and saw a very pretty redhead behind the wheel.

But we had a good time in our little self-contained world. And we were making serious money – a hard-driving team can make six figures a year, but at a cost to their health and sometimes their sanity! Single drivers were not as fortunate, as government regulations dictated that they could only drive eight hours, then had to rest for eight hours. Without a co-driver, they were limited to how many miles they could legally drive a day and they get paid by the mile. Every driver has to meticulously keep a log book showing how many miles they'd driven each day and where they rested. But there were tricks to get around it and some drivers would drive ten or twelve or fifteen hours at a stretch – there are a lot of doped-up, tired truckers on the road.

And it's a very dangerous job, one of the most dangerous in the country. Around 3500 truck drivers are killed each year, an average of ten a day. The combination of deadlines, vehicles weighing forty tons, exhaustion and arrogance is a recipe for disaster. Throw in the fact that most car drivers have no idea of how difficult it is to maneuver these behemoths, or how long it takes to stop them and every truck is an accident waiting to happen.

Joell and I were pretty conservative drivers and drove very defensively. There were times when we'd be berated over the CB for driving cautiously in poor visibility by other truckers who'd go screaming by in a torrential downpour when the wipers couldn't clear the water fast enough.

Two months into this chapter of our lives, we were heading west on I-40 in Colorado. It was bitter cold on a dark, snowy night. Coming out of the Eisenhower Tunnel, the highest point on the road at 11,100 feet, a blizzard blew in, bringing gusty winds and blinding snow. I downshifted to third low gear and crept down the mountain at ten miles an hour, fiercely concentrating, 60,000 lbs. of cargo pushing us, with Joell rigidly sitting next to me, barely silhouetted by the dim lights of the instrument panel.

"Oh, I don't like this, Jon," she said quietly.

"Neither do I," I replied tensely, gripping the wheel and tapping the brakes. I could feel the trailer wheels sixty feet behind me skid and could vaguely see the back of it slide a little to the left in the side mirror. "I think there's a rest area just ahead. Let's pull over."

It was difficult to see with the thick, swirling snow and Stygian night, but there was a feeble glow ahead, pale yellow overhead from the rest area lights and hundreds of dim red taillights from trucks already parked. I inched my way off the road, past trucks

85

illegally stopped on the entrance to the small rest area.

"Oh, oh – this is not good," I muttered rhetorically.

And it wasn't. There was not an inch of tarmac that wasn't covered by a truck and its trailer. I carefully edged my way out the other side and there were no spaces anywhere.

"We've got to keep going, love. We'll just do it slow and easy and hopefully find a truck stop at the bottom."

It was hell. Not only was it difficult to control the truck, visibility was just a few yards, the wind was buffeting the trailer alarmingly and there were other obstacles to contend with. The snowploughs were doing their best to keep this vital commercial link open and occasionally I'd see their dull yellow spinning lights ahead in the whirling blizzard. I'd follow them, inching along behind until they would stop and I'd need to get around them.

But this was not easy. For coming down the mountain, treacherous enough in good weather, were convoys of trucks-five, ten, fifteen of them-going forty miles an hour, trailers sometimes sliding, throwing waves of snow and muck that covered our windshield. We had the CB on, listening for road and weather reports and the crazy truckers laughed and derided us:

"Hey, England – doancha know how to release yer parkin' brake, haw, haw."

"Yo, England, y'all afraid uv a lil' snow, yuk, yuk?"

Well, yes, we were afraid of losing control of 72 feet of metal and two hundred gallons of diesel fuel and careening off the road or into another vehicle. So we continued to crawl down the slick, slippery interstate at ten miles an hour. The posted speed limit for trucks in perfect weather is 30 mph going down the nine-mile descent. But these cocky, stupid drivers didn't give a damn about anyone else on the road and eventually some of them paid dearly for their arrogance.

After nearly an hour, keeping in a low gear, tapping the brakes, staying in the right lane, we made it to the bottom of the steep 7% grade at the small town of Dillon. I was exhausted, my hands hurt from clenching the wheel, my shoulders ached and my head pounded. Joell was calm and quiet, although later she told me she was afraid, very afraid. So was I.

"Look darling, I don't care how far off the interstate we have to drive, I'm finding somewhere to pull over in Dillon," I said.

"Good, yes, let's get off this road before some nutcase driver slams into us. I'll bet you're beat," replied Joell.

I turned on my right blinker and edged onto the exit ramp. Other truckers had the same idea and both sides of the exit ramp were lined with semi's and occasionally the small, snow-covered hump of a car, engine on and exhaust permeating the air. I drove for half a mile on Hwy 6 and found a gas station with a big lot behind it. There were a few trucks lined up there, and I swung around and pulled up alongside the last one in the line.

I peeled my hands off the steering wheel and slowly, painfully eased off the seat and stood up in the sleeping area. It was three in the morning, cold, blustery, snow pelting down and I had just had one of the most intense driving experiences of my life. I started shaking. Joell helped me into the bed and wrapped warm blankets around me, then lay down next to me. I fell asleep, arms around her, finally calming down, letting the adrenalin disappear...

The next morning was brisk and clear, a piercingly light blue sky with brilliant sunshine bouncing off the snow covered mountains surrounding us and glistening on the nearby lake. The blizzard had blown through, and there were piles of snow drifted around the trucks in the lot. I bundled up and trudged to the convenience store to get us some coffee.

" 'Morning, hell of a night!" I said to the young guy at the counter.

"Yessir, sure was. You with one of the trucks out back?"

"Yep. What's the chance of a plough coming through and getting me out of here?'

"My friend'll be here in an hour or so with his Jeep and he'll clear the snow for you guys. Didja hear about the crash?"

"No, we've been asleep," I replied as Joell came in, clouds of frosty breath preceding her.

"Yeah. Happened a few hours ago a couple of miles west on the interstate."

"Trucks?" I asked, already knowing the answer.

"Yessir, four of them. Real bad, three drivers killed they say. Interstate's closed - probably won't open for a few hours yet."

I looked at Joie and a shiver went through me. It could have been us...

"Well, we'll just go back to our truck and rest up some more. You have a good day."

We slogged back to Margaret which was streaked with road dirt, packed snow in her grill from the night before. We held hands and both of us were thinking the same thing. I patted Margaret fondly on the fender, we climbed aboard and went back to sleep...

Mid-afternoon we woke refreshed, had more coffee and eased Margaret through the ploughed lot back onto Interstate 70, heading west for San Francisco. The road was clear, with piles of snow lining each side where the ploughs had pushed it during and after the blizzard. Traffic moved sedately as we merged on. The CB radio was unusually subdued, with little banter. In five minutes we saw why. Traffic ahead slowed and I switched on my four-way flashers. There were dozens of pulsing blue lights and the road ahead narrowed down to a single lane.

We slowly edged by in silence. Giant ten-wheeled tow trucks had dragged the wreckage to the side, leaving one of the three lanes open for traffic. But to the left were the smoking, blackened crumpled carcasses of four semi's, twisted metal sculptures, grotesque and silent. Three men had died there just a few hours before, leaving families bereft.

I looked at Joie and she looked back at me. We both knew it was most likely one of those convoys barreling heedlessly through the black night, through the blinding blizzard until someone had made a slight mistake, maybe hit his brakes a little too hard, maybe lost control for an instant, but that's all it took...

Sadly, it's not just accidents that kill drivers. A combination of long hours, high stress, poor diet and lack of exercise contribute to some drivers just dying in their sleep at truck stops and rest areas. Sometimes it will be days before it's noticed that a truck has been sitting with no one getting in or out. An inspection will find some poor soul lying in his bed in the cab, eyes staring, body cold...

We did meet some really nice drivers out there, even some intellectual ones. One middle-aged driver had been a teacher, but gave it up for the 'freedom' of the road. Another couple saw themselves as highway pirates and their truck looked like a pirate

89

ship, with skulls on the grill and pirate flags flying from the antennas!

And so, month after month we crisscrossed the country from Maine to Florida, Texas to Washington. We traversed all the forty-eight contiguous states, sometimes having a couple of days off to relax and sightsee. We stopped at Niagara Falls on one trip, parked the rig and walked over into Canada for the day.

Once, inching through a weigh station in Louisiana with a load of Florida frozen orange juice, we were told to pull over for inspection. This was always a pain, just another way for the authorities to hassle drivers and try to separate them from their hard-earned money. A burly officer climbed onto the cab step and leaned in through the window.

"Wayll, whatcher carryin' back they-uh, drahver?' he drawled in a thick southern accent.

"Er, orange juice," I replied.

He said something in French to me, expecting me to stare at him uncomprehendingly. But he was taken aback when I responded in French! His eyebrows went up and he said something else in French. This started a conversation that went on for five minutes. I don't think he'd ever had a trucker who spoke decent French, although his language was sprinkled with patois words!

Eventually he reached in and shook my hand with a big smile on his face.

"OK, vouz avez un bon jour," in a Creole French accent, as he waved us through without checking our load or paperwork.

Our fourth month of driving we received a Gold Award from C.R. England and were written up in their monthly newspaper. Our dispatcher John was very pleased with us as we were rarely late for a pick up or delivery and he could also have an intelligent conversation with us! It was the goal of a lot of drivers to get a dedicated run, which meant they drove the same route over and over. Although it could be monotonous, it enabled drivers to know when they'd be home and they could plan their lives with more regularity.

In July, John provided a run which brought us back to the base at Salt Lake City. There he invited us to lunch in the cafeteria and asked if we'd like a dedicated run! Normally it takes a couple of years with a good driving record to be offered this, so we were quite flattered.

"So, what's the run, John?" I asked.

"L.A. to Hoboken, just outside New York City. The trailers will be loaded when you arrive and they're usually not very heavy."

This was good because the lighter the load, the better fuel mileage and the more money in our pockets!

"OK, what's the running schedule?" I asked.

"Well, it's 2800 miles and you'll have three days out, turnaround, three days back then one day off. Then you do it again," he replied looking at us steadily.

"Wow, that's quite a schedule," I said, looking at Joie. "What's the pay?"

My eyebrows shot up when he told us.

"Why don't you finish lunch and talk about it. I've got to get back upstairs. This is a good run, guys. Let me know ASAP."

We were pleased that John had offered the run to us and the guaranteed weekly pay was definitely an enticement. The past few months we never knew how much money we would make each week, as it depended on how many miles we were given. Sometimes we'd drive three thousand miles a week, sometimes half that. Now we'd be covering over fifty five hundred miles each week and could plan our lives a little more. But we both knew it would be demanding, with little time to rest.

"Here's my thought, love. Why don't we take the run and see how it turns out. If we can't handle it, we can give it back to John and do what we were doing before."

"Yes, that's what I was thinking. OK, let's do it!"

John was happy with our decision and the next day gave us a trailer to haul out to L.A., where we would pick up our first load for Hoboken. We found the place in an industrial section of Hawthorne, south of L.A. There was our trailer and I backed up, connected and cranked up the landing gear. By now I had a pretty good idea of the loaded weight of a trailer after pulling just a few yards. This one felt almost empty which meant more speed up gradients and higher overall fuel mileage.

We fought the morning rush hour traffic and within two hours were barreling down I-10 leaving the smog and hubbub of L.A. behind, heading toward Las Vegas. Passing through Sin City, we switched driving and Joell drove through the night up Highway 15. The next two days we drove and drove, stopping one night in a big restaurant parking lot at the 'Piggy Palace' for three hours somewhere in Iowa. Our route took us over the Rockies, across the midwest, skirting Chicago, through beautiful Pennsylvania and to Hoboken. We did it in sixty-eight hours averaging 42 mph, quite respectable!

We unhooked the trailer, slept deeply for five hours until our return trailer was ready. And back we went, retracing our route. We arrived in L.A. three days later, buzzed and tired. C.R.England had a satellite base nearby and we unhooked the trailer and 'bobtailed' over there. We took a shower and crashed for ten hours straight. The next day, back to Hawthorne and we did it again...and again...and again. By the time we had completed the 5600 mile round trip sixteen times, we were getting burned out!

Early in November we were just outside of L.A., heading to Hawthorne after a cold trip across the country, with snow in the Rockies. For a few days we had discussed ending this chapter of our lives. We had little chance for exercise and were both out-of-shape and overweight. We had tried to eat healthy, but it was very difficult. And the nightmare of the trip down the Rockies a few months before was always in the back of our minds. The decision to quit was made for us in the morning rush hour crush.

We had been driving in the left lane and a sign came up that said 'No Trucks in Left Lane'. I put on my blinker, but we were hemmed in and couldn't move over. I tried but with no luck. After two minutes I heard a siren and looking in my mirror saw a Highway Patrol cop with his lights flashing right behind me. Now the cars on the right opened up and let me slide across to the shoulder, the cop right on my bumper.

"License, insurance and log book," he said brusquely.

"Sure, no problem. Look, I was trying to get into the right lane, but no one would let me in and I didn't want to do anything that might cause an accident," I said politely.

He sneered at me and said, "Too bad, you can tell the judge. Stay in your truck, driver."

What a nasty cop. Joell and I looked at each other.

"You know, love. I'm fed up with this. These bloody cops all across the country look for truckers to hassle and give them big tickets all the time. I think this is a message from the universe.

93

That's it. We quit."

Ten minutes later, this soulless officer gave me a $250 ticket, smirked and waved us on. We drove to Hawthorne and detached the trailer. I called John and told him sorry, we quit. He was disappointed, but this happened all the time in the trucking industry.

We drove back to Salt Lake City and turned Margaret over to the company, paying a small fee for terminating the lease early. In ten months, we had put over 130,000 miles on our trusty, gleaming Freightliner and she had rewarded us with exemplary service.

We rented a one way car, loaded it with our personal belongings and drove to my brother Grant's home near San Francisco. We stayed for two months, then bought a ten year old VW Vanagon, which we named Vanna White (yes, we're sometimes a bit sentimental about our numerous vehicles!) and drove her to 'JoJo', our 32' cruising catamaran which had been in storage on the hard in central Florida. All the way across the country, we gave wide berth to and treated with respect each semi that we passed or passed us. For all we knew, the person driving it down the road could have just come out of truck-driving school, be near exhaustion or doped up on amphetamines...and possibly a combination of all three...

* 'Truck Driving School', 'Everyone Said I Should Write A Book'

BOATS, BIKES AND AUTOMOBILES

(Joell suggested I share my love affair with cars. Initially I thought I would write a couple of pages, but it has morphed into the longest story I've written! Within the following pages are short stories surrounding some of the cars, motorcycles and boats I've owned over the years).

My parents told me that the first words I uttered were "cah-cah". They assumed because of my very early fascination with toy cars, that I was referring to vehicles, rather than manure! Ever since I can remember, I've been enamoured of cars. By the time I was about seven, I could identify all the cars on the roads in London – as this was in the fifties, there wasn't the huge, gridlock-forming number of look-alike econo-boxes that there are today.

I remember the stately Bentley, the Humber, the Armstrong-Siddely and Wolseley. The various Austins and Morrises, Riley, Vauxhall, MG's and Triumphs, the XK 120 and 150 Jaguars. The introduction of the Mini in 1959 that paved the way for all the small cars of today.

My father, an American, shipped his huge 1949 Oldsmobile 98 convertible to London in 1950 when he married my mother and drove it for many years - it caused a stir wherever we drove! Pale blue with a dark blue soft top and acres of chrome, it stood out amongst the dark, somber cars the English were producing in those days. I remember people stopping, staring and pointing one day as we drove down Piccadilly and Dad activated the windscreen washers – no one had seen them before!

When he would come home from visits to family in Philadelphia, my father would always have a model hot rod kit for me to build; my room was full of them. In 1963 the British Drag Racing Association was formed and an ersatz drag race was held at the venerable Brighton Speed Trials fifty miles south of London. A friend and I took the train down there and we were wide-eyed at the motley and rather pathetic collection of British 'dragsters'. There was a supercharged Allard, several new E-type Jags and a few home-built cars, based on the American rail dragster.

But the hit of the day was a real dragster shipped over from the U.S., complete with its champion owner/driver, Mickey Thompson. I knew about him from reading American Hot Rod magazines, which my family in the U.S. sent me. I was a shy twelve-year old, very British, quite reserved. I found myself standing behind him in line at the snack bar. When he gave his order, he was told the cost was two and thruh'pence. He turned around to me with a puzzled look on his face and said,

"Hey kid, whad she say? Two an' whaht? Kin you pick out the right amount for me, son?" as he thrust his palm toward me, full of different sized English coins.

"Er, yes, certainly, Mr. Mickey Thompson." I stammered back, picking out a florin and a threepenny bit. He thanked me, shook my hand and walked off with his coffee and sandwich. The first 'famous' person I met...

When the family moved to Philadelphia several years later, I got my driving permit at age seventeen. Dad bought a second car, a huge 1957 Plymouth two-door, with giant tail fins and a ton of chrome. It was christened the 'Purple Monster' and in it I learned to do doughnuts in the snow and burn through rear tyres peeling rubber! That summer a friend of mine from London came to spend a few weeks at our new home in Elkins Park, a suburb of Philadelphia. I asked Dad to let Roger and me take the Purple Monster to Atco, N.J. one Saturday evening to watch the dragsters – yes, he said, but we had to be home by midnight.

This was a huge adventure for two proper English teenagers and we were enthralled by the smell and the smoke and the speed.

After an hour of sitting in the bleachers watching fire-belching race cars zoom down the track, I suggested to Roger that we see if we could get down there, next to where the cars were starting their quarter-mile run.

" 'Ow're you going to do that, then?" he asked.

"Come on Roger, I have an idea."

Reluctantly, he followed me to the announcers' booth in a small two-storey building next to the track. As I started to climb the outside stairs, he held back.

"You can't go up there, Jon," he protested.

"Why not, the worst that can happen is they'll tell us to leave. Don't say anything, just nod and agree with me. OK?"

He looked pretty miserable, but followed me up. Inside were three men, one of them sitting at a table with a panoramic view of the track and the bleachers – there must have been a couple of thousand spectators there that night. The man at the table had a sheaf of papers in front of him and was announcing the next race, which boomed over the loudspeakers to the crowd below. One of the others turned and asked me what we were doing here...

"Ectually," I replied in my finest British accent. "Ectually, we're from the British Drag Racing Association and we're visiting drag strips in the area for a story in our magazine," I brazenly fibbed.

Roger became increasingly uncomfortable and tried to hide behind me. I didn't blame him as here were these two spotty teenagers without any press credentials, presenting themselves as reporters – he was mortified!

'Ya doan say! Hey Bill, these guys are from Engiland and they're doin' a story 'bout drag racing here. Whaddya think of that!"

97

Bill, the announcer, called us over and shook hands with us both, Roger shuffling from foot to foot.

"Well, that's mighty interesting. What type of cars they race over there?"

"Er, Allards, some rails and there's a now a bunch of modified English saloon cars, but they're not nearly as fast as the cars here," I replied, hoping we had got away with my charade.

"So, you boys want to go down on the track, hear these monsters off the line?"

"Well, yes, please, Bill – that would be super!" said I, not believing our luck!

And so we were led into the pits and to the 'Christmas Tree', the series of lights that start the race. I was smiling, in earnest conversation with Tom who was escorting us there. Roger was grim and silent, as he shuffled along behind, expecting our cover to be blown and to be thrown in jail!

Our friend left us there after talking to an official who came over and told us where we could stand. Two dragsters drove slowly to the starting line, snorting and yapping, flames coming out of their exhaust stacks. The cars peeled rubber for a few feet, warming up their tyres to get a better grip. It was so loud, so powerful, so full of energy. Darkness had set in, the track was lit with huge lights but the flames from the dragsters outshone them in a brilliant explosion of high-test fuel, as they shot down the track like bullets from a gun. The smell of the burning rubber, the sound of hundreds of horsepower unleashed, the roar from the crowd was very heady!

After they had made their run, while there was a few minutes to wait until the next two cars came up, it was the announcers job to keep the crowd informed and engaged.

"Lay-dies and gen'lmen, boys and girls!" he called over the booming loudspeakers."We're real privileged this evenin' to have two young fellers here from the British Drag Racing Association in Engiland. They're doin' a story 'bout real dragsters here in the U.S.A. Give 'em a big round of applause, please – there they are, down by the 'Christmas tree'!"

A spotlight was turned on Roger and me and thousands of spectators clapped and whistled. It was the most embarrassing moment of my life and Roger tried to sink into the ground! We politely waved back and hoped there wasn't a real representative of the BDRA in the stands...

For an hour we stood there, next to the cars, chatting with drivers who came over to shake our hands. Our ears were shattered each time two cars let out their clutches, just feet from us – we also smelled of burning rubber! And then at ten o'clock I said to Roger that we needed to get out of there and back home before my 'pumpkin' driving permit expired at midnight. We edged ourselves away and made a beeline for the parking lot, jumped in the Purple Monster and sped out of there before anyone could see us or ask any questions...

Over the next few months, my interest in cars changed and I found a greater appreciation for the quality and diversity of European sports cars. I stopped reading 'Hot Rod' magazine and subscribed to 'Motor Sport', a fabulous British monthly. I saved up my money to buy my first car and sent it to my Uncle Lewis in London. I asked him to buy me a 1940's MGTC and ship it to Philadelphia. He knew nothing about cars, was busy growing his restaurant business and his family, but he located one, a 1946 model and somehow got it to the docks. The car cost $600 and another $200 to ship from England to Philadelphia. I couldn't believe it when I saw the classic car at the docks - British Racing Green, with a red grill and tall 19" wire wheels. I fell in love with my first car and it started a love affair with vintage cars that continues to this day. I drove it that summer all over Bucks County and to the Jersey shore. It wasn't fast, but it was definitely fun and everybody smiled and waved.

After I sold that car – it just wasn't a good idea to drive it to Temple University and park it in the questionable neighbourhood – I had a series of British cars over the years, including an MGA and five MGB's, Triumph TR3, TR4 and TR6. A swooping red Jaguar XK 120, a nightmare of a car – but breathtakingly beautiful. A glorious 1963 Morgan +4 four-seater, three Sunbeam Alpines, Mini-Coopers, three Rovers (including the delightful 2000TC), a ponderous, two-tone 1949 Bentley MkVI, which I bought in London and shipped to San Francisco in the 1980's. That was a fun car to drive around the Bay area. Cops would always stop traffic for me, I never had a problem getting the best parking spot at a restaurant and my Dad once commented, sitting beside me in the high, stately car:

"Now I understand why royalty drive Rolls and Bentleys – you really do look down on other people!"

I derived huge pleasure from my Bugatti replica which I owned for fifteen years and was, for many of them, my only car. It didn't look like a typical fibreglass replica. I paid a lot of attention to detail, down to the turned-aluminium dashboard, four-spoke steering wheel and custom 72-spoke wire wheels, originally built for an early Lamborghini. One day I drove it to the Briggs Cunningham Auto Museum in Costa Mesa, CA. The curator came running out when I parked and asked me if I was crazy driving a 1927 Type 35 Bugatti on the streets. It took him a minute to realize it wasn't real! I drove that car cross-country-twice – between South Carolina and San Francisco, epic journeys each. I called it my 'happy car', because it always made people grin and wave.

There was the unusual 1933 Frazer Nash TT Replica which I completely restored when Joie and I lived in Sonoma in 2007. I participated in several parades in that lovely car and got to race it at Sears Point Raceway.

There have been many more over the past fifty years, including a venerable 1947 Dodge that I drove around Philly delivering pizzas when I was in college! Five Jaguars, four VW buses, BMW's, a 1963 Maserati 3500. Fiats, a rare Matra, a cherry red Porsche 356 convertible, a Renault 17 Gordini, two Volvo convertibles, two Miatas and two hybrids, one of our current cars being a 2000 Honda Insight, the funny looking two-seater that heralded the beginning of the hybrid era in the U.S. At last count, I came up with sixty-eight cars, although I might have missed a couple!

I sat down with Joell to figure out how many cars the two of us have owned together in the seventeen years we've been married. Remembering that we've spent years cruising on various sailboats, when we didn't own a car, we came up with twenty-nine, including three pick-up trucks, five Volvos, two BMW's, a lovely Mercedes station wagon, a Gazelle, a second Bugatti replica, a Daewoo Musso SUV that we bought in Panama, and many others! And the interesting thing is that I rarely lose money on the cars, in fact, we usually make a few bucks!

I bought my first motorcycle in 1969, in January, in Philadelphia, with snow on the ground. I was living at my parent's house and Dad told me if I bought a motorcycle, I would have to move out. I was very rebellious in those days, a suburban hippie who thought he knew everything. Through an ad posted on the bulletin board at Temple University, I met a tall, gangly man named Thomas Firth Jones who was selling a 1957 Zundapp 250 dirt bike.

From this chance meeting, a friendship developed that spanned many years, involved numerous hair-raising adventures and had a powerful impact on my life. Tom became a mentor to me, introduced me to catamarans, was opinionated, sometimes imperious, but always a friend. Tom, his wife Carol and I spent hours riding dirt bikes in the cranberry patches in New Jersey and experienced many sailing adventures, including sailing the Atlantic on his home-built 27' catamaran.

It was freezing cold, I wore my WWII leather flying jacket and a psychedelically painted crash helmet, when I rode the bike up the path to my parent's front door. I rang the doorbell and revved the engine – they were not impressed and closed the door on me! Shortly after that I rented an apartment in the Germantown section of Philadelphia, an area where many students at Temple University lived. The neighbourhood was famous for its great parties and I threw many at our place.

Riding the Zundapp to college each day in the snow and rain was a challenge to say the least and I soon tired of it – that's when I sold it and Tom gave me his huge, four-door 1947 Dodge. Driving down Broad Street to college every day, I would cram half a dozen hitchhikers inside. It was always a great way to start the day, sort of like Sean Penn stumbling out of the VW bus at Ridgemont High!

Over the next few years I owned a series of British bikes, three Triumphs including a 650 Bonneville, two BSA's, and, when I moved to Santa Monica in 1977, a Norton 750 Commando. I soon discovered that riding the L.A. freeways on a motorbike was just plain dangerous and sold it!

For a while in college I worked part-time for an auto wholesaler named Dick Restifo. He'd buy trade-ins and cars at auction, always foreign cars. Then he'd send three or four of us out to pick them up and drive them back to his place in Philadelphia. Sometimes it was to the Jersey shore, sometimes to New York, once to Virginia. It was always fun and occasionally damn scary! We never knew what we'd be driving - lots of MG's and Austin Healeys. Porsche's, Opel GT's, Triumphs, Jags. Sometimes they'd run great and we'd race back to Philly. A number of times they'd break down and we'd try to jury rig a clutch, or limp back with minimal brakes.

But there was one delivery drive that still stands out forty-four years after it happened - I consider it one of my major driving adventures. My mother was leaving on the 9:00 pm flight from Philadelphia to London to see her parents and she really wanted me to be at the airport with the rest of our family when she left. I promised her I'd be there...

When I showed up for work at Dick's that morning, I was the only one there.

"I sent the others off to pick up some cars a few minutes ago, Jon. I've got a great trip for you, but you'll have to hurry. You're going to fly to Butler, near Pittsburgh and drive back a practically new Mercedes Benz 350SL – it's about three hundred miles. I've got a cab ready to take you to the airport and promise me you'll drive it carefully and don't put a scratch on it, OK!"

"Oh, right, Dick. This'll be a fun trip. Can I keep the car overnight if I get delayed?"

"Yes, I don't expect you to be back today. Off you go and drive that car carefully..."

I caught a late-morning flight to Pittsburgh and then a bus up to Butler and a cab to the car dealership where Dick had bought the Mercedes sight unseen. It was around 1:30 pm when I arrived and I expected to jump in the car and make it to Philly airport in plenty of time. But the car wasn't ready – a mechanic was playing around under the bonnet and as time wore on, I got more uptight.

103

Even though the drive was mostly turnpike with a 65 mph speed limit back then, I'd still need to allow around six hours to get back and then through Philadelphia to the airport south of the city, in order to meet the family at eight o'clock. So, I needed to leave immediately.

In spite of my urgings, which fell on deaf ears, the afternoon wore on. At 3:30 pm, I called Mum and told her I was over three hundred miles away and probably wouldn't see her at the airport, but I'd try. She told me not to worry and certainly she wouldn't expect me now...

Finally, at 4:00 pm, the beautiful sports car was ready to go. They'd just been introduced and this was the first one I'd seen – and now I had an epic drive in front of me. Today, as I recall this, it makes me feel that all those years ago, I was the precursor to Jeremy Clarkson, of the hit British TV show 'Top Gear'! I was determined to be at the airport to see Mum off. I climbed into the two-seater and adjusted the comfortable leather seat way back. I took three joints out of my pocket and laid them on the console.

I shifted into 'Drive' and carefully maneuvered out of the car dealership. And then I turned onto Route 8 and put my foot down. I passed every car on that eleven mile stretch until I made it to the Pennsylvania Turnpike. I took my ticket, tightened my seat belt, had a hit and stomped on the accelerator - the V8 made a glorious rumbling whine and in less than thirty seconds I was doing over 100 mph! In the left lane, my fingers flicking the high beams to get slower cars out of my way, I kept the gas pedal to the floor. At 125 mph, I backed off the throttle and held it there. Occasionally, when a car was in my way, I'd obnoxiously blast him with the air horns and he'd scuttle over to the right. I was focused, seat back, both arms straight out, as was the fashion for high-speed driving back then.

Jethro Tull blasted from the Bosch cassette player, then the

Allman Brothers, the Stones - I always carried good music with me when I was working. And still I drove fast, 100 mph, 110, 125. I kept my eyes peeled for cops getting on or off the turnpike. Once, oncoming cars were flashing their lights and I trod on the brakes, slowing down to 70 as I flew past a cop on the side of the road with a radar gun aimed at me. I kept looking in my rear-view mirror, but apparently I had slowed down just in time!

At Carlisle, outside Harrisburg, I stopped for gas, as I was burning through it at this speed. It was now six o'clock and according to the trip odometer, I had covered 227 miles, since leaving Butler two hours before. A quick gulp of coffee and I zoomed out of the gas station and squealed back onto the turnpike. Up to 125 mph and holding it, I crested a hill ten miles down the road and my stomach dropped – the rest of my body tightened!

Sitting in the wide median strip were two black and tan highway patrol cars, side-by-side, facing opposite directions. By the time I hit the brakes and slowed the car down I was already past them, doing well over 100 mph! I lowered the electric window and threw the remaining two joints out. I figured I'd have flashing red lights in my rear view mirror in about two minutes...

But they never came. I don't know if they were too busy talking to each other, or if their heads were down or if they even had their radar on – I'll never know why they didn't both come screaming after me, but they didn't...one specific muscle relaxed!

I kept watching in my mirror, and when they were out of sight, both still sitting in the median, I stuck my foot into it and took off. By seven o'clock, I was just west of Morgantown and had another sixty miles to go. Leaving the turnpike at Phoenixville, I decided to take the shortest road and hopefully it wouldn't have too much traffic. But it did, late rush-hour traffic and my speed dropped to 35 – had my pulse-racing, intense, marvelous, mad drive been in vain – would I miss seeing Mum off? Then, onto a four-lane highway, and headlights on, high beams flashing, I shot down the road, blowing my horn when necessary. Ahead was I-95 and I squealed around the on-ramp and moved to the left lane, putting my foot down. The clock on the dashboard indicated 7:55 as I screamed into the airport, searching for the British Airways departure terminal.

There it was and there was my family, standing outside. In a screech of brakes, the yellow sports car skidded to a stop right in front of them; they all gaped, wide-mouthed! I leaped out of the car, my whole body shaking from the intensity of the past four hours. But I had made it and hugs all around as Mum headed for her gate. The only sound I could hear as my sister Louise joined me for the drive home, was the loud ticking of hot metal as the car sat there, almost panting...

The fastest I've ever driven was just over 140 mph in a 1965 Aston Martin DB5, the car made famous in the early James Bond movies. A friend of mine in the auto business, Donnie had just bought a used one for the then-princely sum of $3500! He was going to the 1969 U.S. Grand Prix at Watkins Glen, N.Y. and asked me if I wanted to join him. That was a no-brainer and on October 2nd we sped along I-476 north. Nothing passed us and we overtook everyone, a glorious red British thoroughbred thundering up the road!

Donnie had reserved a hotel room and after we checked in, we drove over to the track. There were lots of admiring looks at the car and for a little while, I got to experience how celebrities must feel! I ran into a friend from college and he was staying at the same hotel. That evening, Donnie was tired and went to bed early. I asked him if I could have the keys to drive into town. He nonchalantly said yes and threw them to me. I was almost trembling with excitement. I knocked on Fred's door and asked if he wanted to go into town in the DB5. Another no-brainer and we excitedly slid onto the comfortable leather bucket seats and I started it up. It still gives me goose bumps remembering the sound of that glorious six-cylinder engine burbling through the twin exhausts...

"So Fred, you want to go into town and get a drink...or see what this car can do?"

Silly question, as we headed out of town on Route 14 north. We drove for about twenty minutes, moving pretty fast until we hit highway 5 in Geneva. I turned left and ambled through the town until we emerged onto the open road. Turning on the high beams, I saw a long straight stretch ahead, with no cars.

"Hold on Fred – let's see what this can do!" as I tromped on the accelerator in second gear.

Up to the red-line on the tach and into third, then fourth, then fifth, as the speedo climbed past 125 mph. Fred was holding on tight and I was in heaven. I kept my right foot hard on the gas as the car hurtled through the night. 130, 135, the speed was climbing, but the tachometer was nearing the red line. At 5800 rpm, I couldn't get any more out of it. The noise inside the car was very loud, the front end was very light and it was time to back off. I glimpsed at the speedo and for a second the needle hovered just over 140 mph.

I knew I was creating a life memory and savoured the exhilarating moment. Then double-clutch downshift to fourth, then third, tapped the brakes and we were doing 75. Both Fred and I let out a big sigh. He was shaking a little and so was I. There were quicker cars out there, some with higher top speeds, but I doubt if they could match the sheer joy of being in control of this magnificent piece of British engineering.

We drove back to Watkins Glen more sedately and had a beer. I crept into our room and put the keys on the dresser. Donnie was snoring and to this day, doesn't know how much fun his car was that night...

There have been many other driving adventures over the years, but none stand out like those two...

In 1973, I was hired to sell cars at a new dealership in Collegeville, north of Philadelphia. It was about thirty miles along twisting country roads from New Hope, where I was living. It was a natural for me, because the dealership, 'The Great Britains', sold Jaguar, MG, Triumph, Lotus, and Land Rover makes - this was when a new E-type sold for $5,000! I enjoyed the job very much, although the owner got frustrated with me all the time because I refused to wear a tie! One of the perks was that I was allowed to pick whatever car I wanted to drive home each night as my 'demo'. Sometimes it was an E-type, or a TR6 or a Lotus Elan. The manager, Bill Hartmann lived near me and many a night we would race home down the two-lane roads, with the tops down, shifting hard through the gears, squealing around corners, hot on each others' tail...

After a few months I became restless – I missed my traveling adventures. Sitting at my desk on a slow afternoon, I wondered if it was possible to buy a sailboat and sail around the world, taking my home with me. I went to a local store and bought a copy of 'Rudder' magazine and read everything in it. It did seem possible, there were a few people doing it, but nowhere near the huge numbers of cruisers today. I called my friend and mentor, Tom Jones and asked if he knew anything about sailboats?

"Well, yes I do, Jon. I'm building a catamaran in my living room. Why don't you come down on Sunday and I'll show you."

Knowing that Tom was a man of many interests and talents, this didn't surprise me at all. I drove down to his small row house in Manayunk, a blue-collar section northwest of Philadelphia. As I walked through the front door straight into his living room, I had to be careful not to kick over cans of glue and paint. Sitting on trestles in the middle of the small room, one end touching the window, the other six inches from the wall was a thin hull, one half of a catamaran!

"Bloody hell, Tom! You weren't kidding. Tell me about this..."

And then over a beer, Tom told me that he had been sailing since he was a lad. He also told me that he came from a very wealthy Main Line Philadelphia family, but had turned his back on them as a teenager and had created his own life as a journeyman carpenter.

"Well, what you see here is the first hull of a 23' catamaran designed by a somewhat eccentric pioneer designer name of Jim Wharram, from England. He designed and built a simple catamaran in the mid-fifties and in spite of dire warnings from 'traditional' sailors, sailed it across the Atlantic to the Caribbean with two women. Then they built a bigger 40' version and sailed it back to England. Since then he's been selling plans for different sizes of his boats from 23-51'.

"Wow- that's pretty cool!" I said, hunching down to take a look under the upside-down hull.

"Yes, once this hull's finished, I'll remove the living room window, carry it through (it'll just fit!) and take it down to the seaplane base south of the airport. Then I'll build the matching hull here, do the same and then attach it with a simple open deck."

"So, it's just two hulls with an open deck in the middle and minimal accommodations in the two hulls, right?"

"Yes, that's right, very basic, but very seaworthy. Here's his design book, you can borrow it."

That is how my interest and appreciation for catamarans began. I searched the libraries for any information I could find about catamarans and cruising. There wasn't much available back then, unlike today.

A few weeks later I drove to Florida with my friend Dennis and took a week-long sailing course. I fell in love with the way the wind interacted with the sails and was amazed that a boat can use the wind to 'pull' it along, rather than just pushing it. I quickly mastered the concepts and at the end of the week was known as 'Speedy Gonzalez' as I out-sailed everyone in the class!

Two months later I helped Tom take the second hull out through his row house window and put the boat together on the shore of the Delaware River. The little white and red catamaran was christened 'Two Rabbits' and I enjoyed many wonderful days sailing with Tom and Carol. They eventually went on to make an epic voyage, sailing this little engineless boat across the Atlantic to Africa and back! In 1979, I joined them in the Azores in the middle of the Atlantic Ocean on their slightly larger 27' Wharram catamaran, Vireo. This boat also had no electronics or creature comforts. There was no engine and no battery. Running lights were battery powered and oars were used to get in and out of harbours. I sailed with them to Portugal, a not uneventful passage...

Over the next few years I grabbed every opportunity I could to crew on different boats. During my time at law school in England, I lived aboard a racing 38' Wharram down in Devon for the summer. I spent some time hanging out with Jim Wharram and his 'harem' of six women who were designing and building more boats. He had an international following and thousands of his plans have been sold over the past fifty years. His designs are sailing all over the world today and he is universally recognized as one of the pioneers of the modern multihull movement. After my year in law school, in 1976, I worked as first mate on a 71' ketch in the Mediterranean and some of my adventures aboard her are told in my second book.

When I moved to Santa Monica in 1977, I bought my first boat. She was a converted WWII lifeboat made of plywood. I found her on a mooring in Redondo Beach Harbour and bought her for $500! I sailed her a few times out of the breakwater into the Pacific Ocean, looking back on it a foolhardy thing to do. This was confirmed when one Sunday, I went down to the harbour and she wasn't floating on her mooring. All I could see was about six feet of mast sticking up out of the water – she had quietly sunk!

Two years later, I moved up to Marin county, just north of San Francisco and bought a 41' Wharram catamaran. I lived in a little-known area called Santa Venetia, where there was a tributary of San Francisco Bay. I built a sturdy dock and tied my boat 'Different Drummer' to it at the end of the garden – it was idyllic...

It became known among my friends that if you were at the boat by 10:00 a.m. any Sunday, you could come sailing on the Bay. I never knew who would show up, but there were usually ten, fifteen, twenty people, sometimes kids and dogs! We'd sail down the creek, past China Camp and south to the Bay. Then a glorious romp on the Bay, with the large, open deck catamaran easily sailing past all the monohulls with the typical 20-30 knot winds blowing.

One particular Sunday morning, a windy, blue-sky, pretty San Francisco summer day, 'Different Drummer' left her dock with seventeen adults, three kids and a dog aboard and by one o'clock was tacking down Raccoon Straights, heading for Sausalito. There were scores of boats enjoying the water, heeling over, a

111

ballet of white, catching the strong winds blowing through the Golden Gate. As we headed from Sausalito toward the City on a beam reach, we could see a yacht race taking place ahead of us off Crissy Field. The wind gathered strength coming under the famous bridge and so did 'Drummer'. As I turned left and sailed past the shore, the wind was over our port quarter and we just screamed! The log showed 13 knots and, because it was a catamaran, it didn't heel over, but sailed 'flat'.

Everyone aboard was having a great time and I had a big smile on my face as I kept her on course. People were standing on deck drinking beer, some holding onto the shrouds, some drinking a glass of wine without spilling a drop! Three friends were laying on the trampoline nets at the bow, squealing with delight as a dollop of water splashed up from the hissing bow wave. The dog barked at every boat we sailed past...

Three hundred yards ahead and just to our right were half a dozen IOR race boats, monohulls about 40' long, heeled over, each one with seven or eight crew sitting on the windward side, feet dangling over, using their body weight to help the boat stay more level. Because the boats were monohulls, they have a theoretical top speed based on their waterline length. They were doing all they could to get another half a knot out of their quarter-million dollar boats! Catamarans don't have that restriction and some can go faster than the wind blows...

It must have been quite a sight from Marina Green where people were flying kites and having picnics, watching all the boats dancing across the Bay. Here right in front of them, were six serious boats, heeled over doing nine knots, obviously racing, each trying to 'steal' the others' wind. How exciting, how thrilling! But wait – what's that behind them? A strange looking sailboat with two hulls (there were only a handful of multihulled boats on the Bay back then) - a catamaran. And it's full of people and kids walking around on the deck, smiling and drinking, standing up! And it's going very fast, faster than the racing boats!

And we were, the sails drawing perfectly, rooster tails behind the twin rudders, the wind blowing over 25 knots, our boat speed steady at 13. To the chagrin of the racers, this home-built, $20,000 cruiser sailed right past them, on their leeward side, just off Marina Green. As we passed each racer, everyone on board 'Different Drummer' raised their beer or wine in their direction and gave a huge cheer! And so did the hundreds of people on the shore!

It was one of those special times that you re-live again and again. But the racers didn't like it and weren't amused! It took us about five minutes to catch up to the leader and sail right past him, our on board dog barking furiously at them! What a glorious day for multihulls, but I feared this kind of brazen 'one-upmanship' would further anger the 'traditional' sailors who saw these 'new-fangled' boats as threats to the status quo. Now, in the 21st century, I have been exonerated, as millions watched the America's Cup race between state-of-the-art multihulls in the same area I had obliterated those slow, single-hulled racers thirty-three years earlier!

If they had read the history books, they would have learned that catamarans similar to the simple design of my Wharram 'Narai', have been sailing the oceans for thousands of years. In fact, they were the boat of choice for the intrepid sailors who colonized the Pacific Islands. Single hulled ships with *internal* ballast were what European voyagers used to 'discover' the world. It was only 150 years ago that the modern concept of moving internal ballast to outside and under the boat by using a keel was introduced. So, the belief that modern sailboats using external ballast are 'traditional' is just not true!

Catamarans are traditional; 'traditional' monohulls are actually fairly recent inventions and those who sail them are taking their lives into their hands! Oh yes, one more thing – get a hole in a monohull, it'll sink like a stone, as almost half its weight is ballast, usually lead. Hole a catamaran or trimaran, it will still float, though it may be a bit wet inside. Having owned all three, my boat of choice has at least two hulls...

Anyway, I'll leave that topic now – I've had hundreds of conversations (sometimes heated!) about this in sailor's bars, on beaches and in boat cockpits. My philosophy is that it doesn't matter whether you sail a single, double or triple hulled boat – as long as you're 'out there, doing it'...

The eighties were very good to me financially and I was traveling for most of the decade as 'The Time Traveler' and then with the SR2 simulator. I crewed on other people's boats whenever I could. When I sold the simulator business in 1989, I bought a 41' Searunner trimaran, named her 'Imagine...' and spent three years sailing the Caribbean islands down to Venezuela and back. After I was towed back to Hilton Head in S.C. when the engine in 'Imagine' blew up*, I bought a brand new, turbocharged parasailing boat and for two seasons I made a ton of money 'flying' tourists over Port Royal Sound.

I sold Imagine to my friend Richard Johnson and bought a Gemini 3000 catamaran on which I lived for two years. It was a perfect time in my life, living on my comfortable boat in pretty Skull Creek Marina, overseeing my two captains and crew running my parasail business and driving the Bugatti all over the island. In the fall when the season was over, I'd take 'Duet', the Gemini, cruising for a few months.

The first winter, in 1992, I sailed her to Belize and Guatemala. One day, early in the trip with my friend Chuck aboard, we were motoring across the Okeechobee Waterway in Florida, a sparsely populated route which connects the east and west coasts of the state between Stuart and Ft. Myers. Duet was powered by a 35 hp Mercury outboard and about two in the afternoon, in the middle of nowhere, the engine spluttered and died. We couldn't get it started, so I raised the sails and took advantage of the slight breeze to keep us inching along the river.

As we rounded a bend a hundred yards up, we couldn't believe our eyes! In the middle of nowhere, no town nearby, on the south side of the narrow river was a tiny marina with an old wooden dock in front. A small building with a rusty tin roof sat back from the dock. There were half a dozen boats in various states of repair in the water and a couple of dozen on trailers behind the building.

But what immediately caught our attention was an old advertising sign hanging under the porch of the building. It said, in large, rust-streaked letters 'Mercury Outboard Sales and Repairs'. We looked at each other with big grins as I sailed up to the dock. What were the chances of my engine conking out practically in front of a small repair shop in the middle of nowhere that specialized in Mercury – not Johnson or Evinrude, but Mercury? The Law of Attraction at work, long before I was cognizant of it...

After sailing through the Keys, we left Key West for the Dry Tortugas, seventy miles away. With the speed of the catamaran it shouldn't have been more than a ten-hour sail. Halfway there the wind picked up and within an hour was blowing 25 knots from the north. The boat handled it well and we were enjoying ourselves. The waves were about three feet, quite choppy. All of a sudden the boat was steering strangely – I had to use much more pressure on the wheel to keep the boat on course.

Each hull had a separate lifting wooden rudder that dropped down into a metal 'cage.' I ran to the back and looked down – the cage on the starboard side had broken and was flopping around, the wooden rudder restrained by a thin line, tied on for just such an emergency.

"Well, we've lost the starboard rudder, Chuck. Let's reduce sail further so there's less strain on the port one."

We rolled up the already-reefed jib and put a second reef in the mainsail. This slowed us down to about four knots and we were still twenty miles from our destination. At this rate, we'd be lucky to drop the anchor in daylight. Because this was the first time I'd been to this small group of islands, I had no intention of trying to find our way in the dark. So we had to get there or spend the whole night at sea in a storm with iffy steering.

"OK Chuck, if we can keep going at four knots, we should make the anchorage in front of the fort just before dusk. But we'll have to take it easy so we don't break the other rudder cage."

Five minutes later there was a slight grinding sound from the port aft and the boat rounded into the wind – we now had no rudders...

"Shit – that's it then!" said Chuck. "We'll have to call the Coast Guard".

"No, I've been thinking about this possibility for the past few minutes. I've got an idea. We'll drop the outboard down and steer using the thrust from the propeller. It might work".

We freed the two rudders from their cages, dropped the heavy outboard down and locked it into place. It started right up and I pushed the throttle forward. If the wind had been still and the ocean calm it would have been easy to set a course and keep it, but the wind was now up to 30 knots and the choppy waves kept knocking us off course. We were leaving a zig-zag wake behind us and even though we were managing five knots, with our uneven course we'd run out of our limited fuel supply before we got there.

"Hey Chuck – furl the main completely, would you. I think if I just use the jib and keep more pressure on the bows we might be able to steer a straighter course. And make sure both centreboards are all the way down."

I didn't know if this would work, but it was worth a try. With the main down and tied, Chuck unrolled the jib halfway. This had a miraculous effect. The boat held her course much better and with the sail out, we picked up speed – now we were doing six knots, directly toward the islands, which we could just see on the horizon. The skies were grey and low, the waves all around were white-capped and light spume was blowing off their tops.

With the engine purring and the jib pulling, I knew we'd make it before nightfall. I still had to pay attention to the steering, but was able to hold it to ten degrees either side of our preferred course. Giving the wheel to Chuck, I went below and put a cassette in the player and switched on the cockpit speakers, before heading back to the blustery cockpit. Just before I went outside, I lit a big cigar and puffed pleasurably. Sitting back up in the helm seat, I focused on our destination, the huge Civil War-era prison straddling the main island ten miles away, now in view.

The next hour and a half were magical – the energy of the storm, the boat steadily closing the gap, the knowledge that I'd risen to the challenge and overcome a potentially dangerous situation, the pleasure of the rare cigar and the 1812 Overture blasting through the speakers – all of these added up to an amazing feeling of well-being and adventure...

We made it to the anchorage and found calm water in the lee of the huge prison, sitting incongruously on a small island surrounded by crystal clear azure water, sandy beaches and a bird sanctuary! The next day the storm had blown through and we went over the side to assess the damage to both rudder cages. The Gemini drew only two feet, so we just pulled her up to the beach and standing in knee-high water, removed the mangled mess of aluminium tubes!

We went to the rangers office and told them of our dilemma – they were very helpful and agreed to let us use their radio to call Tony Smith, the builder of the popular Gemini boats in Maryland. After an hour, we managed to get through (this was before the widespread use of cell phones) and Tony said he would build two cages and ship them out to us in two or three days.

There are no stores in the national park and catching fish is strictly prohibited for visitors. We didn't have a lot of provisions aboard and after a couple of days Chuck, a professional fisherman, made friends with one of the rangers and was given permission to catch fish for us to eat!

The fifth day we were there, a seaplane landed in the anchorage and taxied up to the small dock. They unloaded some supplies and mail for the rangers and also two easily identifiable packages which contained brand new cages for our rudders. Within two hours we had installed them, dropped the rudders in, said goodbye to our ranger friends and headed out the anchorage. I set a course southwest for Isla Mujeres, a small island near Cancun, about a three-day sail.

The second day we could see Cabo San Antonio, the westernmost point of Cuba to our left and I made sure we stayed at least ten miles offshore, so as not to upset the U.S authorities. I really wanted to visit Cuba, but at that time, if we had strayed into their waters and been apprehended by the U.S. Coast Guard, I could have had my boat confiscated, be fined $250,000 and spent time in jail! (In 2011, I made a paid delivery of a new Gemini catamaran to Mexico and spent a week in Cuba on the way. I was sadly disappointed by the crumbling infrastructure, the sense of desperation and the continuing repression and fear of the people, not just in Havana, but also in the small towns we stopped at).

After an uneventful sail (the best kind!), we arrived in Isla Mujeres and spent a few days relaxing and enjoying the laid-back atmosphere. We decided not to stop in Cancun, but head south down the coast of Mexico towards Belize. Sailing past Cancun, one sunny, beautiful morning, about a mile offshore, we could see hundreds of tourists on the beach as the dozens of tacky, high-rise hotels receded behind us. The chart showed a long reef running parallel to the coast just south of Cancun. After an hour offshore, I decided we should sail between the reef and the beach if we could, which would give us smooth waters without the waves that were starting to build. I checked our GPS position with the chart in front of me and saw there was a break in the reef about a quarter mile ahead.

"Hey Chuck," I called out. "Looks like there's a gap ahead. I'm going to get closer to the reef and then we'll sail through it to the other side. I don't know how deep it is, so crank up both centreboards, please. Then go on up to the bow and keep an eye out for the opening, OK..."

With the centreboards up, we now drew only two feet, and with Chuck on the bow, I edged closer to the reef on our right side, until we were about twenty feet off, sailing parallel to it at about four knots. In the clear water, the reef was quite visible, with the waves washing over semi-submerged rocks and thousands of tropical fish swimming everywhere.

"I think I see the gap about a hundred yards ahead," called Chuck from his position on the bow, one hand shading his eyes.

"Well, the GPS says it's about three hundred yards ahead," I called back, eyes darting between the reef and the chart.

"No, I'm pretty sure it's just up here, Jon."

I remembered my experience going up on a reef in Venezuela a few years earlier and the fact that even modern charts can be off by a few feet or several hundred yards.

"OK, it's right here. Turn to starboard!" Chuck yelled back to me.

I looked to where he was pointing and could see a gap between the rocks, a clear, sandy bottom leading toward the beach. Even though the chart showed it two hundred yards ahead, I trusted my eyes and turned the wheel to the right while letting out the mainsail. A small wave lifted the stern up, rolled under the twin hulls and set them back down gently, as Duet sailed between the rock-strewn reefs on our right and left. We were committed now, could not turn back.

"Oh shit!" yelled Chuck from the bow, just as I saw what he was yelling about. "Stop the boat, there's reef ahead!"

"I can't stop the bloody boat! Hold on tight, we're going to hit!"

The gap that we had entered wasn't the uncluttered pass through the reef – the chart was correct and we should have waited another minute. We were very close to the beach now and about a dozen tourists stopped and stared at the apparition of a catamaran under full sail, hurtling through the reef...

I saw Chuck grab hold of the bow pulpit in front of him and crouch down, while I gripped the wheel so hard my fingers hurt. The sandy little passage we had taken was coming to an abrupt end and twenty feet ahead I could see submerged rocks rising to about a foot below the surface. There was only five feet of the reef ahead blocking us, before it dropped off into calm water about a hundred yards from the beach. But those few feet could have been a mile. We didn't have enough clearance to go over the rocks and as I quickly looked from side-to-side, I couldn't see a clear path anywhere.

I flicked the main and jib sheets off their winches and braced myself to slam into the rocks just ahead at a good four knots, expecting big holes in both bows. But as we were about to hit, I heard the sound of water breaking right behind us. The stern lifted as a wave, larger than the rest, perhaps a small rogue wave, surged across the reef. It lifted Duet, lifted her up and carried her forward in a welter of foam and spray, bow down, stern raised, sails flapping and swept us across those five feet, depositing us gently on the other side of the reef, in deep clear water.

I was stunned and just sat there, sails clattering above, Duet bobbing a few feet beyond the reef, the beach a hundred yards away, astonished tourists riveted to the spot. I looked behind and could see the reef line running north toward the distant hotels of Cancun. South the reef continued on, but now I could plainly see the passage we should have taken, just a hundred yards further down. I adjusted the sails and turned the boat slightly left, my whole body shaking. Chuck slowly made his way back to the cockpit, eyes wide, mouth open.

"Oh my God, can you believe that! I swear Jon, I saw little fish darting out of our way as we skimmed the rocks – they looked as startled as me!"

"Bloody hell, I thought we'd had it that time, mate! If that wave hadn't rolled over the reef at just that moment..."

We were both coming down from the adrenaline rush and were very aware of how close we had come to having the bottom ripped out of each hull, if the wave had subsided before carrying us across. It was time for a beer – no two beers...

Chuck left the boat a couple of days later, while we were anchored off the ancient Mayan ruins at Tulum. He had an offer of a paid captain job on a large private sport fishing boat and headed to the Bahamas (a mistake, as it turned out later). Another friend Pete, not a sailor and prone to sea-sickness, flew out and joined me and we sailed down the coast of Mexico, had some fun in Belize and cruised up the magical Rio Dulce in Guatemala. This is when we were 'attacked' by 'jaguars' in the jungle at night at Tikal, a huge Mayan city inland in the mountains.**

Pete left in Cancun and I single- handed Duet for the next month, arriving back in Hilton Head in March for my second season of parasailing. At the end of that summer, after making a lot of money, I sold the parasailing boat and business and bought another catamaran, a 30' Stiletto, which was as sleek and fast as its name suggests.

Now I had two 30' catamarans, but they were very different. Duet was a cruiser and my comfortable home. 'Cotton Candy', the Stiletto, was my new business and in the summer of 1994 I took tourists sailing in the waters off Daufuskie Island. (I was also one of the captains aboard the 'Spray', a total contrast to the Stiletto!)***

There was a huge nationally televised golf tournament at the prestigious Harbor Town golf course that summer. On the Sunday of the tournament about a hundred spectator boats were anchored in the quiet waters off the course and two helicopters buzzed around photographing the event. My friend John, from whom I had bought Cotton Candy, did large charters on board a 40' ex-racing catamaran he had bought a few years earlier.

This was a fearsome machine, a giant, sophisticated 'Hobie cat', that could carry thirty people on the huge trampoline between the hulls. It was very fast and on one occasion, when neither of us had passengers aboard, we raced up Broad Creek, side-by-side

122

and as we approached the marina, we each tightened our mainsheets and got the windward hull of each boat to lift high out of the water. We must have been doing fifteen knots and friends later told us that it was a glorious sight!

Back to the golf tournament...John sailed his boat down Broad Creek and out into Calibogue Sound, with me following closely on Cotton Candy. John had worked out a deal with NBC and had a huge banner with 'NBC Sports' displayed on each side of his boat. The plan was to sail near the tournament and NBC would get some advertising exposure. But John, who was an excellent boat handler, spiced it up for them and we put on a show...

He sailed alone under full main and jib, as did I aboard Cotton Candy, following a boat length behind his big blue catamaran. We could see a helicopter with NBC emblazoned on it nearby, a large camera aimed at us. Then John turned abruptly left plunging into the hundred or so boats anchored nearby, all partying and supposedly watching the golf! He steered his boat perfectly, weaving in and out of the spectator craft, adjusting the sails as needed after each turn.

There was scant wind, about five knots, enough to keep both lightweight catamarans moving as we turned left, then right, gybed the sails, turn left, tighten the main, tighten the jib, turn back, ease out the sails. I sailed behind him like a little puppy dog, sometimes holding my breath as he squeezed between the stern of one boat and the anchor chain of the boat behind it. His catamaran was about ten feet wider than mine, so I knew I could go anywhere he did...

The people on the spectator boats stood and cheered, raised their beers and drinks as we glided silently by. The helicopter hovered nearby, far enough away so that its rotor wash didn't disturb any of the boats or us. We did this for a full fifteen minutes, a little ballet amongst the sailboats, powerboats and sport fishers

123

anchored out together on this fine sunny afternoon, the golf tournament an excuse for a big party. And then the wind picked up a few knots, as it often does on a summer afternoon, we sailed out of the anchorage, hardened in our sheets and shot off up Broad Creek, with dozens of boat horns tooting behind us.

Later that day I got a phone call from my dad in San Francisco. He told me he had been watching the golf tournament on TV. Was that me he saw on a sleek catamaran, following a big blue cat through the boats anchored off Harbor Town? He said it looked like me and he knew I had just bought another catamaran! So apparently John and I had been on TV all over the country, possibly internationally as well! And my reputation as a skilled sailor was reinforced enormously that day amongst my friends in the boating community there. Looking back on it with pride...I wouldn't do it again!

I sold the Stiletto in September of 1994 to a couple from Portland, Maine. I agreed to deliver it to them and set off late that month from Hilton Head, alone. It was about a thousand miles and I sailed some in the Intracoastal Waterway and a lot out in the ocean, a couple of miles off the beach. It took me almost a month and was a wonderful, introspective time, as I had also sold my Gemini and had decided to leave Hilton Head after three years and head back to San Francisco to be with my family.

Dad's cancer was getting worse and I wanted to be there at the end. After I had delivered Cotton Candy, they flew me back to Hilton Head. Within a week, I had sold or given away anything that wasn't personal and as the weather started to get cooler, I climbed aboard the Bugatti and headed south to drive I-10 across the bottom of the country, then up the coast of California to 'home.'

My father died in 1996, a seven-year cancer survivor and we flew with his body to London, where he wanted to be buried. Three

124

months later I met Joell in Marin county, just north of San Francisco – we were married the end of August, 1997. As recounted in my other books, we bought JoJo, our Catfisher 32, just before we were married. She became our home for six years and carried us safely from San Francisco to South Carolina, through the Panama Canal.

JoJo was sold in Ft. Lauderdale in 2003 and we bought and restored the magnificent 64' trimaran 'Ladyhawke', which we sailed back to Panama and chartered in the San Blas Islands.**** We found ourselves living in Sonoma, north of San Francisco in 2007, after we sold Ladyhawke and the charter business to a young Dutch man and doubled our money.

As Joell is an accomplished artist, we decided to open an art gallery on the Plaza in Sonoma, which was an instant success! I bought a custom-built 17' trimaran on a trailer and we named her 'Swallow'. I had her for just that summer, as the art gallery took up all my time. I only got to sail her once, on a lake up north, then sold her for a thousand dollars more than I paid!

After we sold the art gallery, Joell found a 37' Prout Snowgoose catamaran for sale south of San Francisco. I made a ridiculously low offer and couldn't believe it when it was accepted! We stayed a year in the Bay area and restored the boat, which we named 'Wild Goose Chase'. We entertained ideas about sailing it back to Florida, following the wake of JoJo a few years before. We did sail her down to San Diego and lived aboard for a few months there, but our hearts weren't into making a two-year voyage at that time.

The 'Goose' was sold (at a profit!) and we headed back to Florida, to an area we hadn't lived in before – Sarasota, on the Gulf Coast. We rented a small Florida bungalow sight unseen from an ad on craigslist before we left California. Turned out the owner was a friend I'd lost touch with for forty-three years! Eventually we bought a 37' monohull in Ft. Myers, fixed her up and cruised across the Okeechobee and up to St. Augustine, where we lived for a little while. After we sold 'Beach Money', our next boat was a trailerable Catalina 25, which was tied up behind a house near our motor home in Jensen Beach, FL in 2013.

As I finish this history, Joell and I are living once again in Northern California, just south of San Francisco, on the beautiful coast. Is there another boat in our future? Oh yes, we have more adventures planned, loosely planned, but there are a few islands in the Caribbean we haven't yet visited and then, when we tire of trimming sails, there are over 5000 miles of canals and rivers in Europe to explore in a motor cruiser in our 'golden years'...

*   'Imagine and the Ku Klux Klan' in 'Everyone Said I Should Write A Book'
**   'Tikal Night' in 'Everyone Said I Should Write A Book'
***   'The Spray' in 'Everyone Said I Should Write A Book'
****   'Charley Horse' in 'Everyone Said I Should Write Another Book'

Email sent from Panama, April, 2005

Hello everyone!

About four weeks ago, I was checking the internet for info on The Pearl Islands, where, if you read our previous email, we were hoping to do more week-long (exhausting!) charters. While checking Contadora Island, I noticed there were two large resorts, with over 420 combined rooms. Looking at their activities list, there was jet skiing, kayaking, sport fishing etc., but no day sailing charters. Our lawyer got us their corporate address and told us the owners are a Colombian family who bought both resorts three years ago. As we were spending a week in Panama City, I made up a little photo portfolio, put on some nice clothes and marched unannounced into their downtown offices, where no one spoke any English!

The secretaries thought I was just a crazy gringo when I told them I wanted to see the general manager with a business proposition! Two hours later, just after 5:00pm, I was ushered into the office of a delightful man, who I later found out was the owner of the resorts (plus two hotels in Panama City, two in Colombia, vast tracts of timber land, a furniture company...) A very wealthy, totally unpretentious man, who, contrary to media hype, does not seem to be a drug lord! He spoke no English, but within two minutes understood what I was offering and asked me where had I been for the past three years!?

He invited his charming 23-year old son, Carlos, to join the meeting, which was a great help as he speaks good English. We all talked for nearly two hours and the energy was just great. Two days later they flew me to their resort on the company plane and gave me the grand tour – what a magic island! It's physically very beautiful, surrounded by beaches and most waterfront property has multi-million dollar estates, including one owned by Oscar de La Renta.

The following week we all had a meeting again, with Joell present this time. They were most gracious and we all hit it off famously. A few days later they provided us with a free ferry ride and a complimentary stay at the resort for Joell to get a feel for the place. We rented an ATV and explored the island, needless to say, Joie loves it too.

So, we are moving to The Pearl Islands, 40 miles south of Panama City in the Pacific Ocean! We will do day charters taking a maximum of fifteen people on a one hour sail to a secluded island (only six of the two hundred Pearl Islands are inhabited), letting them swim, sunbathe and snorkel. We will provide a nice lunch and rum punch then sail back. Most of our business will be in the busy, dry months, Dec-April. I also have a management contract to market, promote and oversee the operation of their 60' Hatteras sport fishing yacht. There is a good chance that Joell can eventually open a small art gallery on the island. In busy season, there are usually 1500 people a week staying on the island, 90% of them at the resorts we will be operating from...

You know, for thirty years I've been looking for an upscale resort to run a day charter business – seems like my ship just came in! If you want, check out the resorts at www.hotelcontadora.com and www.puntagaleon.com . And, of course, you're all invited to visit and "survive" here in paradise....

Much love, Jon, Joell and Sailor

THINGS THAT GO 'THUNK' IN THE NIGHT

We rested well after Joell's first night at sea sailing down the coast of Northern California in a gale.* Waking around noon, I was glad we had decided to seek shelter from the storm, in the anchorage off the beach in Monterey. My confidence in our little catamaran had grown immensely during the high winds and large seas and my wife of one year had overcome her justifiable fear of unpleasant weather.

Lounging around the cockpit drinking coffee, we discussed the long night before and the uncertain future ahead. Our assets comprised $900 cash, our 32' catamaran JoJo and my Bugatti replica, sitting under a cover at my brothers home near San Francisco. Our idea was to head south, probably to San Diego where I hoped to get a job selling boats. We expected to work a couple of years to build up our cruising kitty and then planned to sail south to Mexico and beyond, through the Panama Canal to South Carolina, where I had friends.

After a couple of days in Monterey, waiting for the gale to blow itself out and tidying up the boat, we got ready to leave. I intended to sail directly to Santa Barbara, keeping about ten miles offshore. With favourable winds we could be there in three days and avoid the necessity of having to find shelter along the inhospitable California shore. There were few anchorages down the rocky and forbidding coast and it would be best to avoid putting in anywhere. The biggest obstacle ahead of us was dreaded Point Conception, the 'Cape Horn' of California, two hundred miles south.

We weighed anchor early on the third morning, as soon as there was light to see. I calculated that with an average speed of five knots we should be rounding Point Conception in two days, in the morning, in daylight. It didn't quite work out that way...

129

We motored northwest along the beach and rounded Point Pinos with its short, squat lighthouse off to our left. The wind was gentle, the seas calm with a long, lazy swell. As the diesel purred and the autopilot steered we enjoyed the morning and decided to stay close inshore about a mile off, watching the hills of Point Sur State Park glide past.

A few hours later the wind picked up and I raised the sails. Turning off the diesel all was quiet, save for the comforting gurgle of water under our keels as we loped along at four knots. But then an unusual sound...

I heard a muffled clunk on the starboard side and thought it was a small branch or some other flotsam we had run over. A few minutes later I heard it again, a distinct 'thunk'. I switched off the autopilot and hand steered. Something was not quite right – there seemed to be a little play in the steering. I turned the wheel hard to the right; under the boat, at the stern, a definite 'thunk'. I spun the wheel all the way to the left and could hear it again. I also felt it through the steering wheel. Even though the boat responded to the twin rudders, one was possibly loose.

"Joie, something's happened to the steering on the starboard side. I'm going to check the steering cables. Turn the wheel when I tell you, OK..."

A little alarmed, she took the wheel and I hurried below, moved our accumulated stores and provisions off the aft starboard berth and removed the bunk boards. The simple, sturdy steering shaft and cables were plainly visible and easily accessible.

"Turn the wheel full right, love," I called up.

The cable tightened and the rudder post turned, but as it did I could see a little wobble and hear something loose.

"Now, spin the wheel left as fast as you can!"

130

This time when the wheel hit full left, there was a definite sound from the rudder, a sound that shouldn't be there. Something was wrong under the boat...

Luckily the wind was steady and the waves were small. I had to look under the boat, to ascertain what was wrong, but I didn't relish the idea of going over the side to inspect it while offshore. I came back up to the cockpit.

"OK, love. We have a problem. Something's loose under the starboard side and it's possible the rudder is bent. I've got to go under and see what's going on."

"Out here?" Joell asked, startled and concerned.

"No, no. We'll find a place to anchor, where it's protected. I'll look at the chart and see if there's an anchorage nearby."

We were about thirty miles south of Carmel and I didn't want to turn around and fight the southbound current or the swells, especially with a possible broken rudder. I switched the autopilot back on and went into the salon to see where we could find a safe haven. The California coast has very few harbours and after studying the chart, the closest port south was Morro Bay, over a hundred miles down the coast. It was late afternoon and I was concerned about sailing another twenty-four hours to get there, especially not knowing exactly what the problem was.

Scrutinizing the chart further and referring to a book about this coast, the closest protected anchorage was a small headland at San Simeon State Park, near Hearst Castle. This was still sixty miles away, about fifteen hours of sailing at our current speed.

"Joie," I called through the open salon window. "Look, the closest place to drop anchor is an overnight sail down the coast. If this wind stays steady, we'll be there at dawn."

"But won't it put a lot of strain on the starboard rudder to sail all that way?"

"Yes, it will. So I'm going to disconnect it and we'll just use the port rudder. JoJo tracks so well under sail, there shouldn't be too much strain for just the one rudder to handle."

Anyway, that was my theory, so I grabbed some tools and disconnected the steering cable. I went back up to the cockpit, where the light was starting to fade. The wind was holding steady and the waves hadn't grown. With any luck we'd have a pleasant night sail down the coast a couple of miles offshore.

And that's what happened. The boat sailed well under just one rudder, there was an occasional 'thunk' from the starboard as we surfed down small waves, but I tried not to worry and just enjoy the dark night and twinkling stars. Occasionally the faint loom of a small town would slowly appear and then recede into the darkness behind us. Where the highway hugged the shoreline we would see dim headlights from US 1 on our left. Joell loved it, dressed up warm, drinking hot tea, watching the phosphorescence in our twin wakes. This was a much better night time experience for her than the gale we had sailed through three nights before!

As the sky slowly lightened over the low hills, we were only three miles from our destination. The wind had dropped an hour before and we were chugging along slowly, not wanting to arrive before full daylight. Nearing the headland, we skirted the rocks offshore and rounded into a small protected bay, just as the sun came up. There was an old pier there, where the Hearst yachts and those of his wealthy visitors used to tie up.

With Joell at the helm, I dropped the anchor and made sure it was holding firm. Then we both slept all morning! When we woke around lunchtime, the weather was pleasant and the sun was shining. But the water was cold, very cold! And I didn't have a wetsuit. I would have to go over the side and hope for the best – I was not looking forward to it!

I stood on the small swim step in my shorts, with goggles and a snorkel. I really didn't think I could stay in the water more than a minute and Joell was ready with big towels and hot tea. I inhaled several breaths deeply, braced myself and jumped into the dark green water feet first. Oh God, it was cold – freezing cold!

I reached for the rudder and pulled myself down. The goggles were useless as there was no visibility. I had just a few seconds to determine the problem by feel. I pulled on the rudder and it didn't move. I pushed and it didn't move. What was wrong under there? I ran out of air and came up spluttering. Joell was looking over the side with a large towel in her hands. Without a word, I gulped more air and pushed myself under again. This time I reached for the skeg, a triangular piece of thick fibreglass in front of the rudder which provided an anchoring point for the bottom of the rudder.

As soon as I grabbed it, I could feel jagged strands of fibreglass. It was a solid piece that should have no movement at all. However, when I jiggled it, it moved alarmingly from side to side. Now I knew what the 'thunk' was. The skeg had broken off and was only held on by the bottom of the rudder! I figured this all out in five seconds, then shot to the surface, shaking with cold.

I hauled myself up the steps into the cockpit and Joell threw the big fluffy towel around me. I was intensely cold and my teeth started chattering. In the salon the diesel heater had created a warm environment and with two steaming cups of hot tea, I was soon dressed and comfortable.

"So, is there anything wrong down there? Did you find the problem?" Joell asked.

"Yes and yes." I answered. "The skeg has broken off and is just being held on by a nut on the end of the rudder shaft. It was a good idea to disconnect it yesterday afternoon, otherwise the skeg could have torn off and would have to be completely rebuilt."

"Can you fix it here?"

"No, no. The boat has to be hauled out and the skeg re-fibreglassed to the hull."

This would obviously cost us most, if not all, of the few hundred dollars we had. But it must be done if we were to continue...

"What do you think happened?" asked a concerned Joell.

"Remember in the height of the storm a few nights ago when we were surfing down those waves. I heard a bang and thought we'd hit something. Well, I think what happened was that we 'fell' off a wave and came down hard on something, maybe a small log. There's no way to know until we can get a look at it out of the water."

"Can we keep going?"

"Yes, I think so – we've made it sixty miles, so we can probably go further. Let me see what facilities there are down the coast. I don't want to put extra strain on the skeg by going north into the swells and waves. We'll have to continue south."

I pulled out my charts and confirmed that Morro Bay was only 25 miles south. It was noon and if we left immediately, we could be there before dusk. I didn't know if they had a marine Travelift there, but it was better than sitting in this exposed anchorage. So up came the anchor and we motored along the coast, the distinctive hump of Morro Rock getting ever closer.

Through the breakwater, past anchored boats on the right and the pretty little waterfront on the left, we motored to the yacht club and tied up. No one was there, so we headed into town to stretch our legs and explore. The next morning I found out from a local boater that there were no facilities there capable of hauling JoJo, but there was a Travelift and boat yard just down the coast in Avila Beach. I called them and they said they could indeed haul out our catamaran and as the yard was do-it-yourself, we should be able to get the skeg fixed fairly cheaply.

We left Morro Bay and later that afternoon anchored a couple of hundred yards from the slipway in Avila. We dinghied ashore and went to the office where they told us we could be hauled out the next morning, as long as there was no swell. I had noticed dinghying in, that even a small swell made the south facing haul out dock unusable as a boat would be slammed into the side of the dock before it could be lifted out. Apparently this was a continual problem here and the timing had to be just right.

After roughly calculating the haul out costs, the daily rate in the yard and what it would probably cost to have the skeg fixed, we would have maybe three hundred dollars left to continue south! But with no option, we arranged to be at the dock at eight o'clock the next morning.

I didn't sleep well that night, worrying about the boat getting damaged during the haul out and where we would get the money to continue south. As always, Joell was very positive and said all would work out. And it did, in a most unexpected way...

Luckily there was no wind blowing in the morning, but there were long well-spaced swells coming into the anchorage. I could see the large blue Travelift trundling from the yard to it's location for our haulout. With the anchor weighed, we motored slowly to the slipway and I hovered nearby watching the swells. It would have to be timed perfectly!

The Travelift was in place, the two slings hanging below under the water. I would need to maneuver JoJo into the slip, the Travelift operator would have to haul up the slings as quickly as he could and JoJo must be out of the water before a swell could push her into the slip walls.

With a wave from the operator, I timed it as best I could, pushed the throttle forward and drove purposely into the slip. Quickly ropes were tossed by two helpers above us and hopefully they would prevent the boat from moving around in the slip. I ran along the deck adjusting the two slings a few inches either way to make sure they were positioned properly under the twin hulls, gave a thumbs-up to the operator, his diesel engine roared and the slings tightened and started to lift. All this happened within a minute and then a swell came in. JoJo was lifted up about two feet and pushed to the left. Even though I had fenders out for just such an occurrence, she moved quickly and alarmingly toward the concrete wall.

I expected a resounding crash which meant more fibreglass work would be needed! But the helper on the starboard side had foreseen this and had wrapped his rope around a bollard. The swell went under, lifted us up, but with a lurch, the tight dock line held the bow off the wall! The operator started winching us up again and by the time the next swell rolled in, JoJo was hanging in the slings, water dripping off, out of harms way. For a second I thought about how we were going to put her back in, but my attention turned to the starboard rudder, where the damage was.

A ladder was set up and Joell and I climbed down from the boat. It was obvious right away that the skeg had massively cracked and we were lucky it hadn't completely broken off. I could see that it could be fixed, but not by me. I can do small fibreglass repairs, but I know my limitations and, as this was a structurally important area, I had to find a professional within our budget.

136

JoJo was driven to the boat yard swaying in the Travelift and set down on blocks. There were about a dozen other sailboats in the small area and everyone was welcoming and friendly. We were told about a very good fibreglass repair man, name of Bill, who when sober did great work and was cheap too!

The next morning a short, grungy guy in his fifties banged on the hull.

"Hey, anyone there? You need some fibreglass work?"

"You must be Bill – I'll be right down."

Together we looked at the damage and, even though he had obviously already been drinking, he inspected the broken skeg carefully and said he could definitely fix it, make it stronger than new. We discussed the price and settled on $200 plus supplies. He would start tomorrow...or the day after!

After subtracting what we had spent over the past few days, Bill's repair job, the haulout and daily storage, we would be back in the water with about two hundred dollars to our names! We really needed to find an income source so that we had some money when we got to San Diego. My plan once there was to find a cheap slip, rent a car and drive to San Francisco to bring the Bugatti down. Then we'd have transportation to find work...

My friend Cindy who, along with her boyfriend Thierry, had spent years selling Brazilian hammocks at fairs around the country, now lived close by, in Pismo Beach. I called her and she said she'd love to come see us and meet my new wife and she showed up two days later. She had left Thierry on good terms and they had a daughter, who was eight. Cindy was now with Bob, who also made his money on the fair circuit. His family only worked four big fairs each year and made a fortune with their cinnamon roll concession, apparently a fixture for over twenty years at one of the fairs – the Kern County Fair, starting in two weeks."Would you and Joell be interested in working with us at the fair? You can manage our outside location and fill in where needed."

I looked at Joell and she quickly nodded yes.

"Sounds great! Where will we sleep?"

"No worries – we have an extra trailer you can use. Give me a call in a week and we'll firm up the details."

And so the law of attraction worked again. Over the next few days Bill stayed sober enough to repair JoJo and he did an excellent job. The yard agreed that we could keep the boat there for another month. Cindy came to get us and a few days later, after helping Bob load all his supplies and equipment, a motley convoy of four assorted trucks, a motor home, trailers and a brightly painted concession booth on wheels slowly drove the 140 miles to Bakersfield.

Bob's cinnamon roll concession was a favourite with the tens of thousands of fair-goers and he had a big corner section of the main hall as well as the outside concession. We worked twelve hour days setting everything up and finally the fair opened on October 7th. Over the next ten days everyone worked very hard, frosting and selling over 70,000 fresh baked cinnamon rolls at $2 a piece! Towards the end, bone tired, I got a little bored asking customers if they wanted their cinnamon rolls plain or frosted.

"Plain or frosted?" I'd ask, over and over again. There was always a line of customers at each of the four cash registers.

"Pepperoni, anchovies, mushrooms?" I'd continue. "Onions, olives, extra cheese?" At least it got a laugh out of some of them, although there were a few times when someone thought I was serious and wanted pepperoni! And then it was over. We helped clean all the equipment, dismantle the booths and towed everything back to Pismo Beach. Bob paid us and Cindy drove us back to JoJo.

We 'splashed' the boat carefully, waiting for a break in the swell to hurriedly drop her in the water and back out of the slings at full speed, before she could be knocked into the wall. We spent two days at anchor, recovering from the previous two weeks and swore we'd never eat a cinnamon roll again!

And then in late October, a bright blue, crisp fall day, I hauled up the anchor and we headed south toward dreaded Point Conception, eighty miles away. We had been listening to NOAA weather forecasts and it appeared the weather would be benign for rounding this feared point, just north of Santa Barbara. It turned out to be an easy rounding, as we cleared it in the early morning hours with thousands of twinkling stars looking down on us. It was bitterly cold and I had two sweaters on under my jacket. The giant oil rigs which lay off this coast glowed ghostly as the gas from their flare-stacks ignited and cast wavering shadows on the sea.

By mid-morning we were comfortably anchored off the beach at Santa Barbara. The weather was noticeably warmer and we had twice as much money in our pockets as when we had sailed out of San Francisco two months before! We left Santa Barbara and spent a couple of weeks in the Channel Islands, exploring coves and little anchorages. This was the first time we really cruised on JoJo, living the cruisers life, with no hurry and no definite destination. Eventually we tied up in Ventura Harbour and again the law of attraction came into play.

I met someone on our dock who said the local Vessel Assist boat rescue and towing company was in need of a captain. I applied and got the job. We ended up staying there for a few months and had many adventures rescuing distressed seafarers in the Channel

139

Islands, an area I got to know very well....**

* 'Joell's First Night', 'Everyone Said I Should Write Another Book'.
** 'Baptism By Gale', 'Everyone Said I Should Write A Book'.

Email published in 'Latitude 38' sailing magazine

JoJo - 32-ft Fisher
Jonathan & Joell White
Acapulco (Sausalito)

We'd only intended to stay in Acapulco for four days, but ended up staying four weeks. That's not such a big surprise, however, as we were going to hurry through Mexico in just four weeks - but ended up enjoying four months! Now that we find ourselves up a lazy river in western Panama for hurricane season, we'd like to share some insights on Acapulco and other topics.

For us, Acapulco had always conjured up visions of continuous parties, Bogie and his friends dancing the night away, wild revelry and fancy yachts. Some of this does go on - especially during Spring Break, when thousands of the more affluent college kids descend on the beaches. But for the cruising sailor, Acapulco offers many different and exciting possibilities.

We made much better time than we had anticipated covering the 135 miles from Zihuantenejo to Acapulco, and arrived off the sparkling, jewel-like skyline about 0230. Normally we don't enter new harbors at night - especially without radar, and our boat is one of the few in the fleet without it. But the entrance looked straightforward, there was a good moon, and we had entered a waypoint route that would take us right to the anchorage. So we made it in without any problem.

The small boat anchorage in Acapulco Bay is tucked around to the left among a myriad of mooring buoys and a dozen unlit boats on the hook. After a couple of attempts to set the hook in the soft mud, we turned in and waited to see what the city would look like in daylight. There's no doubt that Acapulco has an exciting skyline, dramatically changed from its heyday in the '50s. In the morning we could see the high-rise tourist hotels in the distance, while the rest of the city seemed to climb up the sides of the surrounding mountains.

Having been anchored between the Acapulco YC and the newer La Marina, we decided that La Marina looked a bit funkier - and therefore more inviting. We squeezed into an open slip - *JoJo* is 13 feet wide and the slip was only 14 feet wide - and then made our way up to the office. There we met Gisele, who would prove to be the most helpful, knowledgeable, and pleasant dock master we've encountered in nearly 30 years of cruising to foreign ports. During the next month, Gisele and her staff went out of their way to help us, no matter if it was with shipping, locating parts, suggesting things to do, or taking care of my mother who came to visit. Gisele does this for all the visiting cruisers, so we can heartily recommend the facility.

The berth fees at La Marina are $0.55/foot. There is electricity, but everyone had to share one water hose. No problema, as all the tenants had a good attitude. The marina's swimming pool was absolutely fantastic, and so were the drinks that were served around it! Transportation to downtown Acapulco was easy on any one of the many 'disco buses', which race around the city while blasting music and flashing lights. The buses cost three pesos, about 30 cents to ride as far as you'd like. The luxury air-conditioned buses, the choice of most gringos, cost four pesos. But we thought it was more fun to ride with the locals in the cheaper buses. One night, after Joell, Mum and I had enjoyed dinner in town, we took the king of disco buses back to the marina. Joell called out "buenos noches" to the driver as she stepped off the back of the bus. Everyone on the bus turned around to her, smiled, and returned her salutation!

Acapulco's Central Mercado area, which is off the main tourist track near the Zocalo (center), offers just about anything the cruiser could need in the way of provisions and supplies - other than boat parts and stainless fittings, of course. The latter are only available at the yacht club marine store at very high prices.

While at La Marina, we had the good fortune to meet Edmundo, whose son-in-law had just put a 30-foot boat into the marina. A retired 81-year-old professor from an old Mexican family, Edmundo was determined to show us an Acapulco that few get to see. One of the best things he introduced us to was the Galeria Costa Club, which is run by Marcelo Adano at 123 Costera M. Aleman. This is a cultural museum dedicated to showing people how the Acapulco region of the Pacific Coast has been developed over the last 500 years. Adano also builds the most amazingly detailed model sailing ships that I have ever seen. If you're ever in Acapulco, don't miss his place. Edmundo also took us to hear his friend Jaime Colin play the guitar outside at the Hyatt Hotel. I've heard Segovia play - and I think he could have learned a couple of things from Jaime!

Other attractions in Acapulco include the wonderful Papagallo Park along the waterfront. The park has a boating lake, children's playground, fun fair, and a huge aviary with lots of exotic birds and monkeys. With its unique ambiance, it's easy to visualize lovers strolling through it for the past few decades.

Later we joined Edmundo for a visit to his home town of Cuernavaca, which was about four hours away in the mountains. It's a magical place. One of Edmundo's 14 children has a horse ranch outside of Mexico City, so after missing our horse for two years, Joell got to ride again. It was more magic! Later, while having dinner with our hosts in a small town near Mexico City, we were served eskimoles, the Mexican equivalent of caviar. It sounds as though they might be little eskimoes, but they're really ant eggs! After a copious amount of tequila, we got up the courage to sample them - and they were delicious. After all that tequila, anything would have tasted fine!

Back at the marina in Acapulco, we hired a small, wiry man -

who spent all of his free time exercising - to clean our bottom. He did a superb job. Later we learned that he is 82 years old! The main reason we stayed in Acapulco so long was so that I could install a new autopilot. As we finally departed, we saw a magnificent looking sight - a big square rigger about a half mile away with her crew furling her sails. After a quick look in the binoculars, I quickly recognized her as the Californian. We raised her on the VHF and were told that she was heading for the Panama Canal and a summer on the East Coast.

After a long, windless trip, we're now in Panama. We'd also intended to go through the Canal, but went up the river to put into Pedregal instead. We've already fallen in love with Panama and her people, and have therefore decided to stay for hurricane season. We're even thinking of doing charters in the San Blas Islands next winter.

We have a few pointers for folks planning to cruise south this fall

- Bring earplugs. Anywhere in Mexico where there is a waterfront hotel, you'll be inundated by jet-skis being operated by tourists who don't have a clue how to operate them. In fact, Joell is now working on an AJSD - Anti Jet Ski Device - that resembles a catapult capable of hurling rotten tomatoes!

- Take the time and make the effort to learn basic Spanish. It will show respect for your host country, and will make your visit easier and more enjoyable. We've been amazed at the number of Americans who come down here without having tried to learn even a few words of Spanish.

- Don't treat Mexico or Central America as an 'American Disneyland'. These are real countries with different cultures and ways of doing things. Respect them.

- Every small town has at least one Internet cafe. They range in price from $10/hour at Cabo San Lucas - what a rip-off! - to just $1/hour here in David, Panama.

- We sailed right by Costa Rica. After talking to our friends who did stop, we apparently didn't miss much. The anchorages were said to be few and far between, and there have been some problems at Puntarenas.

- If it's isolated tropical paradises that you're looking for, mainland Panama and her nearby islands may have what you want.

- Jonathan & Joell 6/7/00

(This is about a business I was involved in that I am not particularly proud of. But the story is so improbable, I thought it worth sharing...).

FURS AND FLOOZIES

The autumn of 1981 found me at a loss, disconnected and unsure of what to do. I had spent the summer living in a small cabin on a friend's land up in Humboldt County in Northern California. It was a beautiful, isolated place, a two hour trek across a river into the hills and I enjoyed the solitude and the 'gardening' for a while.

I eventually found myself on a Greyhound bus, heading south to Newport Beach where another friend, Merv lived. He had just started a business and offered me a partnership to help expand it. I didn't really like the what he was doing, but it was a lifeline and who knew where it would lead, what doors might open up from it. In fact, it lead me serendipitously to my next idea that changed my life, put me on dozens of TV news shows across the country and eventually created huge financial abundance.

Merv had found a supplier of fake fur coats in the garment district of Los Angeles and had established a large line of credit. He had a van and traveled southern California working festivals and events, setting up a booth with racks of coats and jackets. I was offered a percentage of the profits if I would work the shows with him and I agreed.

The next few weeks were entertaining and exhausting as we traveled to small weekend shows and big outdoor street festivals. We drove north to San Francisco and south to San Diego and made a decent living, nothing more. One evening late in January, 1982, having dinner at a Denny's after a mediocre weekend show near Riverside, Merv told me he had a great idea. He had recently obtained his small plane pilots license and was eager to fly whenever he could. I had gone up with him once and we had flown around Orange County and a little way out over the Pacific. I don't like small planes and prefer to be a thousand miles offshore on a sailboat than five thousand feet up in a Cessna!

"So here's my plan, Jon," he started off eagerly. "I'll rent a plane, we'll load it with furs and fly to Las Vegas. I've got a friend there with a big Cadillac and she's agreed to drive us around Nevada and we'll sell the furs to the working girls at the brothels! What do you think, could be a blast and make us a lot of money..."

I was speechless. I didn't know if he was serious or not. But he was, as he continued...

"Most of the little towns have at least one cat house and I don't imagine the girls get many chances to shop for furs – we'll bring the furs to them! Well, are you in?"

I sat there, still speechless... Merv ordered coffee and looked at me, waiting for a response...

"Er, um. You're saying you want to fly a rented plane over the desert to Las Vegas, then cruise around the state in a Cadillac visiting hookers by the dozen and selling them furs?"

"Yes, we could charge top dollar and have some fun. But no trading furs for favours – this is strictly business, heh, heh!"

I slowly drank my coffee, playing this scenario out in my mind. I had nothing else to do, although an idea for a business had been playing in my mind since we had sold furs at a carnival a few weeks earlier. It seemed like a ludicrous plan but at the least I'd have a tale to tell in my older years...

"Well mate, it's such an outrageous idea, it will probably work. OK, when do we leave?"

"Day after tomorrow," said Merv, excitedly. "I've rented a Cessna for a week and my friend Lucy will meet us at McCarran General Aviation in Vegas at noon. Tomorrow we'll drive up to L.A. and buy a bunch of jackets and coats. We'll load them on the plane early the next day and leave as soon as we're done. It's only a two-hour flight, so we'll have plenty of time."

"Right, Merv. But why don't we drive the van? It'll be cheaper and we can carry more inventory..."

"Oh, come on. I know you're adventurous, Jon and I want to get more flying hours. Anyway, it'll be more fun driving around in a Cadillac than a Dodge van!"

Adventurous I was, but I wasn't too sure about being a passenger in a small plane loaded to the gills, with a novice pilot flying over the barren desert. Turned out my misgivings were justified...

The next day we drove up to L.A. and stuffed the van with furs. There were fake rabbit and fake fox, faux beaver and faux lynx. Even though they weren't real, I was growing less comfortable with what I was involved in and less comfortable with my partner Merv. I should have listened to my gut feeling.

Back to Newport Beach and I packed a small bag, enough for a week. Merv had told me to bring as little as possible, as the plane had limited carrying capacity – we needed the payload to be merchandise, not clothes. I was somewhat concerned about this as he was a large man, 6'3" and about 275 lbs., but as he now had a pilots license, I figured he knew what he was doing. Not necessarily...

We drove the van to the general aviation area of the recently renamed John Wayne Airport, where there were a few dozen small planes and a number of corporate jets parked on the tarmac. In those days the airport terminal was a small, one storey affair, not the large complex it is today. It was fun driving right up to our airplane in the van and parking next to it – I felt like a hundred thousand dollars. If we'd been in a limo, I would have felt like a million dollars!

Our rented aircraft was a single-engine Cessna 172, red and white, typical of tens of thousands around the country, one of the most successful private planes in the world. I opened the door and looked inside – there were four seats and an open area behind; it wasn't very big.

"Hey Merv! Where's the luggage compartment on this plane?" I asked.

He came over and opened a small door on the side. It just led to the area behind the seats, the small empty space I had seen looking through the passenger door.

"Here it is," he replied casually.

"You're kidding, right!" I exclaimed. "We can't get all those furs in there – it's tiny..."

"Well, we'll use the two back seats as well and just stuff as much as we can in," he said forcefully and a little nervously, I thought.

Merv tended to sweat a bit when he wasn't sure of things and I noticed alarmingly that he was starting to sweat now. Once again I felt a little uncomfortable with what we were about to do and once again I should have paid attention to my feeling.

We carefully loaded the two rear seats and the area behind with as many coats and jackets as we could until they touched the ceiling and there was room for not one more. Merv parked the van and locked it – there were a bunch of furs left in the back, but we had managed to stuff a lot on the plane. I climbed up and squeezed into the right-hand passenger seat, my small bag for the week on my lap.

Merv walked back to the plane and proceeded to do a pre-flight check, starting from the outside, reading from a manual. Then he climbed aboard, put on a pair of headphones, checked his instruments and tested the flaps and rudder. Satisfied that all was well, he licked his lips and started the engine, concentrating fiercely. I was a little concerned, but again found comfort in the fact that he wouldn't have been issued a license if he didn't know what he was doing, right?

He talked to the control tower, gave them our destination and was given clearance to proceed to a specific runway. Some of the dialogue was aircraft-specific, but Merv seemed to know what it meant. I decided to sit back, relax and enjoy the ride.

I must admit it was exciting to taxi around the other planes, wait for a commercial airliner to land, then move to our position for take off. Merv applied the brakes and revved the motor. The plane shuddered. I gripped my armrests as permission to take off came tinnily through the speaker and he throttled up. We trundled down the runway as he applied more power. I could tell the plane felt a bit sluggish with all the weight aboard and this was the first time he had flown this particular rented Cessna. My stomach tightened...

With a little bump we left the runway and the plane started to climb slowly. I looked out my window and could see a line of cars backed up on the 405 Freeway heading for Los Angeles It was just after nine in the morning and we were off on an adventure! Merv banked the plane onto its course for Las Vegas, less than three hundred miles away. He wasn't so tense, had stopped sweating and wasn't licking his lips now. I felt a little easier, the plane seemed to be handling the weight well. I don't like heights, am much more comfortable at sea level, but I had committed to this and decided to savour it.

He took off the headphones, checked the gauges and jiggled the joystick from side to side. The plane flopped around and so did my stomach!

"Cut that out, Merv. Not funny." I said above the drone of the engine.

He grinned and relaxed his hold on the joystick, unclenching his fingers. I slowly eased my grip of the armrests and looked down. We were still climbing and I found the altimeter – it showed five thousand feet, a mile up. Our airspeed was 120 knots, so if we continued at that speed we should be there in a little over two hours – wrong!

We hummed along for a while, sometimes bouncing around in an updraft. The landscape below was mostly beige desert, an occasional small town, black strips of asphalt highway, some mountains off in the distance to our left. We didn't say much, I was lost in my thoughts until Merv said "Oh shit."

I was instantly snapped out of my reverie, looked up and out the windows. To the right a few miles off were large black clouds, getting bigger, seeming to continually unfold and grow. If we had been at sea on a small boat, I would have reefed the sails and prepared for a storm. Up here, being a passenger, there was nothing I could do.

"OK, Merv, do you want to find a small airstrip to put her down, see what this is going to do?" I asked cautiously.

"No, we'll head away from it, more north and see if we can skirt around it." He started licking his lips.

I have always been a conservative sailor (the only area of my life where I'm conservative!), which is probably why I've survived storms, gales and the fringes of a hurricane. As the plane started to be buffeted by winds from the gathering storm, Merv changed

151

course away from it and toward the north, off our course.

"What's the range for the plane?" I asked as we headed into a more remote area.

"With the added weight of the furs, we can fly for about three hours," he replied, licking his lips. "Enough fuel to get to Vegas. I'm not going to put it down out here. We'll just keep flying north until we can get around the edge of the storm."

Even though he sounded confident, I wondered if he was trying to convince himself more than me. I was concerned about our situation, but worse was yet to come...

We flew for about fifteen minutes and left the storm behind. There was some relief in that, but not for long. Ahead of us appeared a low mountain range. I didn't know exactly where we were and I don't think Merv did either. There was no GPS on the plane, it wasn't available back then.

At 120 m.p.h. the peaks were upon us quickly. Perhaps we had been pushed more northwest than expected, maybe it was the southern tip of the Sierra Nevadas. I wasn't too worried about what they were called; I was more concerned that they were in front of us and looking taller every minute...

"Merv, I think we should turn around and put down somewhere and figure out exactly where we are."

"No, no, we can make it over this range, there must be a pass somewhere," he said, not too convincingly.

Obviously he was determined to get over the mountains. I was afraid his determination would be our undoing – especially as he had amped up his lip licking.

He applied full throttle and pulled the joystick back; the loaded

152

Cessna struggled to climb. I kept my eye on the altimeter, on the rapidly approaching mountains, back to the altimeter. Merv was not only licking his lips, he was sweating and it certainly wasn't hot up there...

We climbed to 6500 feet and I could feel the plane straining to go higher. The mountains were filling the windscreen now and we were only a few miles away. I looked to the left, almost frantic. He should have turned back and put the plane down, even if it was on a deserted highway. There was no way through them, especially in a plane that I now realized was overloaded...

"Merv, over there!" I yelled above the noise of the straining engine. "Off to the right, there's a pass in the mountains. Turn right, now!" I commanded.

He was licking his lips constantly, fiercely concentrating, willing the plane to climb higher. It did, up to 7000 feet. He pushed the rudder pedal and moved the joystick and we turned toward the gap. He was still trying for height when the most awful noise reverberated around the cockpit.

'HONK, HONK, HONK!' went a startling alarm and a large red light began flashing on the dashboard.

"What the hell is that?" I yelled, scared to death.

"We're about to stall, dammit," was his curt response.

I had a vague idea that meant the plane couldn't climb any higher and I just hoped it wasn't about to fall out of the sky - judging by Merv's lip licking and the sweat pouring off him, it seemed like that was a likely scenario...

We were just upon the narrow gap and I could see that he was trying to line the plane up to navigate through it. I prayed there weren't more mountains beyond the pass. With that persistent beeping, the red light flashing, the engine straining, the poor plane trying to maintain altitude, Merv lined the wings up and Whoosh! - in a second we shot through the narrow pass in the mountains.

I could see the ridge next to me, about three hundred yards to my right, towering another thousand feet above us. It was one of the scariest moments of my life, worse than having a huge freighter bearing down on me in the middle of the night...

The empty desert spread out before us, there were no more mountains, we had escaped. Merv dropped the plane and the noise and flashing light stopped. The tension eased. He took out a handkerchief and mopped his brow. I slowly unclenched my hands from the armrests and let out a long breath. He looked at me with a weak smile.

"See, no problem, Jon. I'm glad you saw that gap, though!"

I didn't say anything – what could I say? My friend had acted incredibly irresponsibly, had put our lives at risk and didn't even apologize. We landed an hour later at McCarran Field and I couldn't wait to open the door and step onto the tarmac. I had made a decision during the past hour, but wasn't about to share it just yet.

A long maroon Cadillac Coupe de Ville drove up next to us and a pretty middle-aged red-head got out. Merv was excited that she was there and obviously expected to share not only the road trip, but the hotel rooms with her. It was apparent from her cursory kiss on his cheek that she didn't have the same expectations. So his attempt to impress her showing up in his own plane hadn't quite panned out...

We unloaded our merchandise from the Cessna into the cavernous trunk of the car and also onto the back seat. Lucy was

154

a nice lady and I soon discovered that Merv had agree to pay for all the gas, food and hotels on this week-long venture, all of which was to come out of our profits. She was also going to get a third of the profits – something I wasn't aware of. I sat in the back as Lucy headed out of Las Vegas, up highway 95. Apparently the plan was to make a wide circle around the state and end up back in Las Vegas.

I looked blankly out of the window, my arm resting on the stack of faux furs next to me. I was still a bit freaked out by the flight and feeling less happy with what I was doing. Yes, this was a bit of a lark, but it wasn't getting me anywhere in my life and I was becoming fed up with my partner.

We stopped at the first cat house we came to in the little town of Beatty, a couple of hours up the road. Merv told me to wait outside, which I was happy to do, while he went in to chat with the madam. Fifteen minutes later he came out with a smile on his face and said we had permission to put on a show. Lucy had put a couple of collapsible racks in the trunk and we unloaded them and set them up in the main lounge. It was rather seedy, lots of red velvet and a few stained sofas scattered around. A bar on one side, the windows covered, soft lighting throwing fuzzy shadows. A couple of bored looking girls, painting their nails, waiting for customers, hoping that's who we were. They watched with little curiousity as we unloaded about fifty furs and hung them on the racks.

"Ladies, ladies," said Merv, almost like a carnival huckster. "It's cold in the desert at night and we have top quality fake fur jackets and coats at wholesale prices, flown in from Los Angeles just for you."

The two floozies looked up and yawned. One pried herself away from her compact mirror and fingered the furs. The other wasn't interested at all. Three girls ambled out of the back, hoping to make some money, rather than spend it. The madam urged them to look, try on the coats, buy a couple each. Merv liked that and winked at her. Obviously, if the girls spent money with us, they'd have to work more to make up for it.

I figured that Merv had agreed to give the madam a cut of whatever sales we made and that was confirmed later when he admitted that madam was getting twenty percent – off the front! Now my proportion of the earnings was getting less and less. What the hell was I doing here?

We left after an hour, having sold two $100 fake rabbit jackets, not the most auspicious start. A hundred miles down the dusty road, we stopped for the night in Tonopah. Lucy insisted on two beds in their room, which didn't make Merv too happy. I went to my awful room and finally fell asleep, exhausted from the long and eventful day.

The next morning we had breakfast together and it was obvious Merv hadn't got what he had counted on. There was a steely silence between the two of them.

We piled into the car and Lucy drove to a brothel outside of town. Merv went in and was told to come back in the early afternoon – the girls were sleeping after working all night. I could have told him that, but I had decided just to be quiet and watch this pantomime unfold.

He got into the car grumbling, consulted his map and instructed Lucy to head north to Fallon, a boring three hour drive. Halfway there, Merv told Lucy to pull over to the side of the road. I thought he needed to take a leak, but instead he rummaged in his bag and pulled out – a gun! I'm not comfortable around guns; growing up in London, they were not a part of everyday life as they are in the U.S. Guns are illegal there, as they are in most civilized countries. I had never held a gun, let alone fired one.

"What are you doing, Merv?" I asked, rather alarmed.

"Thought I'd practice some target shooting," he replied over his shoulder as he walked a few yards into the desert. There was a battered road sign just down the road and that was his target.

He acted like he knew what he was doing, held the gun in two hands, arms outstretched, squinted and pulled the trigger. Bang and a small hole appeared in the sign. Again and again, bang, bang, bang, he was like a man possessed. I looked at Lucy and she looked back at me, her face a little tinged with fear and questioning. I was not happy with this, but let it go as we all got back into the car. No one said a word.

That afternoon we found a small brothel and the madam let us set up right away. Some tired looking girls came out and one of them latched onto me. She took me back to her room and wanted to know if she could trade her favours for a jacket. I told her definitely not, and she sulked and told me to basically bugger off, which I gladly did!

Merv was selling a few jackets and I helped him, though not with much enthusiasm. Lucy sat at the bar, having a well-deserved drink. We finished our business and sold just under a thousand dollars of coats and jackets. Merv was beaming. I was still freaked out about the gun...

That night we stayed in a motel in Fallon and after we had gone to bed a whole bunch of high school kids took over the rest of the hotel. They were obviously on some kind of road trip and were full of typical teenage spirit. Merv couldn't sleep and I heard him come out of his room and bang on the door next to him. He loudly told the kids to be quiet, and they were...for about fifteen minutes.

Soon I heard Merv stomping around in his room next to mine.

Thirty seconds later I heard his door slam open. I got up and went into the hall. He was pushing open the door to the room next to his where a few rambunctious kids were partying. But what unnerved me was that he had his pistol in his hand...

I was about to grab him when he forced his way into the room and stood at the end of a bed where three young guys were sitting joking around. There were a couple of cute girls sitting on the other bed. Merv stood there, his feet apart, the gun raised in his straight-out arms, pointing right at the head of one of the boys.

"I told you to shut the HELL up. Now I mean it." he yelled at the petrified boy. There was a smell of urine as the kid's bladder let go. He went pale and I couldn't believe what I was seeing.

The teenagers didn't say a word, they were totally freaked out and the girls started crying.

"Hey man, what the hell are you doing?" I yelled at him. I wanted to grab him, but I also didn't want the gun to go off accidentally.

He lowered the pistol and backed out of the room, a look of anger and hatred on his face, replaced by a smirk as he slammed their door behind him.

"There's no bullets in the gun. I took them all out," he said, as if that exonerated him.

"Yeah, but the kids didn't know that, man. I mean, come on, you don't just barge into someone's room and point a gun at them. Shit, if they call the cops, you just committed an assault with a gun. That's a felony."

"Nah, they're too scared. Go back to sleep."

I went back to my room and locked the door. Sitting on the bed, I tried to understand what had just happened and what the hell I was doing in the middle of Nevada with a moron. I felt like I really didn't know this man who I had first met five years earlier through a mutual friend. I also felt really uncomfortable associating with someone who thought it was acceptable to point a gun, loaded or not at a seventeen year old.

My life was not going anywhere doing this and I had an idea germinating that I thought could make a lot of money and be a huge amount of fun. At 1:00 a.m. I packed my small bag, put on my jacket and slipped out of the room. The air was crisp and cold, millions of stars twinkling in a vast desert sky. A few blocks away was an all-night diner. An early breakfast, lots of coffee and at dawn, a Greyhound took me away from this madness.

I felt much safer in a big metal bus firmly on the ground than in a small plane piloted by an inept jerk. As we rumbled down the highway toward San Francisco, I gazed out at the scenery and excitedly planned in my mind how I would create 'The Birthday Chronicle'*, my next venture, which became wildly successful...

I never saw Merv again.

*'The Time Traveler', 'Everyone Said I Should Write A Book'.

RUN JOIE, RUN!

The Hotel Chu was a faded turquoise colour, with coral accents–it had been built a very long time ago and looked like it was ready to fall down. There was a wide and inviting veranda out back that offered a view down to the beach and across the wide bay. About two miles offshore was a small island, enveloped in a light, white mist, like a thin veil of fog. If you leaned over the wooden rail and looked right, you could just see some of the cargo ships waiting at anchor for their Panama Canal transit.

When the wind blew toward Tabago Island there was a distinct smell of guano, fertilizer, as the offshore island was a loading point for this rich and odiferous commodity. JoJo was anchored behind El Morro Point in a protected bay and we putt-putted around in our inflatable dinghy. We bumped ashore on a sandy beach, near the rusty, covered ferry pier and knew the tide was falling.

It was about 11:00 a.m. when we stepped over the dinghy thwart into warm water up to our knees. I carried the small anchor a hundred feet toward the beach and buried it deep. We were already sweating in the humidity of the hot summer day as Joell handed me our day pack. This was the first of many visits to this historical island, both aboard JoJo and four years later on Ladyhawke. The tides on the Pacific coast of Panama can be over six feet and the water moves quickly. We planned to spend a few hours exploring the main town, giving the dinghy time to float again on the incoming tide, as it flowed back in. Didn't quite work out that way...

We had left San Francisco on our 32' catamaran a year and a half earlier and were looking forward to transiting the Panama Canal and sailing to Colombia. It would be about a month before our transit date through the canal from the Pacific to the Caribbean and we had decided to explore this pretty little place, known as the Isle of Flowers.

Joie and I splashed through the water and felt some rocks under the surface. Soon we were walking over the sandy beach to a low wall and then onto a meandering street. The small town of San Pedro sits nestled below the verdant hills, with homes looking down on the town and its central plaza. The streets are barely wide enough for one car and there are very few of them on the island. It is a place to amble slowly, up gentle inclines, around easy corners, stopping to look at old buildings, some preserved, some crumbling.

The town boasts less than a thousand residents and its only source of income is from the tourists who take the ten-mile ferry ride from Panama City to enjoy the beach and crystal clear water. It gets crowded on the weekends, but today it was empty, and the streets were barren except for a few locals going shopping or sitting in the shade. We rambled up a winding road, stopped at a small booth to buy ice cream, then found ourselves in the central plaza, typical of many towns throughout Central and South America.

It was dominated by the whitewashed Iglesia de San Pedro, supposedly the second oldest church in the western hemisphere. Inside it was cool and quiet and we could feel the energy of centuries of prayer. There were the typical garish statues with white-skinned saints condescending to a conquered brown-skinned populace, a concept we always found hard to reconcile.

Leaving the coolness of the church, we emerged into the plaza and the heat and continued our slow amble up and down the narrow, winding streets. Lemon trees, orange trees, bright, vivid bougainvillea, exquisite orchids, climbing, flowering plants, lush ferns, everywhere was colour as the Isle of Flowers lived up to its name. We came upon the remains of a sanitarium with a small plaque stating that the artist Paul Gaugin had spent time

161

recuperating there after his stint working on the construction of the Panama Canal. Isla Taboga was a place where French and later Americans workers would rest and recover after the strenuous and dangerous excavations in the malaria-ridden swamps – but many died, over thirty thousand, mostly from disease.

We were thirsty now and hungry. Heading up a street along the beach, we strolled past an old, faded two-storey building overlooking the water, with a weather-beaten sign announcing the Hotel Chu. It had two large doors which were closed. I turned the door handle and pushed - it moved a couple of inches, stuck on what was probably a warped floor board then opened fully as I pushed harder. We could see a couple of people inside, so in we went, hoping to get a cold beer and maybe some lunch.

An ancient oriental man shuffled over to us and pointed through a large room set with rickety tables to the outside veranda, where a few people sat at more rickety tables under large fans which sluggishly moved the hot, muggy air. Then he scuffled off somewhere in the back and we heard a door close. Always open to new experiences, we looked at each other, shrugged and walked across the dining room, the old, uneven floor creaking at every step.

Onto the veranda we went and leaned on the balustrade, looking down on the beach and the receding tide. To the left, a mile down the beach, the old ferry pier jutted out into the sparkling water and our dinghy was now probably high and dry close to it. I leaned further over and saw the veranda was supported by old, rotted wooden beams crudely held together with criss-crossed pieces of various-sized lumber. Judging by the antique molding in the dining room, the old bar and uneven floors, Gaugin himself may have rested here and sipped an anisette at the Hotel Chu a hundred years ago!

162

We sat at a long table covered by a greasy plastic tablecloth with benches on both sides, gazing out at the bay. A disinterested Panamanian waitress came over and took our order looking blankly everywhere but at us. I glanced around at the other couple of tables; one had a group of locals in the corner, drinking beer, eating noodles and playing dominoes. The only other occupied table had a lone guy, muscular, in his mid-thirties, blond, a bottle of Stolichnaya and a glass in front of him. He was looking at us and I nodded; he smiled back and raised his glass.

Occasionally we caught a whiff of guano and I pulled my binoculars out of my pack and focused them on the little island a couple of miles away. There was a battered old freighter tied up to a battered old dock and an ancient crane was turning, dipping, turning back and dumping great quantities of fertilizer into the hold. A white coating of guano dust hovered over the island, reminiscent of Pigpen in the Charlie Brown comics! The man who had acknowledged us picked up his bottle and glass, pushed his chair noisily back and, uninvited, weaved over to our table and plonked himself down on our bench, next to Joell.

He was tall, probably 6'4", Slavic looking, muscular, tattooed, drunk.

"Allo," he slurred, "Spik Eengliss?"

I nodded slightly, not wanting to encourage him. Joell looked straight ahead, uncomfortable with his proximity.

"Me name Ivan, frum Roosha." he informed us proudly, raising his glass and gulping a shot of vodka. "You like wodka?"

Before I could answer, he yelled at the waitress in rudimentary Spanish to bring another bottle of Stoli and two glasses. I started to protest, but he didn't care – he wanted to party and he wanted to party with us. As Ivan edged closer to Joell on the bench, I got

163

the feeling he'd prefer to party with Joell, without me...

He slopped some Stoli into two glasses for us and in the spirit of detente, we smiled, toasted something in Russian and chugged them down. Our beer and lunch arrived and we hoped he would have enough sense to go away, but, of course he didn't.

"See sheep dare?" he asked, pointing to the freighter loading guano offshore. "Dat my sheep, I da mate on sheep," he said proudly.

We didn't want to encourage him, but I also didn't want to piss off a tall, muscular, drunk Russian...

"Oh yes. Guano?" I asked, rhetorically.

"Da. Guano, ver' good cargo. Smeyl bad, ha ha!"

We nodded our heads. The smell of bird crap wafted around him, reinforcing his comment.

"Now ve drink, hev party, da?" as he edged closer to Joell and put his arm around her shoulder.

His eyes were unfocused, glassy and also steely; he looked dangerous and with his boxer physique undoubtedly was. He inched closer to Joell, right up next to her, acting as if I wasn't there.

Joell glanced at me questioningly – Ivan had taken a shine to her and the fact that she was with me fazed him not. He squeezed her shoulder. I opened my mouth to say something that would have led to a confrontation, when Ivan stood and put one of his legs over the bench, holding onto the table with two shaking arms. I thought he was going to attack me and started to get up, my legs like jelly, but not from too much vodka.

"I go toy-lit now, you drink, drink wodka, ver' good, da," he said as he stumbled to get up.

"OK, Ivan, take your time," I said with a smile on my face.

He slapped me on the back as he staggered by, looked at down at Joell and gave her a big wink. He hiccuped and bounced off the doorjamb, heading inside to find the men's room.

"OK Joie, this could develop really quickly into a dangerous situation. I don't want to get into a fight with this asshole."

"No, you're right. We could spend the night in a Panamanian jail until they sorted it out. And they're so corrupt here it could cost us a bunch of money. Let's get out of here, now!"

As Joie stood up and pushed it back the bench fell over, making a loud clatter - I hoped it wouldn't alert our Russian protagonist. I hurriedly reached into my pocket and removed a crumpled wad of money, pulled out a twenty dollar bill and stuffed it into the hand of the implacable waitress, who was passing by. I grabbed Joie's hand and pulled her toward the front of the hotel – she didn't need any encouragement!

There were four doors along the hallway, two of them restrooms on the left and a staircase along the opposite wall, leading to rooms above. We could hear someone in the room labeled 'Hombres' and hoped the door wouldn't open as we tiptoed past. The double front doors were ahead and I pulled on the handle - it didn't budge! Someone had locked it, which I thought was pretty strange as the hotel and restaurant were still open. I let go of Joell's hand, turned the knob and pulled again. The door moved a few inches, then stuck on the warped floorboards again. We heard the sound of a toilet being flushed – Ivan was finished, and we were just feet from him, trying to get out.

With a noisy screech I yanked the door wide open and pushed Joell through, following quickly and leaving the sticky door open. She turned right and started running down the narrow street. I heard a door open behind me just as I made the first step and turned right – Ivan was done and I hoped he hadn't seen me disappear through the entrance. I didn't stop to look behind, but took off after Joell.

She was moving as fast as her flip-flops would allow, not looking behind.

"Run Joie, run!" I yelled unnecessarily as I caught up with her. We zipped past the small stand where we had bought ice-cream cones a couple of hours before. There were a bunch of people under the small awning, staying out of the heat, gossiping. They watched in amazement as we ran past them down the little street. No one ran on the island in this heat and humidity, except two crazy gringos!

I looked behind, expecting to see a large, angry Russian seaman chasing us, but perhaps it hadn't dawned on his drunk brain yet that we had not stuck around for his idea of a party. We turned a corner and the street went uphill, slowing us.

I pulled a bottle of water out of my pack as we now trotted along and handed it to Joell. She took a swig and we picked up our pace. We were heading for the beach and the dinghy we'd left anchored there on a falling tide two hours earlier. Now we were on the beach road getting closer to the pier and I could see our dinghy ahead, high and dry, sitting on the sand, a hundred yards from the water – not good.

We still didn't know if Ivan was after us and didn't want to stick around to find out. Skidding to the right onto the sand, we stopped briefly to take off our sandals. I thought I saw someone back up the street running toward us.

"What'll we do now, Jon?" Joell asked, a little panicked. "The dinghy's so far from the water, maybe we should just leave it here and run down to Playa Restinga and swim out to JoJo?"

"No, we're not going to leave our dinghy and outboard here," I panted, as we pulled up next to it. I bent over, breathing heavily, sweat pouring off me, then straightened up and looked behind us. Someone was on the promenade, looking toward us. I didn't want to waste time pulling out my binoculars to try and identify him. I just assumed it was a large Russian...

I sprinted to the small anchor which had buried itself deep as the ebbing tide had floated the dinghy toward the sea. I yanked and pulled and wiggled it and it broke free.

"OK, Joie! I think that's him back up the beach. Hurry, grab the rope on the port side and I'll grab the starboard. We're going to lift it a few inches off the ground and run it down to the water. I don't want to get into a fight with Ivan, 'cause I'll probably come out the worst!"

With the thin rope in our hands we hefted the eight-foot dinghy with its four h.p. motor attached to the transom and started down the beach, shuffling under the weight. Sweat streamed off us as we plodded across the sand, heads down, occasionally tripping over small rocks. The rope cut into our hands and the dinghy swayed in between us, bumping our legs and throwing us off balance. The sun burned down and it felt like we were struggling through molasses. It was fear that kept us moving forward. Not just fear of what that big moron could do, but what the Panamanian police might do if they got involved.

We reached the water and kept on going until the little grey dinghy was bobbing in a foot of water.

Joell was panting heavily and so was I, as we flopped over the thwarts and tumbled onto the slatted floorboards. I looked toward the beach and Ivan was running fast, weaving a little, only a hundred yards away...

"Shit, it's him and he's pissed!" I said, as I hurriedly tilted the outboard down. It was still too shallow and it wouldn't go down all the way – it was useless until we could get further out into deeper water.

I jumped out of the dinghy and started pushing it frantically, my feet slipping, my breathing heavy. At least it was a tiny bit cooler in the water! Joell was leaning over the bow paddling madly with both her hands. The bottom dropped off and I clambered back in, as the little motor tilted down and locked - I yanked the starting handle and it sprang into life. Ivan was now at the waters edge, just fifty yards away, deciding whether or not to plunge in after us. He then made a drunken decision as he kicked off his shoes and waded quickly toward us. He was yelling something at us in Russian and it didn't sound flattering...

I pushed the gear lever forward and twisted the throttle wide open. All four horses took off as quickly as they could with me looking back at him. At that moment I wished I had a bigger dinghy with a 15 hp. Yamaha! Ivan the Terrible was splashing around in four feet of water waving his fist at us. I didn't think people actually waved fists at other people, thought it was something in a bad Hollywood movie, but perhaps they really did that in Russia? I steered straight off the beach until we were a hundred yards away, then turned left and skirted the end of the pier, dodging an incoming ferry.

As it was low tide, we had to travel around the end of El Morro point at the tip of its own tiny islet; when the water was in, there was just enough depth for us to get the dinghy through the shallow cut between the islet and the beach. But now it took longer and I was worried that this maniac would see where we were heading and cut us off, as he ran along the beach.

168

"OK, love," I said over the sound of the straining little engine."He's probably figured out we've got a boat anchored off the beach. He seems to be fixated on us – no, on you – so we need to get away from the island. As soon as we get back to JoJo, you climb aboard and start the engine. I'll tie off the dinghy and get the anchor up, OK."

Joell nodded and got ready to scramble up the swim steps. JoJo was in sight a hundred yards away as we rounded the little hill on the left. I looked along the beach and saw a figure loping toward where we were going. JoJo was only a hundred feet off the beach, anchored in about six feet of water. It was slack tide, so she bobbed around with what little wind there was coming from the bay, which meant she was facing out of the small anchorage.

I drove up to her twin transoms in a welter of spray and throttled back. Joell reached over for the grab bar and quickly climbed from the low dinghy onto the swim platform, then up the three small steps and tumbled into the cockpit. She scrabbled around in a small locker and pulled out the engine key, which she put in the ignition and turned. The Yanmar diesel faithfully burbled to life, as it had hundreds of times before. There was a loud yell from the beach and Ivan was there, wading into the water toward us...

I clipped the dinghy onto a cleat, leaped up the steps and raced to the bow. We didn't have an anchor winch, so I signaled to Joie to put the transmission into forward and pointed to where the anchor rope disappeared into the water, leading to the anchor, now buried deep in the sand six feet down. We had pulled the anchor up so many times together, we didn't need words. I hauled it in rapidly, looking behind as Ivan swam toward us with a powerful crawl stroke. I didn't know how he swam so fast, but maybe the run had sobered him up. Whatever it was, although still a bit rattled, I was quite impressed with his persistence...

The anchor rope piled up behind me on the foredeck, as my arms

169

pumped and my hands pulled. Joie steered toward the anchor, following my hand directions. Now the rope had changed to chain, fifty feet of which was shackled between the rope and anchor. It was quickly straight up and down, right over the buried anchor and I took a turn around a cleat to break it free as JoJo motored over it. There was a momentary dip of the bows as the anchor broke loose. I whipped the chain off the cleat with one hand and signalled to Joie for full speed ahead with the other. I pulled in the rest of the chain and the anchor settled onto the bow roller, where I pushed in the retaining pin.

Joell was calling to me and I ran back to the cockpit.

"What's the matter – is it Ivan?" I asked. I looked behind and he was now a hundred yards back, the gap widening.

"No, it's not him. It's really low tide and there's rocks near us!"

I pulled the throttle back and we slowed down.

"OK, you did good – I'll take over now," I said as she moved out of the way and let me behind the wheel. "Why don't you grab us some cold water from the fridge," I suggested.

I turned around to see Ivan treading water, again waving his fist at us, a couple of hundred yards back. I stood on my seat and gave him a one-fingered salute, turned away from Taboga Island and set a course for Panama City, ten miles away...

Four years later in 2004, we were again anchored off Taboga Island, having made our third passage through the Panama Canal aboard Ladyhawke, our 64' luxury trimaran. We were going to be starting our day charter business in conjunction with the Contadora Hotel in Las Perlas Islands, but had a couple of weeks to hang out. We dinghied ashore and went for a walk, thought we might finish those beers we had started four years earlier at the

Hotel Chu! We strolled along the narrow street and bought ice cream at the same little stand. We continued our quest, catching the drips as the cones rapidly melted, licking the tasty treats. As we rounded the corner, we expected to see the Hotel Chu, but it no longer existed – just a big, empty space. The old hotel with all its memories had been torn down and nothing had replaced it yet. Or maybe it had just fallen down!

Joell and I sat on a low wall across from the ex-Hotel Chu and finished our ice creams. A gringo came ambling down the road, deeply tanned, wearing a tattered straw hat. He stopped and we got into conversation. He was an American and told us he'd been living in a little house on the other side of the island for a few years and was on his way to town to buy some provisions. He seemed like an interesting character and we offered to buy him a beer. As we sat around a little bar talking, we told him we were on the big trimaran anchored off the beach.

"First time in Panama?" he asked casually.

"No, we were here four years ago on our catamaran JoJo. In fact, when we just met you, Joell and I were heading for the Hotel Chu to finish a couple of beers we had to leave in a hurry back then!"

His ears perked up.

"Wait a minute, was your catamaran painted green?" he asked.

"Yes, yes it was."

"Did you guys leave in a hurry because a drunk Russian sailor was chasing you?"

"Yes indeed – how do you know?" was my surprised reply.

"Are you kidding! Everyone on the island knows that story – you two are legendary here..."

OUR SCHIPPERKES...

To quote the AKC: The small, foxlike Schipperke (pronounced 'Skipper-key') is known for its mischievous expression and distinctive black coat. This enthusiastic, joyful, and sometimes willful dog has a thickset and cobby body, and lacks a tail. The Schipperke is extremely active and loves to be involved in what is going on around him. The Schipperke originated in the Flemish regions of Belgium in the early 16th century. They were bred as watchdogs and ratters on the river barges, which is where they got the name "Schipperke" since the Flemish word 'schip' means boat. Another common nickname for the Schipperke is 'Little Captain.'

'CHARLEY'

Frenchman's Creek Marina is a peaceful, semi-wild refuge tucked in amongst the upscale homes and condo towers of Juno Beach, near Jupiter in south Florida. JoJo, our 32ft. British catamaran, bobbed gently in her slip, 'resting' after the previous three years carrying us safely from San Francisco. We had been at the marina for about two months and were busily starting our 'Natural Awakenings' health magazine in August, 2001.

Joell handled the production end with the franchise corporate office and I drove around Palm Beach and Martin counties in the Bugatti replica or our classic Jaguar XJ6, 'Miss Kitty' (when it was running!) selling advertising space. It was a rather frantic, yet enjoyable and creative period in our lives. Every day, when I would leave the boat and then return, a small black dog with pointy ears, like a little fox, would run up and down the deck of the sailboat it lived on and bark excitedly at me. It was a pretty little dog with lots of high energy, although its owners, a young couple, were gone most of the time and it appeared the dog was starved for attention.

Early one September morning, we were trying to call some contributors to the magazine and nobody was answering their phone. I went out to the cockpit and a neighbour hurried by and called to me that there was a new world order coming!

"What are you talking about, Seth?" I asked.

"Turn on your television, man!"

"We don't have a television, don't want one!" I responded almost jovially.

"Well turn on your radio or go somewhere there's a TV. Looks like we're under a huge terrorist attack in New York. They've destroyed the World Trade Towers. This is nuts! 'Bye."

And he was gone, hurrying up to the parking lot. I went back into the salon and told Joie to sit down.

"Look, I don't know what's going on but apparently something drastic is happening in New York. I'm going to the office, they have a TV in the little lounge. I think you should come with me."

We walked quickly up the dock to the office, the little black dog on the nearby boat whining as we hurried past. In the lounge, there were half a dozen people, silent, staring at the unfolding scene on the screen. We sat down, grim-faced and watched in horror as scenes of the planes crashing into the Twin Towers were played and re-played, with confusing reports coming in. After fifteen minutes, we went back to the boat, shaken and concerned.

"Well, we don't know what's going to happen, could turn into total war," I said quietly to Joell, holding her hand. "If that happens, I think we should leave and sail to the Bahamas. Let's go to the market and buy a bunch of staples, rice and beans and stuff, just in case."

When that was done, we went back to the TV and watched for the rest of the day. Like everyone in America we tried to make sense of what had happened and searched for clues as to what could or would happen next. Over the next week, it became apparent that this was the work of a handful of men, two of whom had taken flying lessons just down the road! Despite the anthrax scare, it didn't seem like war on an international scale was going to erupt.

Two weeks after the attack, it was linked to Osama bin Laden – we thought it more than coincidental that there were verifiable reports that the only flight to leave right after every plane in the country was grounded, belonged to the bin Laden family, old friends of the then-President's family...

We had put the publication of our first magazine on hold, but now the deadline was a few days away. We decided to go ahead and I re-wrote the editorial to reflect the massive changes going on in the country. The next few days were quite frenetic as we finalized all the ads I had sold and the small corporate office helped with the layout and printing. When it was ready, and we received our first 5000 copies, we were told by the founder of the magazine that it was the 'thickest first issue' they'd ever had!

Then I spent three days driving all over the area in the old, non air-conditioned Jag delivering copies, because I was not only the sales department, but distribution too! The magazine was received very well and we prepared to print the second edition of the monthly.

One day in October when Joell and I were walking down the dock, I passed the boat where the little black dog would normally plead for attention, but he wasn't there. As we continued past, all of a sudden there was a frenzied barking and whining from under the dock. I looked over and the black dog was in the water, frantically trying to climb on the dock, which was too high and too steep for him. He had obviously fallen from the deck of his boat and was splashing around, trying to claw his way out.

I was instantly concerned as there were two big alligators that called the marina home. They usually kept to themselves, but I was afraid the noise and disturbance of the terrified dog would attract one. I looked over to the bank where they normally laid out in the sun and only one of them was there. But there was a ripple near the bank and I could see the two ancient eyes and the snout of its mate slowly heading our way...

174

There wasn't time to come up with a plan. I immediately dropped my bag, told Joie to watch the approaching alligator and jumped down to their dock. These were not floating docks, as there was only a couple of feet difference in the tide and they weren't necessary. It was about four feet down to the water and I got flat on my stomach and leaned down as far as I could. The little black dog became more agitated - something, maybe the vibration in the water of the giant amphibian, spooked him. But I couldn't reach him.

And then, without thinking, I jumped into the water, grabbed the dog by the scruff of his neck and literally flung him onto the dock. I reached up and kicked my legs, got my hands on the lip and with Joell reaching down and holding my arm, I rolled up and onto the decking. The dog was shaking the water off him and ran up and licked my face. It didn't have a tail, but waggled its rump in a most comical way.

The weather was typically warm and I wasn't concerned about being wet. Out of the corner of my eye, I saw the alligator stop and submerge until only its eyes were showing, about a hundred yards away. I picked up the little dog and carried him down to JoJo and dried him off in the cockpit. We kept him all day and he was very grateful to me, happy on our boat and stayed pressed against my legs. When we saw the kids who owned him return to their boat, we couldn't believe what they had in their arms – two skinny little puppies!

We walked up to them boat as they were preparing to go below.

"Hey, I've got your dog here, a Schipperke, right?"

"Yep, what are you doin' with him?"

I explained what had happened, that they'd left this nice dog on their deck and it had fallen into the water. They were nonchalant about it, said thanks and took him from me.

"Did you just get two more dogs?" I asked incredulously.

"Yeah, two miniature Doberman puppies. Cute, ain't they!"

No, I didn't think they were cute, neither did Joie, but we didn't say anything. From then on, every time I walked past their boat, the little black dog would run up to the bow, stretch his head out as far as he could and paw the air at me. He whined and trembled.

A few days later the couple were sitting on the lawn near the parking lot, the little black dog tied short on his leash. The two skinny, unattractive puppies were cavorting around, their ears grotesquely taped up. It was obvious that the couple were enchanted by their yapping brown dogs and were paying scant attention to the Schipperke, who leaped up and strained to get to me. Without consulting Joell, I made a command decision. I reached into my pocket and pulled out my wallet.

"What's the name of the black dog?" I asked.

"Him? His name's Harley. Why?"

"Because I've been watching you the last few days and I don't think you give a damn about that nice dog." I pulled a bill out of my wallet. "Here's a hundred bucks. You keep the puppies, my wife and I will give Harley a good home."

Without waiting for a response, I thrust the bill into his hand, unclipped the dog from his leash and carried him back to JoJo, my wife right behind.

"I can't believe you did that, Jon...but I'm glad you did!" she said.

The dog jumped up onto the cockpit seat and was trembling with excitement.

"Well, I don't like those kids and this dog is being neglected. I don't like his name, either - reminds me of the loud motorbikes. Let's add a 'C' and call him Charley."

And Charley was a wonderful dog. He seemed to know that I had helped him and he was very loyal. He behaved well on his leash and sat upright in the passenger seat when I'd take him for a drive in the Bugatti – he loved it! And everyone loved him. Wherever we took him, people would ask what kind of dog he was. We had

176

met several Schipperkes over the past few years on different boats – they are very popular with cruising sailors as they're small, smart, don't shed much and are fiercely protective.

He had a distinct personality (as did all of our Schipperkes), but Charley made us initially realize just how special these bright, intelligent little dogs are.

A few months after we made him a part of our family, we decided to sell the magazine and go to truck driving school.* Here we were publishing a natural health magazine and we were getting out of shape and unhealthy!

Joell's sister Lois and her husband Fred occasionally fostered stray dogs while a home was found for them. Their Schipperke, Taz, had died recently and we called them up in Oxnard where they lived, north of L.A.

"So Fred, we're going to truck-driving school for six weeks. We can't bring Charley with us. If we send him out to you, would you and Lois take care of him for a couple of months 'till we can come and pick him up?"

They were very agreeable and a few weeks later Charley was put in a special kennel and flew from Florida to California by himself. After we had finished training, we were flown out to Salt Lake City to get our truck. I called Fred and wasn't surprised when he said Charley was a wonderful dog and had bonded with their other canines and was now part of the family.

"So we're not getting him back, right?" I asked.

"Well Jon, he loves it here and we love him. We'd like to keep the little bugger..."

Joell and I thought this might happen and had discussed it before we called Fred. Much as we loved little Charley, we had concerns about how he would handle the restrictions of the cab of a truck – we didn't think it would be fair to him. Joell nodded in silent agreement.

"Sure Fred. Charley's yours. We know we'll get to see him occasionally..."

And so Charley found a warm, loving new home and lived a full, happy life, totally devoted to Fred. We did see him a few times over the years and coincidentally were visiting Fred and Lois on the day Charley died in 2012...

'SAILOR'

After an exhausting year of truck driving, we headed back to Florida and JoJo was moved from the storage area to the work yard at Glades Boat Storage on the Okeechobee Waterway. We had been able to visit Charley a few times when we had time off in the L.A. area. He had seemed pleased to see us, but it was obvious he had bonded with Fred and Lois and we knew he'd stay there.

Joie and I had talked about rescuing another dog and we knew it would be a Schipperke. While we worked on the boat during the day, we searched the internet at night, looking for Schipperkes. We found a Schipperke rescue organization in Ft. Lauderdale and they said they had a dog they thought would be perfect for us. Three days later we drove our VW Vanagon to Ft. Lauderdale, two hours away.

In a modest suburban home, in a labrynth of large cages and connecting wire tunnels snaking around the dining room and kitchen were eight Schipperke rescue dogs. Which was one ours? We had been told on the phone that we would be looking at a neutered male, about five years old that they had named Taylor. Apparently he had been found wandering the streets of Orlando and his skin was sunburned – the authorities who picked him up off the street thought he had been a breeding dog in a puppy mill, who had been tossed out on the street about three weeks before they got him. He had wandered around in the blistering heat of the mid-Florida sun and when caught, he was taken to Animal Control, in Florida a euphemism for a kill facility.

We didn't know it at the time, but there are a number of different organizations, mostly manned by unpaid volunteers, who go into kill facilities and find dogs that are of the specific breed they care about. Then they pull the dogs out and care for them until they're adopted – Paula was one of those angels.

"No, none of these are Taylor," she told us as she closed the doors and they stopped barking. "Your dog is in the far room down the hall. If you wait here I'll let him out. We'll see what y'all think of each other!"

Joie and I sat on our heels as the door was opened. A black bundle of fur raced down the wood floor, skidded to a stop and rolled over on his back right in front of us, eyes sparkling, tongue out happily. After rubbing his belly, it was a love fest all around!

We moved into the living room and sat on sofas around a coffee table to complete the adoption process. Taylor trotted in after us, climbed on the couch between Joell and I, turned around, placed his two front feet on the table and proceeded to intently watch the paperwork shuffle – it was very endearing!

"There's something you need to know before the final signatures," said Paula. "We're pretty sure he was kicked out of a puppy mill, one reason being he wasn't neutered when he was found. Some of these awful people will cut the vocal chords of any breeding dogs that bark a lot. Taylor hasn't barked once in the four weeks he's been here, so he probably never will. Is that an issue for you?"

Joie and I watched the handsome, earnest little dog, sitting expectantly between us, ears perked up, eyes not missing anything; we looked at each other and turned to Paula.

"No, it's not an issue," we both said at the same time!

We left a few minutes later and Taylor sat on Joell's lap, his front feet on the dashboard, enjoying his ride home. I couldn't keep my eyes off him, he was not only a good looking little guy, he already had a distinctive personality as well.

"So Joie, here we are heading back to our sailboat with a dog named Taylor. I think we need to make a small change to his name so it's more apropos. What do you think if we substitute an 'S' for the 'T'?"

"We do think alike, Cap'n! I was just thinking the same thing!"

When we arrived back at the boat yard, I tucked Sailor under my arm and climbed the tall ladder propped up against the side of the boat. We introduced him to his new home and he happily explored every inch of it before deciding the starboard settee was his spot.

That evening there was to be a large party in the boat yard for all the people working on their boats. Around nine o'clock, with a bonfire lighting up the yard, I carried a curious Schipperke down the ladder and started introducing him to everyone. He was friendly and got along with the half dozen other dogs that were wandering around the party - Sailor stayed on his leash. Paula had told us that one day while he was in their yard, he had dug a hole under the fence and she caught him just as he was about to make his escape! She recommended we keep him on a leash at all times – apparently, like us, he had the wanderlust!

Eventually someone pulled out a guitar and sang a Jimmy Buffett song and everyone clapped at the end. Sailor leaped up and to our delight and amazement, started barking at the applause! It was a gruff, harsh bark, as indeed his vocal chords had been cut, but not completely. We were thrilled that he had his own voice and several times over the next few years we'd hear that special bark when he had something important to say...and always when he heard applause!

He adventured with us for years, sailed many miles and went through the Panama Canal on our 64' charter trimaran. He shut down a TV shoot for a Spanish novella we were hosting, when he ran away in Colombia and the whole film crew and actors, about a hundred people and us, combed out and searched for him! We met a lot of people through Sailor, especially in Spanish-speaking countries and made a lot of friends..

Besides being very intelligent, Sailor was usually a most dignified little dog – except around children, he loved children! There were many times in different countries when he'd be in the middle of five or ten or fifteen kids all eager to take him for a walk. He was pet of the week in the Sonoma newspaper, with a photo of him 'cranking' on a jib winch in the Caribbean! He drove cross-country with us four times, always up for an adventure, never complaining, always having fun with us.

He was reserved around other dogs, would sniff politely and then move on. Except for one dog he fell in love with the moment he saw her... It was while we were staying in Ft. Myers, Florida aboard JoJo and I had my one and only construction job helping build a Joe's Crab Shack next to the marina where we were living. We were strolling in the lovely riverside park, heading for our evening walk through the small, eclectic, mostly empty downtown.

Ahead down the path a man was walking a pony! That's about the size of the animal that was approaching us, but it was in fact a gigantic Great Dane, the tallest one I'd ever seen. As they got closer, we moved off the path to let them by, but the owner and the dog stopped to chat. Well, Sailor looked up, way up and liked what he saw – he immediately started humping the left back leg of that majestic creature, much to our horror! He'd never done that before and the big dog did not approve. He took off down the path, Sailor gruffly barking his affection in dismay as the Great Dane dragged his owner after him!

The following evening we were walking down the main street and ahead saw the Great Dane heading toward us. Sailor saw her too and pulled on his leash. It was comical to see; our little black dog who weighed about fifteen pounds in love with a Great Dane about four feet tall! The owner was not amused and immediately crossed over to the other side of the street, pulling his dog with him and hurried away. Sailor was most disappointed, never taking his eyes off his love until she disappeared down a side street....

After several years, Sailor started to have mild seizures, which eventually grew much worse. Joell researched what it might be and discovered that Schipperkes are prone to epilepsy. It was heart-wrenching to watch his little body go rigid and arch backwards, his soft brown eyes wide with fright as he struggled to breathe for two or three minutes.

Finally, in 2009, while we were staying for a couple of months at my brothers house, Sailor started to rapidly decline and one Thursday morning he looked up at us and in his eyes we could see that he was tired, in pain and had had enough. The vet was very empathetic as I held my little friend in my arms and she inserted the needle. He jerked once as the drug entered his veins and in a second he was put out of his pain. For those of you who have gone through this, you know how we felt, how we cried...

Sailor is buried under a pear tree in Grant's orchard, a peaceful, beautiful spot. But he left us a living legacy. Three years earlier, just after we had opened our art gallery in Sonoma, Joell and I took a break on Earth Day. We went to a small pet store in town and while I was paying for Sailors food, she had wandered over to a cage in the window that held a lovely chocolate brown cat. As I prepared to leave, Joell had Sailor in her arms and was standing by the cage, which was at shoulder height, near the door. I watched, entranced, as the cat, which was laying on its side, reached her left front leg out through the bars and rested her paw on Sailors' cheek. He didn't get upset, just let her interact with him, looked at her and seemed to approve.

Two hours later we had adopted the female Chantilly from the local rescue group who sometimes placed their cats in the pet store. We named her Terra Cat, as she became part of our family on Earth Day. Sailor and Terra got along famously and they both flew, sailed and drove thousands of miles with us.

As of 2014, Terra is healthy, happy, very talkative and demanding! She has lived with three of our four Schipperkes and is quite pragmatic about dealing with her various 'brothers'...

'JACK TAR'

A year after we buried Sailor, we were back in Florida, living in a small house in Sarasota. We had a nice sized, fully fenced back yard and no Schipperke! Through the Ft. Lauderdale rescue we discovered there was a woman nearby in Tampa who was about to give up her fathers' Schipperke.

We talked to her on the phone and she told us the dog, 'Buddha' had been bought by her two years earlier as a gift for her wheelchair-bound father. He had died recently and she wasn't able to properly take care of the dog. It was a bit overweight and needed a home where he could be properly taken care of. She drove down two days later and we met at a local dog park.

When she opened the car door, this fat, wriggling ball of black fur tried to jump down, but was so obese, it was afraid to make the leap. She helped Buddha down and he waddled over to the park and sniffed around. Joell and I were horrified at the neglect this dog had suffered. Apparently, her father couldn't exercise the dog and it had spent most of its life in a cage. When the daughter got the dog, she kept it in the cage in her apartment all day while she worked.

There were a couple of dogs in the park, but he didn't want anything to do with them, in fact he growled when they approached him. Joell and I excused ourselves and went for a walk to discuss whether we should take him or not. Looking back over our seventeen years together, we've rescued many things: five sailboats, several cars, four dogs and a cat! Obviously, this was a dog that needed to be rescued and brought back to health...

On the way home, with a fat, concerned Schipperke in the back, we couldn't help but compare him to Charley and Sailor. With his black fur and pointy face, he looked like a gross caricature, hugely obese.

"First thing we need to do is change his name," I suggested to Joell. "How about something nautically related?"

We went through and rejected a litany of nautical names until I suggested 'Jack Tar', 19th century slang for a British seaman. Jack was introduced to Terra and immediately chased her around the house - this was probably the most exercise he'd ever had! We separated them and proceeded to work on getting Jack back to health. It appeared he'd been fed table food and wasn't too thrilled with the strict diet we kept him on.

I took him for daily walks and on the first one it was apparent he had socializing issues. Whenever he'd see another dog, he would go into a rage, barking, snarling, straining on his leash, teeth bared. Picking him up (which wasn't easy as he weighed over thirty pounds) didn't help as he struggled and writhed to break free – he also nipped at my hands. We watched videos of Cesar Millan and tried different ways to get him to calm down around other dogs and were successful to a degree.

Over the next few months he lost about ten pounds and enjoyed himself tremendously racing around the yard, playing hide-and-seek with me amongst the bushes and trees. But he always looked for a chance to growl at Terra, who, being a smart cat, had learned to move around the house using tables and furniture to stay out of his reach. In mid-December we moved from the house into a lovely second floor condo, just south of Sarasota near the beach.

Joell had not been feeling well for a few weeks and on Christmas Eve I took her to the emergency room. After two cat scans, the doctor pulled me aside and told me she needed emergency surgery immediately. They pulled together a team at midnight and the best Christmas present I ever had was when the tired surgeon came out and told me she would live. When she came home a week later, it was obvious she wouldn't be able to get up and down the stairs by herself to take Jack for his walks. I was working every day and we really couldn't give Jack the care and attention he needed. We decided it would be in his best interest if he went to a loving home with a big yard so he could run and play. Now that we had got most of his weight off he was sleek and fast and needed to go out at least three times a day.

I talked with Schipperke rescue and one of their foster homes up in Georgia said they would take him and had someone with a farm they could adopt him out to. It wasn't an easy decision, but it was the right one. One morning, just before dawn, Joell hugged him and said goodbye. Jack and I traveled six hours in our Mercedes station wagon and the last two hours, he lay across the seat with his head in my lap, my hand ruffling the fur on his head – he knew something was happening and was sad, as was I.

But when we arrived at the small ranch, he leaped out happily and ran to greet the other dogs playing in the front yard. I met Barbara and we chatted about Jack and the family who would soon adopt him. I told her about his socializing issues, but perhaps that had changed as he was rollicking and running with the other dogs. He was a far cry from the fat, waddling, aggressive dog we'd rescued six months earlier...We hope he's happy – we've never heard anything more about him.

"PEG-LEG PETE THE PIRATE"

In 2012, after moving back to California, we bought my second SR2 simulator, setting it up and eventually selling it in Tucson.** Joell and I then bought a large motor home and drove to Jensen Beach, a small town on the Atlantic coast in Florida. We spent a hot, humid summer living on a unique island next to the beach. I sailed a Catalina 25' sloop we bought and rebuilt a second Bugatti replica.

We swam each day in the lovely pool next to the Atlantic ocean waves, went for long walks and got healthy. But there was something lacking in our life there - we just felt this area, although very pretty, didn't have the right energy for us. In September we decided to move near St. Augustine, where we had lived a few years earlier on our 37' sloop 'Beach Money'. We drove up in the Miata and found a small, quiet RV park across from a glorious miles-long walking beach.

The following week I hooked up a U-haul car trailer to the motor home and carefully drove the Bugatti onto it. With Joell following in the Miata, we drove up A1A for four hours to our new 'home' in St. Augustine Beach on Anastasia Island. That's one of the nice things about living in a motor home – it takes half an hour to disconnect from the grid and move your home!

We had really enjoyed St. Augustine when we lived there for a few months. It's the oldest city in America and once you get beyond the tacky tourist places, is full of old (for America!) homes and buildings, oozing history. There is a pretty waterfront, an ancient Spanish fortress and lots of connections to pirates! And we were enjoying it this time, too, although neither of us were quite sure why we were there or what we were going to do...

A month after we arrived, Joell told me over our morning coffee that we needed to talk. I tried to think if I was in trouble for something in particular, but couldn't think of anything...

"I was surfing the internet last night and it seems there's a Schipperke up for adoption, right here on the island..."

We had talked occasionally about getting another dog, but I saw it as way in the future, when we had a little more direction in our lives.

"Wow, I wasn't expecting that, Joie!" relieved that it wasn't about me! "Are we ready for a dog right now? I mean we haven't talked about it for ages..."

"Well, I don't even know if they still have him. He's at that little rescue place down A1A a couple of miles. Can we go and look at him...please?"

I couldn't say no, so an hour later, on a lovely Sunday morning we found ourselves sitting in the office of S.A.F.E., a small, private rescue shelter with about thirty dogs in large cages in the next room There were a few volunteers from the neighbourhood who came and took the dogs for a walk. It was quite casual and comfortable. Before we met the Schpperke, we sat down with the lady in charge and talked about adopting the dog. When we told her we had already rescued three Schipperkes and understood their idiosyncrasies, she was delighted.

She then told us that S.A.F.E. was an all-volunteer operation that would go to the Animal Control (kill) centre in Jacksonville and take as many dogs out as they could handle. They had seen this dog, called 'Crash' two weeks earlier, an unusual dog, obviously a pure-bred. Apparently he had been given to Animal Control because his owners had been kicked out of their apartment and were homeless. They figured he was about eight years old, he was overweight, had rotten teeth and also a cough. She thought the dog had been neglected, probably physically abused.

I felt a little uneasy about rescuing a dog with these problems, but Joell had no such qualms. He was let into the room and walked over to us, coughing slightly. He was docile and friendly, but was about ten pounds overweight and had the worst breath of any dog I'd ever met! They clipped on a leash and we took him for a walk, a slow walk...he just had no energy.

At one point he started coughing and he looked up at us sadly, humiliated, embarrassed as if he was thinking to himself that there's no way they'll take me home with them now. I hunched down and went to look in his mouth. Before I could reach it, he licked me gently on my hand and peered up at me with questioning brown eyes, ears up, head tilted to the left.

He opened his mouth for me and it was a horrible sight inside. His teeth were green and yellow, with big red and yellow infected sores on his gums, some covering his molars. He looked mortified and started coughing again, trying to close his mouth so we couldn't see his wretched condition.

"Phew, I don't know, Joie. He's a real mess – maybe we're taking on too much? But he is a nice dog, isn't he..."

"I think he really needs us, Jon. He jumped out at me from the computer for a reason – there aren't any Schipperkes right now for hundreds of miles and here he is, just down the street. We can fix these problems – Barbara said that S.A.F.E. will pay half the dental, and we know how to deal with weight and coughs. Please,

187

he needs someone to save his life and we're perfect for him..."

Of course, we left an hour later with the coughing dog and the phone number for their vet. 'Crash' didn't work for us as a name for a dog, we hoped it wasn't a reflection of the household he'd come from. We tried 'Skip' or 'Captain' or 'Dick' or 'Buddy' – but none of them worked. And then I came up with what I thought was a great name: Peg-Leg Pete the Pirate!

"Well, it's different...but it's really long!" commented Joell.

"I agree. How about we shorten it to Peg-Leg Pete the."

"Hah, hah – very funny! O.K. We'll call him Pete."

And so it was. When we got home, he tried to get up the two steps into The Duchess, our motor home, but it was all he could do to get his front feet onto the first step. I lifted him up and he sniffed around inside. Terra let out a pissed-off 'Miaowww' and Pete trotted off to say hello to her – it was very cordial.

We drove to the vet the following day and as she had put him on antibiotics to get rid of the cough, she said we had to wait two weeks before extracting the five teeth that needed to come out. While doing a quick examination of his mouth, she touched one of his molars and it just fell onto the table!

Poor Pete wasn't much for exercise. We took him to the beach every day and initially he would walk about fifty yards and stop, out of breath. His cough got better and his breath got worse...

The vet pulled his teeth and he looked most miserable as he came out of the anesthesia. Two days later we took him to the beach and he walked his normal few yards and stopped. He had lost a little weight as we fed him only good dog food and his breath was much sweeter. His eyes were also brighter and he had more energy; the infection was going away and his mouth was healing.

A few days later on the beach, he was walking slowly next to me and he started to run - he was on a long leash and I ran next to him. We ran a hundred yards – he stopped, panting, smiling and we ran back to Joell.

"Wow – where did that come from?"

Over the next few weeks he became a totally different dog than the one we had first met. Some of his fat turned into muscle, he loved to run and jump, his eyes sparkled and he made us laugh – a lot! He was well-behaved and, unlike any of the Schipperkes we'd had before, I could let him off his leash on the beach and he would come when I called him. We were delighted to have him as part of our family and he and Terra established an uneasy truce.

But as he became the dog that had lived inside him, there were also some troubling issues. He was deathly scared of any men, including me, who had something, anything in their hand. If he thought we were angry at him (we never were), he would cower on the ground, whimpering. Walking behind him, it's easy to see his spine is way out of alignment – his back legs 'crab' slightly to the right. It's obvious he was abused, probably beaten by the morons who had no idea what an intelligent, funny, loyal, thoroughly enjoyable little rascal they had.

We love him very much, he makes us laugh at least once a day and there's no doubt he loves us. Sometimes in the morning, as I'm slowly waking up, he'll feel me stir and quietly, so as not to wake Joell, he'll inch his way forward on the bed until his head is next to mine and I can feel his breath on my cheek. As soon as I open an eye, he stretches forward and gently licks my cheek. Petey is the sweetest, kindest, funniest dog I've owned and having him in our lives completes our family.

We're discovering he also has a lot of similar traits to Sailor. He looks like him, more than Charley or Jack did. He has the same little bump on his nose. He stands like him, runs like him, laughs like him and we both find ourselves sometimes inadvertently calling him Sailor. He also has epileptic fits every few weeks...

We believe they're related, is he Sailor's grandchild (grand pup?!) or great grand pup? After all, Sailor probably fathered hundreds

189

of dogs and St. Augustine is only a hundred miles from Orlando...

* 'The Open Highway', This book.
** See 'The Amazing Simulators', 'Everyone Said I Should Write
  Another Book'

AFGHAN DILEMMA

I sat in the back row of the rusty, creaking Japanese minibus as we bounced our way across the bleak Afghan desert from Kandahar to Kabul. In front of and next to me, their turbaned heads brushing the roof were seven Afghan tribesmen replete with ancient carbines and crossed bandoliers.

They talked amongst themselves and occasionally cast a glance back in my direction. Although there were a number of young westerners on the 'hippy trail' in that fall of 1971 this was probably the first time that a lone 'ferengi' with bushy beard and long hair traveled beside them. I was on my way to meet up with my friends who were already in Kabul. Foregoing my usual hitchhiking as the weather was turning cool, I had found this minivan in a small market area in Kandahar a couple of hours before. For two dollars I would be in Kabul soon. By now I was immune to the pervasive odour of unwashed bodies and uncured, dirty sheepskin coats emanating from my traveling companions.

It was the beginning of Ramadan, the holy month for Moslems; for thirty days they don't eat from dawn to dusk. I knew this but reached into my pack and brought out some crusty bread and goat cheese. Seven long, gaunt, slightly hostile faces turned toward me...

"Oh", said I, slapping my forehead, "Ramadan!"

I made a big deal of putting my food back into my pack, the tension was gone and they smiled good-naturedly.

These were the descendants of some of the fiercest warriors the world has ever known. They had withstood invading armies from Genghis Khan to the British Empire and would eventually defeat the Russians. It was said that if you were wounded in battle against the Afghans, it would be much better if you died, because when their women scoured the battlefield afterwards they would do unspeakable tortures to an enemy left alive. They were tall,

191

fierce-looking, proud, dirty and looked capable and very eager to protect their barren lands.

Suddenly there was a loud bang, the bus lurched to one side and we rolled to a stop. Everyone piled out to inspect the flat tyre. The driver cheerfully threw the baggage piled in the back onto the roadside, rummaged around to find his tools and the spare and went to work. It was cold in the desert and within three minutes one of the men had built a warming fire, made with dried camel dung patties found beside the road.

Perhaps because of my gesture with the food they seemed to be comfortable with me; one of them spoke a few words of English. Using hand motions and a stick in the sand I tried to explain to them how big a skyscraper is and that there are tubes under the ground through which people hurtle in metal trains. Supermarkets, redwood trees, sailboats, these and more were 'discussed' and marveled over with looks of wonder and disbelief.

A few minutes before we were ready to squeeze back into the van we stood around smoking, as I shared my cigarettes with them. One man, the one who spoke a few words of English pointed to himself and told me his name was Ali. I told him mine. He then pointed to himself again and said clearly,

"Ali, Moslem – Jon, Christian?"

A defining moment in the life of a twenty-year old! How do I answer this question here in the middle of nowhere, no one knowing where I was, surrounded by these gun-toting tribesmen?

In a sudden flash of insanity I decided to be truthful. Standing tall, with them waiting expectantly for an answer, I looked Ali squarely in the eye, pointed to myself and said one word: "Jew".

After I said it I had this momentary vision of seven ferocious Afghanis gleefully dismembering me with their deadly knives and leaving me to rot in the desert.

192

A startled look came into Ali's eyes and he walked quickly around the fire toward me. I stared back at him unflinching as he rushed up and stopped inches from me.

He studied me up and down, an intense look of disbelief on his face. I glanced behind hoping for an escape route but the others had moved closer to me, their eyes unwavering. For ten seconds no one moved. My mind raced as Ali raised his arms at me. I expected a blow and automatically started to shield my face.

Instead of hitting me, he threw his arms around me. He hugged me tight and his bad breath overpowered me.

He stepped back and spoke only one word,

"Bruzzer!"

I was taken by surprise and immensely relieved. He talked rapidly to his friends who looked at me with amazement, all gesturing wildly with their hands. One by one they shook my hand, told me their names and smiled at me. We sat down around the fire, joined by the driver who by now had replaced the flat with a bald spare tyre. Ali explained haltingly in a few words his reaction to my confessing to being a Jew in this apparently hostile environment.

"Abraham, Moslem father; Abraham, Jew father - we bruzzers."

Here at the ends of the earth, warming ourselves by a camel dung fire was this simple man's profound understanding of mens real relationship to each other. He wasn't concerned with the rhetoric of modern politicians; he probably couldn't even read a newspaper. But he did know that five thousand years ago, we both came from the same patriarch and in spite of our vast differences we were indeed brothers…

193

THE BEST LAID PLANS

o' mice an' men gang oft a-gley...

Well, our plans definitely 'gang a-gleyed' (went astray)! The morning of Friday, May 28, 2003 was spent running around Isla Mujeres, a few miles from Cancun, Mexico, getting ready to leave for our voyage south to Swan Island. Last minute provisioning, clearing out with Immigration and the Port Captain and spending our remaining pesos at the fuel dock. The weather forecast called for ESE at 10 knots, so it wouldn't be too uncomfortable - or so we thought...

Motoring through a narrow, winding, aquamarine creek, we emerged into a large bay with the concrete ugliness of Cancun a mile in front of us. Setting course, we motor-sailed toward Swan Island, 280 miles out in the Caribbean Sea. The wind was a bit fresher than projected and the waves a little higher. Three hours passed and the wind was blowing at 15-20 knots, the seas had grown to 3-5 feet, short and closely-spaced, right on the nose. The sails were luffing and useless, so down they came. This was the first time since we had bought this huge 64' custom trimaran four months earlier that we had encountered 'bouncy conditions'.

We motored on at about 4 knots, fighting a strong current. Our autopilot, which relies on its own internal compass to keep us on course, decided it didn't like these conditions and would steer 'Ladyhawke' radically off course every ten minutes or so. It was becoming clear that this may turn out to be a difficult passage.

With the autopilot basically useless no matter how I adjusted it, we would have to take turns hand steering continually to Swan Island. This was a discouraging prospect – it is tiring enough to make long passages without having to steer the whole time; with no autopilot, it was daunting for just the two of us. Then a further three days and nights to Isla Providencia, a small island owned by

Colombia, but inhabited by English-speaking descendants of English pirates...

It was now mid-afternoon and we decided that discretion was the better part of valour, so we discreetly altered course for Cozumel, twenty miles away on a course which would enable us to sail, rather than motor. We made it to a deserted anchorage on the north coast of Cozumel just as the sun set...

The next morning, we both dinghied Sailor ashore for his run, swam in the crystal clear water and discussed what we should do. The autopilot, a strong, expensive unit which came with the boat, had handled calm seas with no problem, but proved itself a problem once the boat was buffeted by waves. We decided the universe was sending us a message and we should forget Swan Island and head for Belize City, where I could have the autopilot checked out. For the most part we could anchor each night, so would not be too exhausted hand steering.

Leaving Cozumel about noon, we crossed gorgeous indigo-blue waters and motored against the north flowing three-knot current, which sped up as it squeezed between the island of Cozumel and the Mexican mainland. The autopilot was working better, keeping her on course for half an hour or so before needing a little adjustment. It was an overnight passage to the Chinchorro Bank, an atoll seventeen miles off the Yucatan mainland, 112 miles south of us. We were now in Mexico illegally, as we had cleared for Providencia, which belonged to Colombia.

As we motor-sailed out of the lee of Cozumel, the 20-knot winds started kicking up large waves which increased the motion of the big, wide boat. The autopilot was working again, only needing a correction once in a while, or when a larger wave knocked the boat substantially off course. As the skies darkened, the wind picked up and the seas got bigger, some of them breaking against the windward hull and sending spray into the cockpit.

195

We motor-sailed on, making only about four knots against the fierce current that sweeps up this coast. About midnight, with the large waves causing the most motion we had yet experienced on Ladyhawke, I heard the engine rev up a few hundred RPM's, then settle back down. Five minutes later, it did it again, this time going to full revs for fifteen seconds before dropping down...

The waves were now 5-7 feet (doesn't sound like much, but believe me, they move even this large, heavy boat significantly), with occasional 10-footers, some soaking the cockpit. Sailor was not happy at all and I was concerned there may be an engine problem. Our 6-cylinder Perkins diesel had just received necessary maintenance and had purred all the way down from Florida. I noticed the tachometer fluctuating wildly, but refused to admit to myself what I knew was about to happen...

Sure enough, five minutes later the engine gave a sigh and died. With the wind direction and the strong current against us, we fell off the wind a little and our speed rapidly dropped to less than three knots. The motion became less agitated, but we could see the large waves approaching us by the moonlight through the low, scudding clouds; it was eerily beautiful and with no engine noise, we could hear the wind whistling through the rigging making plaintive music that matched the night.

Leaving Joie to hand-steer under sail and keep us close to our course, I disappeared into the hot, cramped engine room, turned on the overhead light and checked the two in-line Racor fuel filters. It was as I had feared - the cartridges were black with dirt and the filters were only half full of diesel. I knew immediately what had happened and saw a frustrating, filthy, diesel-covered night ahead. The violent motion of the yacht as it battled the seas had shaken up years of accumulated sludge and grime from the bottom of the two 150-gallon fuel tanks.

The paper canister filters had soon become clogged with the crud and wouldn't allow fuel to pass through, that's why the engine was acting up. There were also three smaller filters before the fuel made it to the injectors - I hoped a speck of dirt hadn't made it through all of them. The engine might never run again without dismantling and cleaning the six injectors, a delicate and painstaking job that would require a trained diesel mechanic and I didn't have one of them aboard just then! Although I'm competent at basic maintenance and minor troubleshooting, cleaning clogged injectors at night in a rough sea was out of the question.

I now had to fill the two filter canisters with diesel fuel without getting air into the system. Squatting between the large, cylindrical fuel tanks in the gloom of the bilge, I unscrewed the small vent pipe. I found a four-foot length of plastic tubing and inserting one end deep into the tank, I stuck the other in my mouth and sucked diesel. As soon as I got a mouthful, I immediately transferred the tube to a small container held at a lower level than the tank. Spitting diesel fuel furiously out of my mouth into the bilges, I watched the little jar fill with the precious fluid. With so much built-in fuel capacity, I didn't have any five-gallon diesel containers.

After replacing the filter cartridges, pouring the fuel from my precious container into the Racor canisters, screwing on the top, scalding my arm on the hot engine, cursing a few times trying to maintain my balance while all this was going on, I wiped myself off, climbed out of the hot engine room and had Joell turn the key. The starter cranked and cranked – nothing...

Then the fuel in the canisters got through. Within twenty seconds the engine was running smoothly. I moved back to the cockpit in the dark, tumbling night, sweaty, hot, covered with diesel and tasting it in my mouth. I assured Joell I could handle the problem, although I didn't know how long the engine would run until more slime stopped the fuel flowing. I cleaned myself up, we got back on course and plunged ahead into the night...

Twenty minutes later the engine revved itself up, then died.. Back I went into the engine room, emerging fifteen minutes later, grimy, sweaty and diesely. There followed one of those dirty, exhausting, exasperating nights that more than counter-balance the azure seas, tropical beaches and perfect sailing weather. It was a long night, a very long night. I disappeared into that engine room a dozen more times, sucking diesel fuel, sloshing it over me, getting the engine running again for a little while.

As the sun came up and showed the large seas, Joell commented that on nights like this, it's better if you can't see what size wave is approaching! The sky lightened and we looked at the awesome majesty of the ocean and watched the serried ranks of waves marching toward us. 'Ladyhawke' handled them beautifully, rising like a gracious swan, heeling slightly to one side, hesitating as the wave passed under the main hull, then tipping the other way...over and over again. Although we never had a doubt about her sea-keeping capabilities, it was still not too comfortable in these kind of seas...

I was also concerned about whether the mast would stand up to this motion – after all, we had bought it used from a boat yard in Ft. Lauderdale and had no idea what type of boat it had come from or how old it was. It had only been stepped on Ladyhawke a couple of weeks before, we didn't know if the rigging was done correctly, or if I had torqued the bolts enough, or if the tabernacle would support it or...

By sunrise we had about 45 miles to go and as it was apparent that the force of the current had slackened, we were now able to sail toward Chinchorro at about five knots, without the engine on. We should be able to drop anchor by mid-afternoon. I filled the filters one last time; we couldn't afford to have the engine die as we came in through the break in the surrounding reef...

Mid-afternoon, tired and apprehensive, we neared the gap in the reef, two small islands directly ahead of us, one with an old lighthouse. On motor, powering through the gap, watching the tachometer and listening for any change in the engine sound. Picked my spot and dropped the anchor onto a hard, limestone bottom, hoping the hook would find a convenient rock to lodge against. Just as the motor spluttered again, having sucked more dirt into the filters, I turned it off; the mainsail was still up and luffing into the wind.

It took me sixty seconds to don mask, snorkel and flippers and jump over the side, swim down the anchor chain and see how well hooked we were – the anchor flukes had found the perfect rock! Back on board, tired from the long night, with the bouquet of diesel still clinging to me. Sailor smelled the land and eagerly awaited going ashore to relieve himself. I started to lower the dinghy and noticed a panga heading toward us from the direction of the lighthouse. I grabbed my binoculars and saw there were four men aboard, all with guns.

Were they banditos? If they were, we were in big trouble as there was no way we could get out of there in a hurry and there was no one else around...

"Joie!" I said nervously, peering through my binoculars. "There's a panga heading for us and they have guns. Get below, now!"

She went pale remembering our encounter with the 'pirates' aboard JoJo a few years earlier and disappeared quickly. I continued to scrutinize the approaching skiff, once more thinking I should consider carrying a firearm on board. Maybe they just wanted some rum or cigarettes?

"What's happening, Jon?" asked Joell from below, fear in her voice.

"Wait a minute, hang on...oh! I can make them out now - it's OK. They're military, I can see their uniforms, I think they're the

Mexican Navy. Come on up, bring some beers and we'll hang some fenders over the side."

We both let out a sigh of relief and the immediate tension drained out of our bodies. Great, we're here illegally, in the middle of nowhere and I have to deal with McHale and his crew!

Joie hung some fenders along the port side and the panga slowly turned and gently bumped alongside. Docking lines were secured and four unsmiling Mexican navy sailors clambered out of their boat and proceeded to leave black streaks on our decks from their heavy boots.

"Buenas dias, Navale Mexicano. Inspeccion, por favor, Capitan," said the one in charge.

They held their rifles loosely and another spoke in halting English.

"Capitan, izz no allow anchor heer. Izz restric' area. You go now, si."

"Oh, I did not know it is a restricted military zone, but I have problema with my boat and must stay until I can fix it."

There is an ancient concept in law dating back to Roman times called 'force majeure' which, when applied to a maritime situation can entitle a boat that is unable to proceed because of a problem to stay where it is until fixed. I hoped this would apply here.

"Que problema?" he enquired.

I made a 'brrm, brrm' sound and he nodded. Now this all took less than a minute and Sailor was wandering around sniffing the land smells on their boots. The men bent down and petted him, but Sailor had other thoughts on his mind. He trotted over to their boat, looked down into it, smelled the dock line tied to our cleat and to my horror raised his leg and made a long and obviously satisfactory pee all over the rope, which probably smelled of the shore.

There was stunned silence aboard as the yellow stream trickled down the dock line and dripped into their boat! Joell looked at me with concern. I had no idea whether they'd be literally pissed of at us...

The four sailors looked at Sailor, looked at each other, looked at us and burst out laughing! We joined in with them as Sailor, obviously much relieved after twelve hours without a pee (his longest time pee-less was forty-three hours – he hated to pee on the boat where he lived), trotted back and smiled up at us!

Any tension that was there had gone and the young captain followed me into the engine room. I showed him the two fuel filters and the two dozen dirty paper cartridges littering the floor – he immediately understood that I had to clean out the fuel tank. I told him I could fix it and would leave in the morning.

"Si, no hay problema. You stay an' feex eet."

When we climbed back on deck, the other three were sitting around the table with Joell, each with a cerveza in hand and a smile on his face. We joined them and chatted for a few minutes. I asked if it was possible for me to bring Sailor ashore so he could stretch his legs. I really wanted to go up the lighthouse and get a good view of the island.

He told me he would ask permission from the base commandant and would radio me on channel 22. With everyone shaking hands, they climbed down into their boat. I rinsed the dock line with a bucket of sea water and cast them off, everyone waving furiously! We now had horrible black streaks all over our decks which took hours to get off!

Thirty minutes later later I received a call on the VHF saying we had permission to come ashore. I lowered the dinghy into the warm water and Sailor leaped aboard, tongue out, eager to be on dry land. We putt-putted along a pretty, deserted beach on our right and tied up at the small dock. Obviously the story of Sailor peeing on their boat had made the rounds and everyone wanted to pet him. The commandant said we could stay ashore for an hour and yes, he would allow me to climb the lighthouse with an escort.

It was indeed a spectacular view from up there – I could see practically the whole island and Ladyhawke looked magnificent bobbing at anchor down the beach. When we left, Sailor was presented with a whole bag of bones the cook had gathered for him!

We rested for a while and then I spent seven hours cleaning the goop out of two cylindrical 150-gallon fuel tanks in the bilge, transferring fuel from one tank to another through a small electric pump I rigged up. When the tank was dry, I inserted a long flexible tube which was attached to another pump. It acted as a vacuum cleaner and sucked up amazing amounts of long, stringy, gummy, nasty, oozy crud from inside the tank. It smelled awful, looked horrible and felt slimy.

Eventually I cleaned one tank, then pumped the fuel from the other tank through a fine mesh back into the empty one and repeated the 'vacuuming'. It was hot, muggy, dirty work, cramped and slippery. I put in the last of my two filter cartridges, filled up the canisters, bled the system of trapped air and turned the key.

Hooray! It started within ten seconds, hiccuped a couple of times, then settled into a purring idle. I jumped over the side with a bottle of dishwashing liquid and cleaned myself thoroughly, listening all the while to the sweet sound of the engine exhaust. I let it run for an hour, charging our banks of batteries and using our small watermaker to produce fresh water.

We both slept for twelve hours and left for Belize the following morning. The engine never troubled us again...and, oh yes, the mast never fell down...

THE TURKISH MOUNTAIN

Jake drove through the night after leaving the town of Mashad in eastern Iran. He was angry and uptight and kept muttering at the injustice of having just spent a night in jail.* I wasn't too thrilled about it myself, but as it was Jake's fault and I had angered him trying to extricate ourselves from the mess he had created, I kept quiet as I lay in the back of the Ford Transit van, trying to keep warm.

We were driving west to Tehran on Route 44, a smooth highway that was the main route between the two cities. It was cold in late December and even with the heater going full blast, it was barely enough to keep the back of the van comfortable. He kept up a steady speed of 50 mph and fourteen hours after leaving Mashad, we pulled into Tehran, a bustling city full of American cars and trucks, donkeys and rickshaws, the modern alongside the ancient.

Jake drove straight to the American embassy intending to let them know how unfairly we had been treated by the local police in Mashad. I told him I thought this would be a futile gesture as he had caused the whole mess chasing some kids and knocking down a lamp post. But he wouldn't let go of it and stormed into the embassy, determined to get 'revenge'. Fifteen minutes later he was escorted out by a U.S. Marine through the courtyard and instructed to keep driving west, out of Iran! This was late in 1971, and the country was governed by the Shah, a brutal dictator, a puppet of the U.S. who had installed him there.

It was early morning and Jake was now more pissed off than ever! He slammed the transmission into gear and drove crazily through the streets, looking for Route 2 to Tabriz. I held on tight as he yelled at other cars and constantly blew his horn. There had been little communication on the drive from Mashad, and he was surly to his girlfriend Mary. I was in the back of a van with a lunatic driving, fifteen hundred miles still to go to Istanbul...

Snow was falling lightly as we reached the highway; luckily Jake was not suicidal and he slowed down and fell in behind some trucks, going about 30 mph. A hundred miles down the road, as they had slept little in the jail and were exhausted, we pulled in to the small town of Qazvin and found a cheap, fairly clean hotel. The next day was grey and overcast and we continued along Route 2 and reached Tabriz, a large city in Eastern Iran, the next evening. Again, a cheap hotel, my own room, a meal of kabobs and rice and a good nights sleep.

The following morning I felt sick, my intestines were acting up again. Jake couldn't care less and I lay in the back, breathing slowly and hoping not to pass out. About an hour north of Tabriz, at Marand, we left the main highway which continued north, in order to head west into Turkey. Now we were on an old two-lane road, 'Highway' 32, which was bumpy with pot holes. Luckily the snow had stopped the day before so Jake could see the road and stay on it. But we couldn't average more than about 35 mph as we were getting into some hills and also had to watch for herds of sheep and goats slowly moving down the road, bleating and crying! The traffic had thinned out and sometimes we wouldn't see a vehicle for an hour. As we made our way west, I lay shivering in the back – my fever had returned.

We bumped and jostled our way over two hundred miles that day. About five hours into the trip, we left Iran and crossed into Turkey, fifteen miles west of the town of Maku. After the border inspection, which went very smoothly, we stopped at a small house by the road. Inside, a family wearing old, dirty, smelly traditional clothes fed us fresh, warm goat's milk and rice. As we sat and ate, about a dozen children shyly poked their heads over the window sill and looked through the ancient low door. They ran away giggling whenever we made eye contact!

I don't know if it was the goat milk but within an hour my

stomach had settled down and I was no longer feverish. We spent the night in Dogubayazit, just over the border, about a thousand miles east of Istanbul. In the morning, as we drank strong, sweet Turkish coffee at a small restaurant, I asked the name of a mountain I could see about ten miles off to the northeast. There were actually two pretty mountains, side by side, covered in snow. I was told the large one to the east was called Agri Dagi, the Turkish name for Mount Ararat, where Noah's Ark was purported to have settled.

The temperature was freezing and we could see our breath as we prepared to leave. More ominously, dark, foreboding clouds were moving down from the north. The past two days we had been steadily climbing and were now at an altitude of five thousand feet, about the same as Denver, Colorado. In the parking lot, I spoke with a truck driver who knew a few words of English. He warned me of a mountain pass just east of the city of Erzurum, about 150 miles away, that would be treacherous if there was snow on the road.

I relayed this information to Jake who gave a disinterested grunt and appeared in no hurry to move on. At this point he seemed to derive some satisfaction in aggravating me – probably because I had shown him to be a moron when he acted so foolishly back in Mashad. Eventually we headed west and should be in Istanbul in three days, if road conditions stayed clear– they didn't...

This was mountainous territory and the road was either climbing up or dropping down into pretty valleys. Within an hour, the clouds rolling in had developed into a storm, the temperature dropped below freezing and snow started to fall. We crawled along, sandwiched between several overladen and wobbly lorries, Jake quiet and focused on keeping the van on the road. It took us six hours to go 140 miles and by mid-afternoon we were only twenty miles east of Erzurum, our destination for the night. The snow was falling steadily, big, wet flakes that stuck to the road. I reminded Jake about the mountain pass ahead and the warning I had received from the truck driver that morning.

"I don't care what he said. I'm a great driver and we'll get over this pass with no problem," was his abrupt retort.

I looked out the rear windows and could barely see the headlights of a big truck behind us through the swirling snow. The conditions were getting worse and half an hour later we were forced to stop on the road. Bundling up as best I could, I slid open the side door and stepped out into a cold, bleak landscape, with a low, grey sky above. Crunching through the snow, I could see dozens of trucks ahead of us, all stopped with their engines idling. There were several groups of men huddled together and further up someone had managed to light a bonfire.

I told Jake I would find out what was happening. As I trudged up the road, past the snow-covered trucks, the storm lightened a bit and the snow stopped falling. It was still very cold and a foot of fresh snow covered everything. The warmth of the fire was comforting; there were about twenty men standing around, talking and gesticulating. I offered them all cigarettes which were received with "thank you's" in Turkish and Persian. One man spoke a little English and told me that the name of the village we had passed through two miles back was Pasinler. It marked the beginning of the narrow road over the mountain that rose steadily another two thousand feet before dropping down into Erzurum, ten miles away.

"Izz ver danj-roos road," he told me. "Zumtime troock zlide (izz correct, 'zlide'?) off road, down mountain. Zumtime ve stay here two, t'ree day."

Just then a heavily laden lorry crept past us heading east, honking his horn.

"Well, he drove over the mountain pass, yes?" I asked.

"Yiz, he ver loocky!"

We moved into the middle of the road and I saw where it snaked up over a ridge and disappeared around a bend about a half mile ahead. It was a very narrow two-lane road with steep drop-offs on either side, as it was built atop a thin ridge.

"How many kilometres is the road over the mountain before it becomes flat?" I asked.

"Izz ten keelomeeter," he replied.

About six miles of treacherous, snaking, slippery road, up over a mountain, then back down the other side. No guard rails, nothing to stop you falling into the valley far below if you skidded off the road.

"Are you going over the mountain?"

"Izz posseebal in one, two hour. I watch wezzer and zee if troock come from vest – tawk to driver."

I walked back to the van, half a mile down the road and relayed the information to Jake, who was keeping warm with the heater on.

"Well, I'm going around these trucks to the front of the line anyway."

He rolled up his window and I followed him back on foot as he inched past the waiting trucks. He pulled over near the bonfire and got out – Mary stayed in the van. She was scared of the storm, scared of the truck drivers, scared of this nasty road and almost seemed to be going into shock. I didn't know why she had gone on this adventure – she certainly didn't have the spirit for it.

We stood around the roaring fire, talking desultorily with the men. Suddenly there was a series of loud horn blasts coming from the pass. We all looked up as a huge truck started down towards us from the mountain pass to the west. It was an old cab-over Mack, probably shipped to Turkey from the U.S. after every mile had been squeezed from it on the Interstate systems. Hooked to the tractor was a beat-up flatbed trailer. And strapped on the trailer was a pyramid of logs, about twenty of them as long as the trailer, which was around fifty feet.

Another blast from its horn and everyone stopped talking and stared intently at the truck, inching down the steep grade in a low gear, engine loud in protest. He tapped his brakes and the rear of the trailer slid a couple of feet to his left. Probably the only working brakes were on the tractor - it was unlikely the trailer brakes were hooked up and if they were, they didn't seem to be working. This was a potentially dangerous situation, as in the best of conditions, it is imperative that the wheels on a trailer are capable of braking, otherwise the trailer can 'keep going' when the brakes are applied.

The truck picked up speed and the driver obviously tapped his brakes again. This time the trailer slid off to the right and tried to overtake the tractor! He took his foot off the brakes, the trailer straightened out and the whole rig sped up. So he was caught between a rock and a hard place. If he braked to slow down, the trailer would slide out under the huge weight of the logs. If he didn't brake, his rig would gain momentum and hurtle down the winding, slick road, going faster all the time...We stood mesmerized, about forty truck drivers from Turkey, Iran, Russia and a couple of western hippies, stamping our feet in the cold, all watching the drama unfold. And then – catastrophe!

The diesel engine was doing its best to keep the truck at a slow speed, straining in what was probably low second gear. About a quarter mile from us, we heard a loud bang, awful metal grinding sounds, black smoke came out of the exhaust stacks and the truck started going faster. The tired old diesel engine had blown up and with it, the braking effect of the engine decompression. Within a few seconds the rig was traveling twenty miles an hour on the slippery surface downhill, out of control...

The driver panicked and stood on his brakes. The wheels on the tractor locked up and the rig started to swerve. The trailer, still going downhill with no working brakes, tried to overtake the tractor and within five seconds was sliding sideways. There was a slick of black engine oil darkening the snow behind the tractor. The trailer was skidding and was now at a ninety degree angle behind the tractor, uncontrollable. And it was heading down the mountain toward us!

Men started yelling and running toward their parked trucks, slipping in the snow. If the runaway rig crashed into the line of trucks it would be a disaster – several of the trucks were carrying gasoline from the oil fields in Iran. And rather than wait in line with everyone else, Jake had arrogantly pulled the van up to the front - it was about to be demolished. Mary had opened the door and was scrambling out. She was in such a panic, she slipped and fell into the slush. Jake was frozen to the spot.

As I ran to help Mary, I heard an ungodly sound – screeching, groaning, snapping. I stopped and looked back at the rig – so did everyone else. It had been maybe five seconds since I had turned away to help Mary, but in that five seconds all hell had broken loose.

The back of the trailer had gone off the road, over the side to the left and was pulling the rest of the rig with it. It was happening less than a thousand feet away and as the grim scene unfolded it seemed to be in slow motion. When the trailer wheels had gone over the edge, the trailer had twisted, which snapped the chains holding the logs on. The loud noises I had heard were the logs freeing themselves from their restraints. The trailer was now more than halfway over the precipice and most of the logs were bouncing down the mountain, making a fearsome echoing noise.

The driver was trying to get out of the cab, we could see him frantically pushing his door open. If he jumped, he would hit the road at over 30 mph. If he didn't, he would go over the side with his truck. And then, like something out of a special effects movie, within a few seconds, the rest of the trailer went over the edge and dragged the old Mack tractor with it...

The sounds of its death throes reverberated around the mountains as the logs tumbled into the precipice, the trailer jounced after them and the tractor shattered into a thousand metallic pieces and burst into flames, tumbling over and over as we ran to the edge and looked down. A group of men raced up the road, slipping and sliding, toward something dark laying still in the road, near the edge.

All of this had happened in less than thirty seconds and I remembered that I had been rushing to help Mary after she fell getting out of the van. I looked toward the van across the road, next to the bonfire. Jake was there and he was holding Mary who was crying and shaking. I let them be and turned toward the pass where the group of men had just reached the bundle in the road. I started up the road toward them, avoiding the trail of oil from the blown-up diesel and the pieces of the engine scattered over the snow – the oil pan with a big hole in it, a couple of battered pistons, some old rubber hoses and numerous unidentifiable bits, steam rising from them.

As I got closer, I could see with relief that the bundle in the road was moving and sitting up with the help of the other truckers - it was the hapless driver and he had managed to jump free before his truck and livelihood disappeared. They had him upright and were slowly walking down toward me, supporting him on either side, with his arms around the shoulders of two men. I joined the group coming down and listened as they talked excitedly amongst themselves.

The driver seemed alright, he was limping and blood was coming from his nose. I imagine the snow cushioned his fall as he escaped certain death. I offered him a cigarette which he accepted with a smile.

Back at the bonfire the men were talking and gesticulating, probably reliving the drama of the past five minutes. I was just pleased that the rig had gone over the side before ploughing into us and certainly causing much damage and probably death...

The injured driver was gently handed into a truck which then turned around and headed back to Pasinler where he could get some rudimentary medical attention. I found the truck driver who spoke English, standing near the fire, heaping more wood on. He was in his fifties, deeply lined face, grey hair and clipped moustache, about 5'9", stocky, with a commanding look.

"Ah, zere you are. Amereecan?" he asked me.

I wasn't about to explain dual nationality, so answered in the affirmative.

"Yes, my name is Jon. What is your name?"

"My name izz Hakan. I am frum Eestanbool."

"So, Hakan, will you go over the mountain today, after what just happened?"

"Yiz, I weel. Zat happen' becoz eet was ole, bad truck, and no brakes on trailer. My troock back zere, is one troock, no trailer. I carry petrol, you call eet gazoleen, yez?"

211

"Yes, that's right – gasoline. You've been over this pass many times, Hakan?"

"Oh yiz, many, many time. I have plan to help get van over mountain, Meester Jon. My troock ver' strong, have good tyres, good brakes. I pull ze van over mountain with chain, yez?"

"Wow, thanks for the offer, Hakan. But it is not my van. I just ride along. It belongs to that man over there, with his woman. I will bring him to you."

I walked over to where Jake was calming Mary down. The spectacle of the log truck going over the side had unnerved her more than usual. I thought that the idea of going up and over the pass in the snow would totally freak her out! Jake followed me back and I introduced him to Hakan.

"Zo, Meester Jayek. Ve haff one hour before ze dark. I zink zere weel be more snow ver soon. I have goood troock and strong chain to pull. We put chains around zee tyres on my truck – ver good for snow. I know zis road ver well. Use strong chain and pull you over mountain. I do ziz for one hunnerd dollars U.S. Yiz?"

I thought it was a brilliant idea and even though it could be dangerous, at least we wouldn't be stuck here, possibly for days. But ornery, arrogant Jake started to object, of course.

"Well, I'll just wait till the snowploughs come and clear the road. And we can go back to the village and find a place to stay for the night. And a hundred dollars is too much. And it might damage the van. And how do I know you can do this? And what happens if you lose control?"

Hakan looked at me, shrugged his shoulders and walked back to his truck, where he lit a cigarette-I thought this was a bit careless when he had a couple of thousand gallons of petrol behind him,

212

but attitudes in third-world countries tend to be more fatalistic. Hakan then started to unload the chains to put around his tyres.

"Look, man," I said to Jake. "This isn't the States – there aren't any snowploughs out here. We're in the middle of nowhere and no one's coming to clear the road. I think Hakan is right, there's another storm on the way and if we don't try it now, we could be stuck here for days, maybe weeks. I doubt if there's any rooms available in Palinser - there must be a hundred trucks behind us now. I don't like the idea of sleeping in the van in the cold tonight or a bunch of nights if we can't get through for days. Maybe we can haggle with the price, if that's bothering you. The other things you're worried about – well, who knows? Where's your sense of adventure, anyway? I think we should take him up on his offer. Otherwise, I'll leave you now and keep the money I owe you. I'll give it to Hakan and ride with him to Istanbul."

"Let me talk to Mary," he replied gruffly.

"OK, but make it quick. He's putting the chains on his tyres and will probably leave in a few minutes," I said, turning my back and walking away.

Jake went back to Mary, who was now in the van and I could see them arguing. I headed to Hakan's truck and helped him attach his chains, my fingers cold and numb.

"Vell, ve do ziss?" he asked.

"I don't know, Hakan. He's not the smartest man and does not like suggestions from other people. If he wants to stay here, can I ride with you to Istanbul? I can pay you fifty dollars U.S."

"Yiz, ve can do zat. Heer koom Meester Jayek."

We finished attaching the last chain as Jake approached.

213

"Mary is really scared, but I think we will accept your offer Hakan. I will give you $50."

Even though the Turks are known for their haggling expertise, Hakan was wily enough to know that we had no option and held firm to his price.

"No, Meester Jayek – zat is ze price, one hunnerd dollars U.S."

A hundred dollars was a lot of money back then, especially in a third world country and to Hakan, was more like a thousand; he wasn't going to miss this chance and I didn't blame him.

"OK, OK, a hundred dollars," said Jake and they shook hands as Hakan pocketed the money.

Hakan pulled his truck in front of the van and attached a stout chain to our chassis, getting covered in snow as he crawled on his back under it.

I slid open the side door climbed into the back. Jake kept the engine on but left the transmission in neutral. A blast of the trucks air horn, the chain tightened and we jerked forward as Hakan released his clutch. Mary was rigid in her seat, her mouth moving, no sound coming out. I crouched by the side door, looking through the front window as snow started to fall. It was getting near dusk and I didn't want to be traversing this horrible road in the dark – neither did Hakan!

I could feel him shifting through his gears as the tow chain slackened and tightened and he stayed in low third, going about 15 mph. Mary had her hand on her door handle and I did the same. My right hand was firmly on the handle on the sliding door and I thought that if it looked like we were going over the edge, I would slide the door back and jump out. Problem was, if I had to do that, I would have jumped right over the edge, as we were no more than four feet from the road to the steep drop-off! And we

214

were going higher...

Now the visibility was dramatically reduced as the snow started falling harder. The van slid to the left and Jake fought to correct it. Mary screamed. She was not handling this well and I didn't blame her – it was insanely dangerous!

There was a puff of exhaust smoke from Hakan's truck and I could hear him downshifting as the road became steeper. My whole body was tense and I squeezed the door handle tighter. Jake's fingers gripped the steering wheel and I will admit he did a good job keeping the van straight behind the petrol truck thirty feet ahead, its red taillights barely visible in the lowering storm.

And the treacherous, dangerous drive continued, Hakan never going over fifteen mph, Mary muttering, Jake oblivious to anything around him except keeping us lined up behind Hakan and me shivering in the back, crouched down, ready to leap out if I had to...

After fifteen agonizing, harrowing minutes, we reached the summit and Hakan carefully pulled over. There were about two dozen trucks behind us, slowly following us up the mountain grade. They eased past, each one blowing its horn. When they had disappeared into the murky gloom ahead, Hakan got out of his truck and walked back. Jake rolled down the window and a blast of cold air enveloped us.

"Vell, Meester Jayek. Ve at top of moontain. Now I unhook chain and you follow me slow, down to Erzurum, yiz."

As he had no alternative, Jake agreed and Hakan crawled under the van again and unhooked the chain.

"I know good, cheap, clean hotel in Erzurum. I go zere. You follow, OK."

And with that, he waved, lit another cigarette, climbed back into his truck and moved slowly down the road. We followed, Jake never getting out of second gear. The convoy of trucks that had preceded us had packed down the newly falling snow and even though their track was wider, Jake managed to keep the van in their ruts. It was scary going down the mountain as dusk drew in and combined with the heavy snow, cut visibility to a few hundred feet. We felt like we were in a tunnel and couldn't see the sides of the road, which was probably just as well...

We skidded a few times, the tyres losing grip, but finally, after half an hour, the road straightened out and we could see the loom of our destination ahead. Into third gear, we followed Hakan's truck through the streets of the ancient city. Soon, he stopped in front of a small hotel and we all walked in to register. The proprietors knew Hakan and they talked for a few minutes, probably about our scary trip over the infamous mountain. Then we were shown to our rooms and a few minutes later, Hakan knocked on my door and invited me to have a hot meal with him. Jake and Mary didn't want to go, so the two of us trudged through the snow on the sidewalk a few hundred yards to a little restaurant tucked away on a side street.

We walked in to a scene from Scheherezade – a warm room with maybe fifteen tables, all full of Turkish men eating and laughing! A band played traditional music in a corner and waiters dashed to and fro with trays heaped with beef and lamb, doner kabobs and vegetables. There was excellent Efes beer and small glasses of raki, an anisette-based liquor similar to ouzo. A big log fire in an ancient and soot-covered fireplace roared and crackled.

At one table sat some of the truck drivers who had followed us up the mountain pass. They called to Hakan and made space for us. Lots of hand-shaking, back-slapping and introductions. As soon as I sat down, there was a heaping plate of food in front of me, a bottle of beer and a glass of raki. And what a night it was, into the early hours of the morning. Everyone was happy to have put the mountain behind them and they all loved to party!

Around midnight there was a hush in the room, the band started playing soft, seductive music and onto the floor swayed a belly-dancer, covered in gold jewelry, face behind a crimson veil. She danced and gyrated, slowly, sensuously, gorgeous painted eyes darting around the room, focusing her attention for a brief moment on everyone, captivating them, making each of us a part of her flowing story. When she was finished, coins were tossed onto the floor and she gracefully picked them up and disappeared.

Sometime in the early hours of the morning, after much shaking of hands and well-wishes, Hakan and I stumbled out into the cold night. The snow had stopped and the stars glistened and twinkled above. We staggered back to the hotel, supporting each other, joking and laughing. A big hug, garlic-breath from both of us and I fell onto my bed and slept for a few hours.

Jake banged on my door and I sat up, kneading my aching head! We had a cup of strong Turkish coffee in the small lobby and I went looking for Hakan. But he had already left, had headed down the road to Istanbul, seven hundred miles away. We climbed in the van and I lay in the back, massaging my head, remembering the loud, colourful, smokey night before, the traditional Turkey that few foreigners get to experience...

We arrived in Istanbul two days later and I gladly paid Jake his fifty dollars and turned my back on him and Mary. It had been an exhausting journey, sometimes boring, sometimes too much the opposite.

My friend Abdullah in Herat, who I never heard from again, a night in jail in Iran, the ominous mountain in the snow. Nearly three thousand miles across a landscape that had changed little in centuries. Old villages where people stared at us unblinking, kids laughing and pointing, shepherds herding their flocks of sheep and goats down the road, causing us to slow to a crawl. Fertile valleys, meandering rivers, ancient mosques and crowded, smelly bazaars. And always the questions, whenever we stopped; "Where are you from? Are you married? What is the purpose of your visit to our country? Would you like some chai?" Usually welcoming, always curious, often gracious...

*   See 'Hard Journey Back' in 'Everyone Said I Should Write Another Book'.

Within a week, I had flown back to New Hope, Pennsylvania, where I had been living before I left on this adventure. I received medical attention and the doctor said he had never seen anything like my intestines – he was amazed I had survived my debilitating dysentery in the Himalayas and was astounded that I had endured the grueling overland trip back.

Four weeks later, I borrowed $5000 and with a leather cowboy hat on my long, curly hair, I boarded PanAm Flight 003 in New York. I got off in Tehran and transferred to a small, old Afghan Air jet which flew me back to Kabul. There I bought all kinds of jewelry in the bazaar and sheepskin coats in Ghazni. I also visited Mazar-I-Sharif, where the best hashish in Afghanistan was made... Besides the jewelry, all the smelly, uncured coats and clothes were bundled into burlap sacks and air-freighted to Philadelphia. It was my first venture into the import/export business. I had just turned twenty-one years old....**

** See 'Busted', 'Everyone Said I Should Write Another Book'.

218

THE VOYAGE ENDS...

The following are emails spanning three months which chronicle the end of our long voyage aboard 'JoJo', our 32' Fisher catamaran. We had left San Francisco in 1998 and arrived in Hilton Head, S.C. in 2001. We stayed there a few months, then sailed down to Juno Beach, Florida and bought a 'Natural Awakenings' health magazine franchise. Below are five little 'time capsules' that I discovered printed out, in a box of photos we hadn't opened in several years...

Email sent December 1ˢᵗ, 2000, The British Virgin Islands

When we sailed under the Golden Gate Bridge on August 29, 1998 (with $900 to our names!), we had no idea where we would end up. We knew we wanted to be on the Atlantic side of the U.S.A. and South Carolina was the hazy goal. Those of you who have been following our exploits know that we have had some adventures along the way!

For the most part you have been regaled with stories of whales and beautiful beaches, exciting landfalls and interesting people. There is no doubt the majority of the voyage has been great, but there are also some downsides to this way of life. Last night Joell and I were sitting in the cockpit discussing what we had done and she feels very proud of our accomplishment.

Joell has proven to be an incredibly adaptable woman, who has put up with some hardships to make this a reality for both of us. All of our laundry has been done by hand by our maid, Joell...dishes have been washed in seawater, wherever possible. We have been on a platform that is always moving, very tiring...we have faced many uncomfortable and sometimes dangerous situations – high winds and huge seas, which made us realize what a great boat we have, but also how small and vulnerable we are out there.

Being a hundred miles out at sea off Costa Rica and having a small fishing boat approach, circle us menacingly and have four piratical-looking men line their deck looking us over, leave and then an hour later come back is a story in itself! The constant uncertainty of being in a foreign environment. Wondering if the anchor will hold, will that incredibly vicious lightning storm hit us, the mosquitoes are eating us alive, the intense heat and humidity can be debilitating! Stuff gets stolen off small boats, so constant vigilance is needed. The never-ending motion at sea, which sometimes makes going to the toilet a marathon venture! The maintenance and repair/replacement of bits of various parts of the boat that this harsh, salt water environment engenders...

No, we're not complaining, we have chosen this lifestyle and are proud of our accomplishment. Would we do it again, keep cruising? Absolutely! But we want you to know that it is not all just laying around on a beach!

The skills necessary to get a floating fibreglass home from point A to point B are many...The captain needs to be knowledgeable about diesel and gasoline engine maintenance, electronics, electrical systems, plumbing, carpentry, sail repairs, all kinds of rope-work, fibreglass repair etc., plus sailing and navigational skills. Joell (the Admiral)does everything else, including laundry, galley work, organizing, fishing (!), cooking under sometimes very uncomfortable conditions, dinghy handling, taking her turn standing night watches (identifying ships by their lights) plus much more, all in a pitching, yawing environment. She does it well, with a great spirit and positive energy.

So here we are in the Virgin Islands. As you know, we just participated in the charter yacht show, but don't expect to see results for a few weeks. We have become good friends with a lovely South African family who operate two catamarans out of Tortola. One is a 44' day-charter boat which takes up to forty

220

people to a small island an hour away for a day of snorkeling and swimming. They have asked me to captain for them and we start tomorrow, with Joell as first mate. Sounds like fun, but the responsibility is huge and Joell will have to provide a continental breakfast for the guests so there is a lot of work involved! We are excited about this, as the owners are looking to change their lives after four very successful years and we may have the option to buy the business next year. Time will tell if this is the road (ocean!) for us to travel, but in the meantime we have become rapidly accepted into the charter community here in Tortola and at least the next few weeks will be amongst beautiful islands, fish-filled waters, friendly people and perfect temperatures...

With love,

The Captain and Joell

Email sent December 20ᵗʰ, 2000, Tortola, BVI

To quote one of Jimmy Buffett's great songs:

"It's Christmas in the Caribbean

Send away for mistletoe,

It's Christmas in the Caribbean

Got everything but SNOW..."

We have plenty of rain though, as it's been very squally lately...Still, the sun does come out and the temp is usually around 80. We went snorkeling yesterday and came face-to-face with a nurse shark – don't know who was more surprised! A minute later, a shoal of squid squirted by, it was very rhythmic, like a ballet...

In a couple of days we will sail to eastern Puerto Rico, where we will spend the few days around Christmas anchored off some small islets, swimming and snorkeling. Then to San Juan where we intend to celebrate the New Year in Old Town. After that, through the Bahamas and in the Florida Keys in early February...

HAPPY NEW YEAR TO ALL!

The Captain and Joell

Email sent January 8, 2001, Turks and Caicos Islands

On a bright, sunny morning, with the trade winds blowing out of the northeast, we raised anchor and set sail along the north coast of Puerto Rico. Our destination was a small group of islands called the Turks and Caicos, nearly four hundred open ocean miles away – the day was Saturday, December 30.

The warm wind blew us along the beautiful coast all day and as night fell, we were out of sight of land. The wind shifted direction and picked up speed. The sails were sheeted in and we romped over steadily larger waves on our northwest course. The next day the winds had backed further and were almost on our nose – on went the 'iron donkey' (our diesel engine).

We brought in the start of the 21st century (really it WAS the beginning of the millenium, the Gregorian calendar started with the year 1, not the year 0!), pounding into four-foot waves, sipping a little celebratory single-malt whiskey, toasting all of you gallant readers...

On the morning of January 2nd we dropped anchor in the southernmost of the Turks and Caicos Islands, a one mile long, pristine, uninhabited island called Big Sand Cay. We dinghied ashore in the afternoon and stepped onto the softest pink sand - a large iguana ran in front of us and bright butterflies flitted around. As we crested a small hill, the lagoon on the other side came into view – it was one of the most beautiful settings we had ever seen – a small island about three hundred yards away, with crystal clear water in between of the most vivid and soft shades of blue and green...We walked along the deserted beach and tumbled in the surf, what a wonderful way to bring in the new year!

The anchorage was exposed and rolly, so at three in the morning we upped anchor and had a boisterous sail to South Caicos, where we set the hook, after it dragged three times, at seven in the morning. Dinghying ashore we found a small, slightly run-down community, which we found out later consisted of about nine hundred souls. We officially cleared into the country and the Customs and Immigration were very pleasant – this always bodes well (stay away from the British Virgin Islands, they are very unfriendly!). We wandered around the town, got bitten by mosquitoes and high-tailed it to a local bar, dodging horses, cows and pigs roaming the streets

After a couple of beers and some potent local rum, we got talking to a couple of local fishermen originally from Cuba – turns out they fished for lobster and after we bought them a beer, they left and came back with five fresh lobster for our dinner! We liked this little island, untouched by tourism, relying on fish and lobster to get them by. After a couple of days, we planned to make the 43-mile crossing over the very shallow Caicos Bank to get to the larger island of Providenciales (Provo). However, a norther blew up and the visibility over the Bank dropped to where we wouldn't have been able to see any coral heads in the way!

So we headed south around the banks, doubling the distance, but it was a lovely night and we had a beautiful sail. We are anchored off the beach at Provo, where there are a number of resorts and a lot of tourists – not really our scene...

So, we will leave here on Thursday and head toward the Bahamas...

Much love from your sailin' friends

The Captain and Joell

Email sent January 24, 2001, Marathon, FL, USA

Where were we...? Oh, yes, the last email was sent from a hotel/resort/casino on Provo Island in the Turks and Caicos – well right after it was sent, we went to the small casino, Joell fed about $5 into a slot machine and won $321! We immediately got a couple of rums and staggered back two miles down the moonlit beach to the dinghy....time to leave, thinks us.

The next day it was blowing strong from the north and we powered our way through the tiny gap in the reef, with waves crashing very close on either side. A bumpy three hour motor followed, after which we cleared some outlying reefs, fell off the wind, hoisted full sail (I love this nautical talk!) and headed WNW towards Cuba and the southern Bahamas. After thirty-six hours, we anchored off a small deserted Bahama island to rest for a night. The next day we sailed eighty miles to Little Ragged Island, as the wind decided to blow from the NW right where we were heading. We stayed for two days until the storm passed, anchored in typical blue-green Bahama water, playing Scrabble and getting ready for the next passage.

We had decided at this point to head for the Florida Keys, rather than spend three weeks or so going through the Bahamas. There followed a wonderful sail as we paralleled the north coast of Cuba, with its mountains in view. The trade winds filled in and we had three days of steady Nor'easterlies, blue skies with puffy white clouds and 2-3 foot waves off the beam. Just a great way to end our ocean-going part of this adventure. Cap'n Jon caught a fine Albacore tuna, which fed us for three days!

Last Thursday morning, we motored in light winds toward Marathon Key, halfway down the chain of islands off the Florida mainland. We were both tired from a three day and night passage and wanted to get the hook down and sleep for twenty hours! Three miles from the anchorage, after two-and-a-half years of faithful service, the diesel spluttered and stopped dead! There was a slight breeze, so I unfurled the jib and we ghosted to the anchorage, where the anchor went down under sail in American waters after two years....

I spent the next three hours getting dirt out of the fuel system (bad fuel in the Turks & Caicos), bleeding the air out and cursing softly under my breath (Joell would disagree with that!). The following day we motored into a landlocked anchorage and dropped the hook amongst about three hundred sail boats! Here we are for the next six weeks and some friends and family are coming to visit. Early March, we will head up the Intracoastal Waterway to our final destination for this part of the voyage-Hilton Head Island, S.C.

Who knows what the store has in future..?? Thanks for following our escapades and special thanks to those of you who have written back to us – don't go away now, we'll be back...

Love from Jon, Joell and 'Stormy Weather' (our new Cockatiel!).

Email sent March 6, 2001, Hilton Head Island, S.C.

This will be the last installment of our voyage, at least for now. We have to 'swallow the anchor' and make some money before we venture out again.

Florida was so cold with northerlies blowing down one after the other. It just wasn't conducive to having guests and as our friends in South Carolina were anxious to see us, we decided to head north, even though everyone said we were crazy! We left Marathon Key and took three days to sail slowly to Ft. Myers on the west coast of Florida. There the Captain's brother Grant joined us for what would turn out to be a delightful trip across the middle of Florida.

We had a few days of warm weather and set off up the Calloosahatchie River to enter the first of a group of locks which would raise us to the height of Okeechobee Lake (the second largest freshwater lake in the country). Unfortunately there has been a prolonged drought and we heard rumours that the lake was very shallow and may be unnavigable. The Cap'n telephoned the Army Corps of Engineers and was informed that the lake could carry a six foot depth, so as we only draw three feet, off we went...

The only restriction was on the opening of the locks, as they had been placed on a strict timetable in order to preserve what water remained in the lake. We motored up the beautiful river and were the only boat in the first locks – after the Panama Canal it looked like a piece of cake, but there was a tremendous surge in the lock chamber and it knocked the bow hard against the concrete wall – JoJo is a strong boat and I think she did more damage to the lock!

Because of the drought, there have been severe forest fires in Florida and as we motored along towards the lake, the land on our left was burning and smoldering – the smoke was thick and intense. It was especially sad for me as I had been this way a few years ago and this particular stretch was magnificent and verdant.

Once we entered the lake, the wind blew up and we started to sail with small waves splashing over the bow. The depth sounder on JoJo is quite temperamental, so I threw our lead line over a number of times and found we had four feet under our keels – no worries! Four hours later we found the east side of the lake and motored into the lock at Port Mayuca. The next day we went through the last lock and motored under clear skies to Stuart, where we joined the Intracoastal Waterway. That night we moored in the pleasant town of Vero Beach and witnessed a space shuttle launch from Cape Canaveral, about 35 miles away - it was absolutely awesome, just spectacular!

Grant left the next day and we sorely missed him, as he is a superb shipmate and a great Scrabble player! (Grant, two nights ago Joell scored 116 with one word!). The next few days we motored north on the Waterway, waving to the few boats headed south – who looked at us as if we were nuts!

We encountered fog and very cold conditions, but JoJo also has an inside steering station and with the cabin heater keeping us toasty, it was a pleasant and beautiful trip. I pointed out to Joell where I had wrapped a crab trap line around the propellor and spent a few days on a small island with a KKK redneck nine years earlier!

Two weeks ago we tied up at Palmetto Bay Marina where the Captain had lived aboard on a couple of different boats several years earlier. Our friends have been wonderfully welcoming and have hardly left us enough time to re-adjust to land life! We had the Bugatti shipped out, so we are mobile, as long as it doesn't rain! Joell has a commission to paint a mural in a pediatrician's office, plus others in the works. The Captain got a job doing 'dolphin tours' – we'll continue to live on JoJo and make future cruising plans...

Jon and Joell, Hilton Head Island, S.C.

(We stayed on the Island for three months, then decided to move down to Florida, where we stumbled upon a franchise opportunity to publish a new magazine called 'Natural Awakenings'. We were quite successful, sold it and went to truck- driving school!).

FRED, THE PUPPET

After the demise of Fiesta International, my Mexican export business, I found myself back in Los Angeles with no direction. I wanted to buy a catamaran and go sailing, but didn't have enough money to do that. So I decided to go to New Zealand...

My friends Mike and Gaynor were planning to move back to her native country in a month and had invited me to visit. We had talked about buying a cruising sailboat together and exploring the Pacific islands. I bought a ticket to fly out of L.A. to Auckland in November, but had three months with nothing to do. I decided to have a hitchhiking adventure and go back east to visit old friends in New Hope, Pennsylvania.

One morning in August, 1980, I stuck my thumb out on I-15 in L.A. and got rides to Barstow, in the desert. It was 2:00 in the afternoon, very hot, when I walked down the circular entrance ramp onto I-40, the highway that would take me nearly three thousand miles to the east coast. As I got closer I could see at least a dozen hopeful travelers standing or sitting resignedly by the dusty side of the road, some with their thumbs hopefully extended. Oh no, fierce competition!

Etiquette dictated that I be the last in line, so I continued past the others, a quick greeting as I tromped down the ramp toward the interstate. I took off my backpack and squatted on the hot concrete, using my pack for support. With this number of hitchhikers and a sporadic parade of cars and semis, I thought I would probably be there for a day or two. I took a mouthful of water, leaned back, closed my eyes and started to doze. Two minutes later I heard the sound of a diesel engine and gears shifting as a semi came onto the entrance ramp. Then the squeal of its brakes as it slowed down. I opened one eye just as the towering white cab pulled up next to me and stopped.

229

I opened the other eye and jumped up! The driver pointed at me. I hesitated for a second and looked at the line of hitchhikers staring back at me. I had been there less than five minutes and the rules of the road dictated that I should back off and let the first person, who had been waiting there much longer than me, have the ride. I looked back at the driver, a young, burly guy with long blond hair, who impatiently beckoned to me to climb aboard.

What if I got in and then further down the road I met up with one of the other hitchhikers who were in front of me? How true should I be to the code of the road? How long did I want to be out in the baking heat of the desert in this god-forsaken town in the middle of nowhere? Three other hitchhikers had hoisted their packs and were running toward me and the truck, obviously pissed off...

I reached up for the grab bar, opened the door, threw my bag in and quickly followed, pulling my hat down so as hopefully not to be recognized by my competition. The driver slammed the gearshift into first, let out the clutch and quickly went through the gears as we trundled down the entrance ramp. I kept my head low, but could see in his side mirror that the others on the side of the road weren't happy at all – several pointed their middle fingers in my direction.

I felt a pang of discomfort at the thought that I was now a pariah to other hitchhikers heading east, but hoped that I wouldn't run into anyone who had seen me. I also felt much cooler as the air conditioning swept aside the oppressive desert heat and sweat. I looked over at the driver and smiled.

"Hey man, thanks for picking me up. Where're you going?" I asked.

"Indiana," he replied slowly. "How 'bout you?"

"Near Philly."

He didn't respond, but concentrated on getting his huge rig up to 70 m.p.h. and then set the cruise control. I looked around the cab and saw that there was a sleeper area behind me.

"Throw yer bag in the back and relax. Mah name's Whitey, Whitey Naas."

"Great!" I replied, a big grin on my face. "I'm Jon."

Now this was very cool - sitting high above the cars, cruising through the desert heading closer to my destination in an air-conditioned big rig! We chatted for an hour and he asked about my British accent – he'd never met an Englishman before and had a bunch of questions. I asked him about the multiple gears and how difficult was it to drive this monster?

"Yah know how to drive a stick shift, right? Well, instead of four gears, yah got ten."

He explained to me that there was a low range and a high range and how you moved the long gearshift and pulled and pushed the knob attached to it to engage the ranges. Then he told me about something called the 'Jake Brake', which used engine decompression to slow the truck down without touching the brakes. He could see that I was genuinely interested and said, half-jokingly,

"Mebbe I'll let yah drive in a while."

I looked at him and laughed. Whitey slid a cassette into the player and Pink Floyd blasted the cab as we headed down the road. An hour later he pulled into a rest area west of Kingman, Arizona and we stretched our legs. As we walked back to the truck, he reached into his pocket for the keys and said,

"Listen man, ah'm really tired, been drivin' fer two days and ah need to sleep. But ah also need to get my load back to base on time. So, here's the keys. You drive..."

"You're kidding, right? I've driven a lot of different vehicles, but never something like this!"

"Well, here's yer chance. Ah'll watch yah for a while, see how yah do, OK?"

"Sure," I replied nervously, unlocking the driver's door and climbing up into the drivers seat. Whitey plopped down next to me and showed me how to start the truck. He pointed out the light switches, the overhead cord that worked the air horn and the turn signals. I started the truck, my hands shaking. I depressed the clutch and shifted into first. He told me that I'd only spend a couple of seconds in each gear before I had to shift and that I needed to let the clutch out smoothly, otherwise the whole rig would jerk and shudder! Now I was really nervous!

He watched me intently. I looked both ways and no one else was moving – I had a clear shot onto the entrance ramp to I-40, once I pulled around the truck parked on my left. Taking a deep breath and trying to stop my hands trembling, I released the clutch, there was a brief shudder and we moved slowly forward. Within a second, I pulled the knob up and shifted into first high, the depressed it and moved the stick back to second gear. Then flicked the knob up and repeated the whole procedure. I glanced into my side mirror and turned the big steering wheel left as I eased the entire 72' length past the truck parked next to us.

"Straighten out," Whitey commanded. "Now, hard left!" as he leaned over to look in my side mirror. I was starting to sweat, but within thirty seconds we were out of the confines of the parking lot and I was shifting through the gears as I moved down the entrance ramp. There weren't too many cars and those heading in our direction quickly slid into the left lane. Within two minutes I was in high gear at 70 m.p.h., let out a huge sigh of relief and concentrated on how the rig handled. Steering was easy and it stayed in a straight line with very little adjustment from the driver – me! I flicked on the cruise control and looked over at Whitey, who had been watching me intently.

'"Hey, this is pretty easy, man," as I relaxed back into the driver's seat, which rested on springs to further absorb road bumps. "I like this!"

Whitey didn't say anything, just sat back and paid attention to how I was doing. Apparently I was doing well, when half an hour later, as the sun was setting behind us in glorious hues of deep red and scarlet, he told me to turn on the headlights, climbed into the back and pulled the curtain closed. He obviously trusted me and told me he was going to sleep. Any problems, just wake him up! This was another surreal event in my life...

And so I drove through the night, the traffic thinning and the truck thrumming. This was great, towering above the small 'four-wheelers', following the path of the powerful headlights. We climbed steadily and sped though Flagstaff toward Winslow and Holbrook. I slowed down using the 'Jake Brake' and pulled over at a truck stop as the fuel gauge was getting low; Whitey slid back the curtain and rubbed his eyes.

"How ya doin', Jon?" he asked sleepily.

"No worries, Whitey. We need some fuel and I could use a cup of coffee if I'm going to keep driving."

"Nah, I got a few hours sleep. Pull next to that pump. There, that's good. Well done, man. Seems like yah can drive this rig just fine."

"Yeah, not a problem. I like it!"

We filled up with a couple of hundred gallons of diesel and Whitey got a large cup of coffee. He climbed behind the wheel and I ducked into the back to 'hot bunk' for the rest of the night. I fell asleep to the soothing sound of eighteen tyres carrying us ever east.

Early the next morning, as the sun rose above the desert near Tucumcari, New Mexico, we had breakfast at a Flying J truck stop.

"So Jon, what're yer plans, why're yah goin' to Philadelphia?"

"Well, I've got three months with nothing to do before I fly to New Zealand. I've got friends there and we're thinking of buying a boat and cruising the Pacific Islands. Now I'm going to Philly to hang out with some other friends before flying out of L.A."

He looked at me like I was a little crazy. I doubt if he knew where New Zealand was or could conceive of buying a sailboat and crossing oceans.

"OK, so yer kind of footloose for a few months, right?" I nodded. "Well, I was watching yah for a while last night and yah can drive a big rig pretty well. My company needs drivers. How would yah like to come to Indiana with me? I'm sure they'd hire you..."

I stirred my coffee and thought about it for ten seconds.

"Ah, right OK..." I stammered. "That sounds cool, but don't I need a truck drivers license?"

"Yeah, but it's real easy to get in Indiana. It's like gettin' a regular license, yah jest take a written test. I know yah can get a license an' if I tell the company yer a good driver, they'll hire you. They need a dozen drivers right now."

I drank my coffee and looked out the window at the row of idling semis parked perfectly parallel to each other. This could be a real adventure and I'd arrive in Auckland with a lot more money in my pocket! I couldn't pass up this opportunity to briefly be one of America's last 'cowboys' and become an over-the-road trucker. Little did I know that twenty-two years later, my future wife and I would attend truck driving school together and spend a year crisscrossing the country in our own big rig!

"OK Whitey, if you think I can get hired, I'll call my friends in New Hope and tell them I'm not coming. I'll go to Indiana with you and take my chances!"

We shook hands over the table and walked back out to the truck. Taking turns driving the 1100 miles through New Mexico, Oklahoma and Missouri we arrived a day later at a small town just south of Indianapolis, where his company was based. It was an old, quiet, typical mid-west town, sleeping in the oppressive heat and humidity. We pulled into a small truck yard with half a dozen tractor-trailers parked in a row on a gravel lot behind a small faded building.

I climbed down and walked inside with Whitey, who introduced me to the owners, a pleasant couple in their late fifties.

"So, yah wanna come work for us, huh?" they asked me pleasantly.

"Well, assuming I can get my truck driving license, yes, I'd like that," I replied, my British accent fairly distinct amongst these mid-Westerners.

"Where you from, Jon?" Mrs Baker asked.

"Oh, originally from London, but that was a long time ago, ma'am. I live in Los Angeles now."

"Wayl, we never had a limey driver before, but if you can git your license, we'd love to have you as part of our company. So you got a California driver license, right? Good, Bill here will drive you down to the Motor Vehicle Department and you can study the manual and take the test right there. That OK with you?"

"Um, right. OK then. See you in a bit..."

Bill drove me through the somnolent, shady town and we pulled up outside a small hut-like structure, more a large shed than a building!

"Ah'll be back in an hour, Jon. Good luck!" as he dropped me off and drove away.

I watched his pickup truck disappear and turned to the little building, opened the door and walked inside. There was a short, middle-aged lady behind a small counter. The whole place seemed lilliputian, nothing like the huge, bustling, noisy DMV's in L.A., with hundreds of bored people sitting on hard plastic chairs waiting for their number to be called, like something from the movie Betelgeuse!

She looked up from her small pile of papers and smiled at me. "Can I help you, sir?"

"Er, yes, right. Well actually I'd like to take the written test to get a truck drivers license, please."

I expected her to tell me to show proof that I'd completed a course in maneuvering a 72' long, 40-ton behemoth before taking the test. But no, she smiled sweetly and gave me a simple form to fill out.

"Now young man, you can study the manual right here if you haven't yet, then answer the twenty questions in this here exam sheet. Then turn it in to me with your driver license and ten dollars and if you pass the test, why, I'll take your photo and give you a new license right now. How's that?"

Well, I thought it was pretty surreal, but I smiled back at her, took the paperwork and sat down on a wobbly chair to study the manual. It didn't take me long to read it, maybe ten minutes. I'm very good at tests, I always do well and this was just twenty multiple choice questions. Within forty-five minutes I had my photo taken and traded my regular California driver license for an Indiana truck driver license! I looked at it, then looked back at Miss Julie Hansen who was batting her eyelashes at me.

"So now I'm legal to drive a semi, right Julie? I mean, you don't even know if I can maneuver one of those things."

"Well now, English Jon, you better be able to, 'cause you got the license!"

I heard a vehicle pull up outside and a horn beeped twice.

"How'd it go in there, Jon?" asked Bill as I climbed into his truck.

"Well, I passed the written test, is there anything else I need to do?"

"Yep, yer gonna drive one of my rigs a couple a miles down the road, jes' so I know yah can handle it, then we're gonna set yah loose!"

And that's exactly what happened. With Bill sitting next to me, I easily jockeyed the rig through the gates of the yard, drove around town for ten minutes then headed back. What I hadn't realized was that he wanted me to back the whole rig between two other tractor-trailers – there was about twelve feet between them and the rig I was driving was eight feet wide! Whitey had neglected to have me back up on our two-day journey and I was concerned - no, petrified!

I had watched him do this maneuver at a couple of truck stops – he had swung wide and positioned the whole rig in a straight line directly in front of the narrow space between two parked rigs, then slowly reversed, using both side mirrors to make minor corrections. So I did the same. There was plenty of room in the yard for me to swing in a big circle and position myself in front of the space Bill had directed me to back into.

He didn't say a word, but watched me intently, which added to my nervousness. I looked in both mirrors, decided I was evenly positioned between the two parked tractor-trailers, engaged reverse, let out the clutch and slowly edged backwards. Over the years, I had driven a few small vehicles with trailers attached so I knew that in order to get the trailer going in one direction, you had to turn the wheel of the tow vehicle the other way. On a rig like this, where the trailer is three times longer than the cab, the principle was the same, but the dynamics were quite different...

I could see the left side of the trailer edging toward the parked rig and turned the huge steering wheel to the left, all the time feathering the clutch. That was better, it moved away and I straightened it out. And back we went, slowly, carefully as I slid between the two parked rigs...perfectly! I pulled out the yellow parking brake knob, there was a hiss of released air, I yanked twice on the horn string and switched it off.

"How did I do, Bill?" was my rhetorical question.

"Yah did fine. Now ah'm gonna send you to Dee-troit, OK?"

"Sure, no worries!"

An hour later I was driving up I-69 by myself with a cargo of steel strapped onto the flatbed trailer behind me. It was a short trip, less than three hundred miles, but it was really cool to be a 'king of the road'. I listened to the CB radio, learning the language of over-the-road truckers, occasionally letting others know where 'Smokey the Bear' was hanging out with a radar gun!

The next three months had me driving mostly around the mid-west and north-east, with a couple of runs out to California. If the journey was a thousand miles or less, I'd go by myself, but more than that and I'd have a co-driver, so we could 'keep the wheels turning' almost 24 hours a day. I met some characters at truck stops and on the regular routes got familiar with a few other truckers who gave me the 'handle' 'Limey Jon' on the CB!

November 6th loomed nearer and I had to be in L.A. at 1:00 p.m. to catch my long flight to Auckland. I told Bill and Mary that I had a birthday to attend in Los Angeles and could they arrange a trip that would get me there on time?

"Sure, no problem, Jon. We'll have a good co-driver fer yah, too," said Bill.

I felt bad that I would be leaving them like this, but they had made a lot of money off me and there's a really high turnover rate in the trucking business, so I knew they'd still flourish without me! On Tuesday, I met my co-driver, we climbed aboard and headed west, hauling a load of beef in the refrigerated trailer.

Howard was a pleasant, quiet, tubby man about my age who didn't say much, but was a good driver. By Thursday morning we were a hundred miles east of L.A. having breakfast at a truck-stop.

"So, Howard, you're pretty comfortable driving this rig, right?" I asked innocuously.

He looked at me a little suspiciously. "Yup, no problem. Why?"

"Well, I'm going to leave you in L.A. and you'll have to drive

239

back yourself," I responded looking straight at him. "I'll call Bill and tell them and you'll either get a co-driver or drive back yourself, take a little longer, but you'll get more pay."

"Sounds fine by me. Where yah goin'?" he asked.

"New Zealand," I replied, matter-of-factly.

"Where zat?" he said.

"The other side of the world..." I said getting up and paying the bill.

We drove to Compton, an industrial part of L.A. and unloaded our cargo at a smelly, disgusting meat-processing facility. By noon we were finished, and I had an hour to get to the airport. I slowly drove along the surface streets and just before 1:00 pm, followed the signs into LAX. Howard wasn't sure what I was doing. He thought I was going to take a cab from Compton to the airport, but I had decided otherwise...

With Howard sitting upright in amazement and 'four-wheelers' angrily honking their horns as they buzzed around us, I slowly and carefully maneuvered 72 feet of over-the-road monster into LAX and pulled up outside the Air New Zealand departure terminal. With a loud hiss of escaping air, I engaged the parking brake and turned on the four-way flashers.

People gawked and stared as I shook Howard's hand, wished him luck, grabbed my back pack from the bunk and climbed down out of the cab. A couple of airport cops came running up and as they ordered me to leave, Howard slid over into the driver's seat. He rolled down the window, gave me a huge grin, blew two blasts of the air horn and pulled majestically away, as I disappeared into the terminal. There must have been a hundred people, as well as the two cops, staring as Howard went through the gears and edged his way out of the airport...

It was a long flight, with a brief stopover in Honolulu and I arrived groggily a day later in the southern hemisphere. Gaynor met me at the airport and guided me to her car, a classic 1959 Austin Cambridge in lovely condition. She drove at a leisurely pace north toward Auckland, skirted the city and then southwest to Titirangi, where they had rented a small house. To the left I could see sailboats dancing on the water, little inlets and bays everywhere – it was very pretty and I looked forward to meeting members of the local Wharram catamaran sailing group.

We made a left off the main road and bounced down lovely, leafy lanes, turned into a driveway and stopped in front of a pretty pink bungalow with an inviting porch and many shade trees. Michael ambled out and grabbed my pack – I just wanted to sleep! Twelve hours later we sat on the veranda catching up and talking about buying a catamaran and sailing the Pacific.

It soon became apparent that their relationship was on rocky ground and the likelihood of the three of us going cruising faded quickly. I planned on staying through the holiday season, then decide what to do. For the next couple of weeks I explored the area and the delightful city of Auckland. I met members of the Wharram catamaran group and went sailing on the bay with them.

New Zealanders appeared to be a thrifty and self-sufficient people. There were a lot of classic English Austins, Morrises, Riley and Wolseley cars from the 1950's and 60's, most in perfect condition and driven daily. Also many old British motorcycles, Triumph, BSA, Ariel, Matchless, bikes that anywhere else would be collector's items, but here they were everyday transportation, lovingly cared for and expected to last a long time. A vehicle was a huge investment for a typical New Zealand family and when they saved enough to buy one, they planned to take care of it and drive it for fifty years!

In many back yards there were makeshift shelters and temporary sheds made of corrugated steel, some like the famous Nissen huts designed during World War I. And peeking out of the front would be the bow of a boat being built. There were small ones and large ones, some motor boats, but mostly sailboats. For many New Zealanders, if you wanted a boat...you built one! In some ways the country and its hardy occupants had a pioneer spirit, similar to what Americans must have been like at the beginning of the 20th century.

A small package arrived in the middle of November from a friend of Gaynor in London. She opened it and pulled out a Christmas card and a small string puppet. It stood about seven inches tall and was made of four pieces of shaped wood – a big piece for the body, a smaller piece in the shape of a head and two flat pieces for the feet. They were joined together with short lengths of coloured yarn. Bright yellow thumb tacks were the eyes. There was a simple X-shaped control bar with four strings - one for the body, one for the head and two for the feet.

It was stained a deep rich colour and was beautiful in its simplicity and appeal. We named him Fred and played with him for a couple of hours - we had him walking, running, climbing onto the furniture and dancing on the table. There was something soothing and playful manipulating his strings and little body. The flat feet clicked and tapped on the wood floor. Fred was very amusing and enchanting!

The next morning I was having a cup of coffee on the veranda and making Fred climb onto the table. 'Click, click' went his feet and his 'body' and 'head' swayed from side to side. I was mesmerized by the puppet, he seemed to have a happy personality, almost seemed alive...

Our neighbour's children, Tom and Sally, curly-headed blond youngsters, called out to me from the driveway,

"Coo, Captain Jon, that's a lovely puppet! Can we 'ave a go?"

"Of course you can, come on in."

For the next half an hour, the two kids took turns manipulating Fred into all sorts of situations! Climbing a small bush, hiding behind a tree, scurrying across the small lawn, jumping up the steps onto the porch. They were fascinated by his simplicity and 'life-like' response to their hand movements.

"Please, Captain Jon, where did you get Fred? Maybe Mummy will buy one for each of us?" said eight-year old Tom, quite seriously. "I'd like one and so would Sally, wouldn't you?" he asked looking at his little sister.

"Oh yes please. He's really fun and I'd love to have one for Christmas. But mine will be a girl and I'll call her Ducky!" she said intently, as if there was no doubt she'd find one in her Christmas stocking.

An idea had been circling my mind over coffee and this had clinched it.

"OK kids, I'll see what I can do and talk to your Mum. Off you go to school now, you're going to be late."

They scampered down the driveway and ran toward their school, half a mile down the road. I absentmindedly drank my cold coffee and looked at the puppet laying on the table. I thought about how intently the children had played with him and how they had laughed at his antics. There was something about Fred that had an enormous appeal. And Christmas was just a few weeks away...

Gaynor sleepily wandered out the green front door, her first cup of coffee in her hand.

" 'Morning," she grunted.

"Hello cheery one," I responded, suddenly energized with the entrepreneurial spirit! "I have an idea that could make lots of people smile and make us some money," I said eagerly.

"What? Are we going to import Mexican stuff to New Zealand? I don't think they'd go for it!" was her deadpan question.

"No, no. I want to stay away from that! But Tom and Sally stopped by on their way to school and were captivated by Fred here. They each want one for Christmas!"

"Well we've only got one and they're not getting Fred," she said adamantly.

"I know that, luv. But what if we made them each a puppet? No, what if we made a whole bunch of puppets and went out to toy shops and stores in Auckland and sold them? I bet we could make them for fifty cents and wholesale them for $2.50. I bet they'd sell a ton of them for $5.00. People here enjoy simple things and Fred is so damn appealing," I blurted out.

"Wait a minute, I need another cup of coffee..." replied Gaynor as she ambled off to the kitchen. I followed her, deep in thought.

"It wouldn't take much, just a jig saw and some yarn and thumb tacks and string. Why, I bet we could make fifty of them at a time. Let's see, if we can make and sell a hundred Fred puppets in a week, that's two hundred bucks profit. If we make twice as many..."

"Slow down, Jon. What are you mumbling about?"

"I think we should make a bunch of Fred puppets and sell them before Christmas. And I think we should go out today to a few shops and see if they'll order some. What do you think?"

244

"Hmmm." Gaynor sipped her coffee, stared out over the garden and replied light-heartedly, "I don't think I've got anything on my social calendar today! Might be a lark. Yeah, let's take Fred out and see if anyone wants to buy some."

And that's just what we did. Into the old Austin and into town. We stopped at the first toy shop we saw and while Gaynor made Fred walk and dance down the counter, I talked to the proprietor about buying a few for Christmas. Luckily, there was a mother there shopping for her kids.

"Ooh, that's nice. I'll buy one for each of my children," she said to us and the shopkeeper.

I looked from her to the owner, who instantly said,

"Roight, Mrs. Watkins, cum back in a week, dear."

He pulled me aside and said, "Roight then, young man, 'ow much and when can oi 'ave 'em?"

He had a distinct Cockney accent and had probably emigrated in the 1950's, when England suffered what was then termed 'The Brain Drain'. Australia and New Zealand wanted to attract talented people to help grow their countries' population. Their governments subsidized the cost of the steamship tickets and I remember seeing newspaper ads offering one-way tickets down-under for just 10 pounds...

"Um, they're $2.50 each and you can have them in five days," I replied, not having a clue how we were going to make them and if we could do it in five days!

"Awright then. Oi'll take two dozen an' oi'll see you on Froiday. Cheerio!" And out we went, Fred running and hopping in front of us.

"Blimey! We've got an order from our first call and I've no idea how we're going to fill it," I said excitedly to Gaynor.

'Well, let's see if we can get some more, then we'll figure it out. This is fun!" she replied, unfazed.

By mid-afternoon we had stopped at half a dozen shops and had orders for over a hundred 'Freds'! Now we had to deliver...We stopped by a small lumber yard and showed them our puppet.

"What kind of wood is this made from and do you have anything similar?" I asked.

"Well, if you want to cut out small pieces like this, I'd suggest radiata pine. It's native to California, but we grow it here. It's easy to work with, but you've got to work around the knots. Here, let me show you some."

We chatted as he took us between piles of neatly stacked lumber. I asked him about the right type of saw to buy and he thought for a few seconds.

"So, you live in Titirangi, right? Well, I know a chap there, retired, not much to do, but he's got a small woodworking shop in his garden. Why don't you stop by, tell him I sent you, maybe he can give you some help..."

We loaded up the boot with four-foot lengths of wood and trundled up the road to the address he had given us. As we pulled into the driveway, a short, smiling man in his sixties, wearing stained jeans and a checked shirt came out of his house.

"Alloo, ah'm Dave. Bill at the timber yard called an' said you might be stoppin' by. 'Ow can ah help you?" he asked, hand outstretched.

"Hello Dave . I'm Jon and this is my friend Gaynor. We'd like some advice as to what saw we should buy to cut this wood into shapes like our puppet? We have orders for a whole bunch of them and we need to start making them right away so kids can have them for Christmas!"

"Hmmm, so there's just the four pieces. You'll need a band saw, a sander and some jigs," he muttered, studying Fred and moving around the side of his house. "And some stain and rags, yarn and drawing pins. This shouldn't be too hard..."

We followed him through a small gate into a carefully tended little garden, with neat rows of vegetables sprouting in the spring warmth - it was very 'hobbit-like'. I had first read The Hobbit when I was ten years old and quickly devoured the Lord of the Rings trilogy immediately after. Many things about New Zealand reminded me of hobbits and I wasn't surprised when the films were shot there forty years later!

Tucked into one corner of the garden was a small, brightly painted yellow shed, with a round window cut into the front! He opened the door and I expected to see Bilbo Baggins fashioning something on a lathe! He could have been, because inside that 10 X 10 space was a perfect miniature woodworking shop with a small lathe, dozens of tools hung neatly on peg board and in the middle a gleaming band saw, which looked like it had been designed and built in the 1950's. Turned out, it had!

"So you want to make a lot of these little puppets, right? Well, rather than going out and buying the tools, I'll let you use my shop if you're careful. 'Ow's that?"

Gaynor and I looked at each other in amazement (law of attraction at work!)

"Er, yes, that would be terrific, Dave. How much would you charge us?"

247

"Ooh no, I'm not looking to make any money, Jon. I'm retired and this would be fun. Tell you what, I'll trade you shop time for a couple of puppets for me grandchildren. 'Ow's that, then?"

"Well, that's terrific! When can we start?"

"No time like the present..."

And so we had an instant manufacturing facility! Within an hour Dave made some jigs and showed me how to feed the wood we had bought through the saw blade. Gaynor drove home and came back with some sandwiches and biscuits.

We worked until the sun went down, Dave and I getting along well, swapping sailing stories amidst sawdust and rising stacks of 'Fred' parts. We swept the floor, he oiled his tools and off we went to the local pub where I bought him a couple of Guinesses. The next morning Gaynor went out and bought different coloured yarns to connect the pieces and different colored thumb tacks for eyes. We set up our small living room as an 'assembly plant' and soon Gaynor, Mike and I had a smooth 'assembly line' where the four pieces of wood were attached by coloured yarn that matched the 'eyes'. We had a stack of control bars and thread cut to size to make them 'move'.

By evening we had built a hundred and twenty puppets and put each one into a plastic freezer bag - our simple packaging! The next day Gaynor and I drove around to the shops that had given us orders, delivered our puppets, put NZ$300 in our pockets and went to shops on the north side of Auckland, where we got orders for two hundred more!

It was pretty easy. Gaynor and I each had a puppet and we'd make them dance and perform tricks on a counter top. Usually a couple of mums would come over and ask if they could buy them. We always walked out with an order for at least a dozen, usually two! The next week we had a regular routine where we'd spend a day at our 'production facility', then a day at our 'assembly plant'. Then a day exploring the shops and stores in Auckland and its suburbs, delivering our orders and getting more.

In all, we sold, built and delivered almost a thousand puppets and made a lot of kids happy. When the local children went back to school after the holidays, we would see many of them walking past our driveway, fiercely concentrating on their 'Fred' puppets, making sure they walked properly in front of them!

By the middle of January, I could see no reason to stay any longer. Mike and Gaynor needed to sort out their relationship and I had some ideas that I wanted to pursue in California. Gaynor drove me to the airport and I left with a thousand dollars more than I had arrived with!

I still have a Fred puppet and pull it out once in a while. Gaynor and I lost contact over the years until the day Joell and I sailed back from our week in Mexico and tied up at the dock in San Diego. It was January 3rd, 1997 and I had proposed to Joell a week earlier, the day we had left for Mexico on our chartered sailboat. I was loading our stuff from the boat into Joell's Honda, when a tall, gangly woman walked by. I didn't pay any attention to her until someone called out "Gaynor, hey Gaynor!"

And it was her, after seventeen years! Big hugs and I introduced her to my fiancee. Gaynor was the first to know that we were engaged. And she had also followed up on her dream of going cruising. She had divorced Mike and was now living aboard her sailboat in the marina. You just never know exactly when and how your dreams will be realized, do you?

ON THE REEF!

The second year of my leisurely cruise through the Caribbean found us anchored off Georgetown in the spice island of Grenada. I had left Hilton Head, S.C. on a chilly morning in November, 1989, one day before my thirty-ninth birthday. Joining me for the first phase of my cruise aboard my 41' Searunner trimaran 'Imagine', was an old college friend, Dennis who had little sailing skill but a thirst for adventure. Having sold my simulator business a few months previously, I had this lovely boat, a bunch of cash and the unknown before me...

Cruising down the Intracoastal Waterway, winding peacefully between the tall grass banks of meandering, isolated rivers in Georgia, we were wrapped up against the chill, brisk weather, visions of sparkling Caribbean seas and hot tropical sun spurring us on. Almost magically, crossing the border into Florida, the weather turned warm and the sweaters came off. We left the waterway and sailed down the Florida coast, about a mile offshore, as 'Imagine' tasted the Atlantic Ocean for the first time.

In Miami, my old sailing friend Jean-Jacques joined us and we three sailed through the Bahamas and left San Salvador Island heading out into the Atlantic, looking for the trade winds to push us to the Virgin Islands. It was a tough sail, mostly beating into the wind for several days, until we were able to turn south, ease the sails and glide to St. Thomas. Jean-Jacques left us there and a couple of weeks later I asked Dennis to move off the boat while we were anchored in St. John, as the close quarters had brought out some personal habits that were difficult to live with. He promptly disappeared into the hills and I next saw him in L.A., many years later!

I invited a woman I had known years earlier when living in New Hope, PA., to come down for a week to sail the Virgin Islands with me. She was recently divorced and readily agreed. Lyndy and I had a wonderful time and she stayed an extra week. She decided the cruising life was for her and we meshed well. A month later, after I single-handed Imagine down to Antigua, she flew in and joined me there, with no time schedule and a small replacement refrigerator as part of her luggage! We spent several months island hopping down the Caribbean chain, exploring all the diverse islands had to offer. Bustling, colourful markets, full of spicy smells and smiling local ladies, offering fresh vegetables and fruit. Lush, tropical jungles with parrots and waterfalls, azure waters with isolated beaches and bright, darting fish on the reefs.

The island of Dominica was especially gorgeous; with no cruise ship dock and a small airport that couldn't handle large planes, it retained its natural beauty and hadn't yet been turned into a tourist trap. For some reason, most cruisers sailed past it, so there were only a handful of boats anchored. We met another cruising couple, rented an old Hyundai and spent a week exploring every road and track I could get that poor car down.

At one point, after a heavy downpour while we were up in the mountains, the car bounced down a muddy, water-filled track, swerving and skidding, the brakes ineffective, the four of us holding on tight, laughing and screaming, until I brought it to a stop at the bottom, using the handbrake and rapidly downshifting to first gear! There were hidden waterfalls, secluded swimming pools deep inside the jungle, friendly, curious locals and excellent lobster. It was here I ate a local delicacy called Mountain Chicken that I assumed was a small, local chicken and it was very tasty. Only after I had finished it was I told by the smiling lady who cooked it that it was a large frog from up in the mountains! We spent a month there, in that Garden of Eden, that beautiful, unspoiled tropical paradise, the embodiment of everyone's dream island …

251

And so down the island chain – Martinique, St. Lucia, St. Vincent, the gorgeous Grenadines to Grenada, where we prepared to sail to our first South American country, Venezuela. Over the course of a few days the anchorage filled up with cruisers preparing to head south out of the hurricane zone. It was a homogenous, friendly group with sailors from the U.S., Canada and Europe eagerly looking forward to the different cultures of the vast continent to our south.

One warm tropical afternoon in October, 1990, about forty of us from sixteen boats gathered for a late afternoon lunch at an outside restaurant overlooking the harbour. Our boats were ready, the weather forecast was perfect and we toasted each other and made bets on who would arrive first at the tiny island of Testigo, thirty-eight miles off the coast of mainland Venezuela. As mine was the only multihull in the group, I was given a handicap and instructed to leave three hours after the monohulls as my boat was faster!

Lyndy and I sat in the cockpit in the late afternoon breeze, waving as the other boats weighed their anchors, raised their sails and one by one sailed gracefully out of the harbour and set a course southwest. Isla Testigo, the first place we could legally clear in to Venezuela, was about a hundred miles away and we waited the three hours. We left at dusk in order to arrive before sunset the following day. With the sun just falling below the horizon and the twinkling lights of the island off to port, we raised the anchor, hoisted the sails and headed out to sea. The temperature was balmy, the wind blew about fifteen knots from the northeast, the stars were twinkling and we glided over a comfortable sea, searching for the boats already twenty miles ahead of us.

There was cheerful banter over the VHF radio, other boats egging us on, some saying there was no way we could catch them and win the six pack of beer, the prize for the first boat to drop anchor in Venezuelan waters! But slowly, after a couple of hours, a scattering of dim white stern lights ahead showed we were catching up to the fleet. Within another hour, her three bows easily slicing through the water at eight knots, Imagine was parallel with the stragglers. The boats were spread out over a couple of miles and it was magical to sail quietly through them, each boat a little world of its own carrying intrepid sailors off to fulfill their dreams.

Ever since I had started cruising back in the mid-seventies (when there were far fewer boats out there), I had formulated a concept about ocean sailors. No matter where they were from, they all had four things in common. First they had a dream, a goal. Most people go through their lives just getting by, never really having a goal. If they did, they rarely focused on accomplishing it or often let other things get in the way – there's always an excuse, a 'but'. Second, the would-be sailors started working toward their dream. Some knew how to sail, many didn't, but took sailing lessons, crewed on friend's boats, read whatever books were available, gained experience. Third, they saved their money, eventually bought a boat. The majority of cruisers are not wealthy people and many had to work long and hard to buy their boats and make them seaworthy. Some even built their boats from scratch, taking years to create their dream in their own back yard. (I admire these people greatly, I don't have the patience to do that!). And finally, they had the sheer guts, the courage to sail over the horizon into the unknown...

No matter where they are from, no matter what flag they are flying, cruising sailors all share these common traits. And this creates a strong bond amongst us, continuing the tradition of the seas, ready to help a fellow sailor, seeing a part of themselves in every cruising sailor they meet.

Having sailed through the fleet easily, loping along with three sparkling wakes of phosphorescence glimmering behind us in the moonlight, I reefed the mainsail and slowed the boat down to about six knots, just a little faster than the monohulls. As the false dawn lightened the skies, we looked around at a spectacular sight. Fifteen sailboats were sprinkled behind us, red and green running lights moving up and down, ghostly white sails spread before the wind, slightly heeled with a small white wave at each bow – one of life's magic moments. As the sun rose, flying fish skimmed over the gentle waves, slapping their tails as they tried to outrun their pursuers. And then, with full daylight, the dolphins appeared! Hundreds of them, some swimming between our three hulls, leaping and playing for the sheer joy of it! The radio crackled to life as excited sailors let everyone know about the dolphin welcome to the day!

Someone must have spotted us a couple of miles ahead. As Lyndy brought me a cup of coffee, my friend Bill called over the VHF radio to the others that there was a weird, three-hulled boat in front of them! There was some good-natured bantering, then I told them it was time for me to get to the anchorage to get some sleep and I'd see them in a few hours. I unreefed the mainsail, hoisted the staysail and we sailed away at a comfortable ten knots, twice as fast as them!

Three hours later we dropped the anchor off a gorgeous, wild island with a smaller island nearby. As we had been up all night enjoying the magical passage, we went to sleep as soon as the anchor was set. A few hours later half a dozen boats had anchored nearby and the rest were straggling in. There was a small military outpost on the island, near where we had anchored. We could clear into Venezuela there, show the visas we had obtained in Grenada and get our passports stamped.

Lyndy and I lowered our dinghy, attached the outboard and

headed to shore. We stopped at a couple of boats and told them we'd let them know how complicated it was to clear in. We ran the dinghy up to the lovely,deserted beach and headed off to a small building about a mile away where half a dozen officials were delighted to see us. We were ushered into a small office with a large fan lazily moving the hot afternoon air around. Lemonade was brought and pleasantries exchanged, my basic Spanish coming into play.

Papers looked at and passports stamped with a flourish and we were legally welcomed to Venezuela for six months. They were excited that so many boats had arrived at once, as they were all bored! I explained that it had been an overnight passage and many of the sailors were sleeping. Would it be possible for them to go ashore this evening and wait to clear in tomorrow?

"Si, si - no hay problema!"

After shaking hands all around, we stretched our legs along the empty beach and dinghied back to the boat. I got on the radio and informed everyone that there was no rush to clear in, the process was simple and they could wait till tomorrow. This was received with cheers and I suggested a party on the beach that evening.

And what a party it was! Driftwood was gathered and a large bonfire built, everyone brought a dish and I ceremoniously received my first-to-arrive six pack, which was quickly dispensed with! A few local fishermen with their families stood shyly on the perimeter listening to Mick Jagger on a boom box! We invited them to join us and eventually they were self-consciously shuffling in the sand. Some of the government staff and a few soldiers arrived and the party grew larger and louder as cruisers practiced their Spanish and taught the locals a few words of English – it was an amazing introduction to South America!

After a few lazy days snorkeling and exploring the main island

and the other little surrounding islets, we weighed anchor and sailed 'Imagine' to a completely different reality. Isla Margarita, a day's sail downwind, was a popular tourist destination for many Venezuelans and South Americans. We dropped anchor off the bustling town of Porlamar, amongst about three dozen other cruisers, some of whom we had sailed down with from Grenada. After days of solitude, it was almost an insult to the ears, with taxis, buses and hundreds of small motor scooters creating a cacophony of noise.

Leaving 'Imagine' in the care of a friend, we took a ferry to Cumana, rented a car and drove to Caracas. After a couple of days, Lyndy and I boarded a small plane and took a scary flight to Merida up in the mountains. From the hot tropical warmth to snow and ice! A wonderful contrast. We rented a Jeep up there and spent two weeks exploring the gorgeous mountain country, then back to the boat and a decision where to go next?

Some cruisers we met at the local sailor's bar said we mustn't miss the fabulous Los Roqes Islands, an aquatic national park about eighty miles off the coast of Venezuela. We had a chart, but it wasn't very detailed. The little information in the cruising guides was quite tempting, so one afternoon we said goodbye to our friends and set sail towards the islands. Today it's restricted as to where you can sail and apparently special permits are needed, but back then you could cruise anywhere.

There are very little supplies in the archipelago; the few families who live scattered throughout the islands survive by fishing and the scarce provisions delivered by an occasional small freighter. We had combed the markets of Porlamar and stocked Imagine with enough food and beverages to last a month.

There are about forty named islands and hundreds of semi-submerged sand bars scattered throughout the azure waters of this remote and little-visited archipelago. It is about two hundred miles from Porlamar to Los Rocques; we weighed anchor in the morning and sailed around the south of Isla Margarita, then set a course WNW with the trade winds blowing from the NE at a steady, warm fifteen knots. Across a sparkling sea with dolphins sometimes accompanying us, the day turned into night and the brilliant display of stars radiated above us.

The next morning, as the sky lightened, the fuzzy shapes of low-lying islands appeared just where they should be. Looking through my binoculars, some palm trees were becoming visible. I studied my chart and headed toward Boca del Medio, a break in the reef that runs up the eastern side of the island chain. The archipelago stretches about fifty miles east to west and about twenty miles north to south and there is a barrier reef along the east and south perimeters. Using my SatNav (this was before the days of GPS) which could take up to an hour to provide a position fix, I found the pass and we sailed between crashing waves, from dark ocean water into a vast area of scattered islands and light green and blue waters. It was very beautiful, breathtakingly beautiful...

We had been sailing for twenty-five hours and were very tired, so turning right, I lowered the sails, and we motored slowly north looking for somewhere to anchor and rest. Behind the protection of the barrier reef, we found a quiet spot with eight feet of water and a sandy bottom. The anchor dug in, we had a celebratory drink and slept for twelve hours...

Next morning, after a swim in the crystal clear water full of fish, like an aquarium, we hoisted sail and with trade winds and calm, protected waters, sailed smoothly to Gran Roque island. Low-lying hills surrounded the small, main community and there was a protected anchorage right off the beach. We cleared in easily with the authorities and were free to explore the island chain, which had been granted National Park status in 1972. There was

257

little going on here, mostly a few tourist fishermen who came for the world-famous bone fishing on the flats.

The next few days we wandered west through the colourful, bright waters, anchoring wherever we wanted, snorkeling amongst thousands of tropical fish. On the sixth day in this magical, tropical paradise, we left an anchorage on Isla Larga, a long island stretching about ten miles and headed west toward Caranero. The waters around the islands were mostly free of rocks and we could usually see any obstructions as it was crystal clear, so the fact that the charts were sometimes a little inaccurate was of no major concern. As we left the anchorage and sailed along the north coast of Isla Larga, we could see Caranero Island a few miles away. Between the islands, the water turned a little darker as the depth increased. There was a reef shown on the chart, running parallel to the north side of our destination, but it was marked as being very close to the shore.

In the early afternoon, with full sail up and the centreboard (a retractable keel that provides better sailing characteristics and can be winched up to provide a shallow draft) fully down, we sailed along the coast at eight knots on a flat, azure sea. I looked down at the sketchy chart laying next to me in the cockpit to make sure we were far enough off shore, when with a horrible screeching sound, like wood being torn off over rocks, we bumped and bounced, rapidly decelerated and ground sickeningly to a halt, sails still pulling. Lyndy was thrown off the cockpit seat and I was pushed into the steering wheel as we stopped quickly.

"What's happened?" called Lyndy in a scared voice.

"We're on a reef. The chart is wrong. Damn!"

I leaped out of the cockpit and looked over the side. We were sitting on top of branching, red coral in about two feet of water, firmly wedged. Looking back, I could see where we had sailed

258

onto the reef about twenty feet back, a trail of broken coral leading to where we now sat, immobile. The centreboard had kicked up into its retracted position when we hit.

"OK, we need to get the sails down now!" I called to Lyndy.

She was already furling the jib on its roller and I jumped back into the cockpit and released the main halyard, the sail billowing out to port. It was quickly gathered and tied. Now at least we weren't being driven further onto the reef. There was no one in sight, we were alone and stranded off an uninhabited island and darkness would arrive in four hours. I didn't want to be stranded on a reef at night!

The tidal range this time of year is only one to two feet, but I didn't have a local tide table and wasn't sure if we were on a rising or falling tide.

I put on my reef walkers and scooted down the boarding ladder to take a closer look at our predicament. The coral was hard and unyielding and ended about ten feet off our starboard side, where the deep, safe water continued between islands. I put on my mask and surveyed the bottom of the boat, scared that we had ripped a hole in her. We had seen three sailboats, high and dry on different reefs, forlorn, stripped of anything valuable and abandoned, lives changed, dreams ended. Was that to be our fate?

There didn't appear to be any holes, just a few gouges under the main hull where the jagged reef had scraped the 'sacrificial keel'. This is a rectangular 'box' about six feet long, a foot wide, and about eight inches deep, through which the centreboard drops. It is built very strong to withstand accidental groundings and in a worst case scenario would tear off before the bottom of the boat was ripped out!.

'Imagine' was sitting on the small keel, leaning to the left, the port ama (float) still buoyant. This is a definite benefit for catamarans and trimarans, compared to deep draft, heavily ballasted sailboats. 'Imagin'e was light enough that she bounced up, onto and across the reef, rather than slamming into it and cracking her hull.

I had to come up with a plan...and fast. There was no way I could back her off the reef using the engine. Trying to tow her off with the dinghy wouldn't work either. I needed strong, continual pressure, something solid to attach her to so she could be winched off. Unfortunately, there was no convenient, sturdy tree nearby – we were half a mile offshore!

"OK, Lyndy. This is what we'll do. I'll get out our big storm anchor, we'll launch the dinghy, and I'll row the anchor out to the end of the reef behind the boat. Then I'll cobble up a way to winch us off. So, quickly now, slide the dinghy off the deck into the water and make sure the oars are aboard..."

I threw open the hatch on the right ama and crawled inside, where I extricated the sixty pound emergency storm anchor and its fifty feet of chain. It was difficult to get it out, but after three minutes, we had carried it to the stern of the boat and loaded it into the dinghy. I was moving quickly, totally focused, sweat pouring off me. I quickly shackled a half-inch rope to the end of the chain.

"All right, I'm going to row like hell to the outer end of the reef. Pay out the chain and rope and make sure the bitter end is attached the boat!"

Within thirty seconds I had rapidly rowed out to the drop-off. I remembered looking at the depth sounder before we hit and I knew we were in twenty feet of water. I rowed another thirty feet in order to provide enough length so the anchor would be pulled at a gradual angle, allowing it to dig deeper into the bottom.

"OK, is the end attached, Lyndy?"

"Yes, no problem," she yelled back.

I heaved the 60-lb. anchor over the side of the dinghy and fed the chain out. When it hit the bottom I gave it a sharp pull and felt it start to dig in. I was quite upset that our keel had damaged the reef and I knew that when strain was put on the anchor, there would be more damage. But I had to get us off, as abandoning the boat would cause much more long-term damage...

Quickly pulling myself back to 'Imagine' along the anchor rope I scrambled aboard, after securely attaching the dinghy. I didn't have an electric anchor winch, otherwise I would have used some pulleys to run the line there and winch us off. But I did have two large manual winches for the jib sheets and I led the heavy anchor rope through a threefold block and tackle, which provided a huge amount of pulling power, to the winch on the port side of the cockpit.

With Lyndy tailing (pulling on the end of the rope as it comes off the winch), I started to grind the handle. I didn't know if it would work. I didn't know if the winch could move a boat that weighed several tons fully loaded. I didn't know if the anchor would pull out, or if I had the strength to keep winching until the job was done. Was the tide going down? Would we be stuck here for the night...or forever?

As I turned the winch handle, the slack in the rope and chain tightened. After anchoring hundreds of times, I could 'read' what was happening to the anchor on the bottom through vibrations sent back up the chain and rope. It was bar tight and it appeared the anchor had dug firmly into the bottom. Now was the test. Would she move, would a link in the gear break, would the winch be ripped off its mounting?

Lyndy looked at me with fierce concentration and smiled. This was our home and everything I owned was aboard.

I wiped the sweat off my forehead and hands, planted my feet firmly on the wide deck, took a deep breath and with both hands on the winch handle slowly cranked it counter-clockwise. It was a two-speed winch with built-in gearing which enabled me to use the reduction to develop more power. It turned and the rope turned with it - about three inches came in. I ran back to the stern of the boat and placed a hand on the rope. It didn't move, didn't vibrate, it was holding!

Back on the winch, I slowly, methodically ground it, grunting with the effort. And then we felt a slight movement. 'Imagine' had moved back a couple of inches! If she could move two inches, then she could move two feet – it would just take time and effort...

I put my head down and turned the handle – the winch revolved slowly, Lyndy tailed and I wound in a little more anchor line. The block and tackle was working! We moved, like a snail, inch by inch, a heart-rending, grinding, crunching sound coming from the sacrificial mini keel. I almost wished it would tear off, for then the boat would float; a new keel could always be built later.

A foot, then two. I stopped, wiped the sweat away, grabbed some water. Lyndy poured a bucket of sea water over me.

"OK," I panted. "We can do this..."

The next hour was agonizing, but the vision of abandoning everything I owned spurred me on. The tropical sun blazed down. I focused on nothing but the shiny winch, rivulets of dirty water running from it across the coaming and down the deck, as the tension in the rope squeezed the water from the strands. 'Click, click' went the ratchet inside the winch, each click another inch of anchor rope coming in, another quarter inch across the reef. My arms started throbbing and my legs trembled with the effort. We were halfway there.

Lyndy ran to the back of the boat and looked down.

"The anchor chain is coming onto the stern roller, Jon. We're getting there!" she called out excitedly.

With the chain coming directly over the stern of the boat I rigged up a further system of pulleys to keep the rope on the winch – you can't wind chain on a winch!

I jumped over the side with my mask to inspect the bottom again. There were flecks of red antifouling paint on the coral, marking our trail. As much as I could see of the bottom of the boat looked good, the rudder wasn't damaged and we were now only five feet away from deeper water. I climbed back aboard and started winching, knowing we would eventually get off. It seemed the tide was with us, as now it was a little easier to winch her off.

Finally, after two intense, exhausting hours, with Lyndy encouraging me, the winch turned a little easier and suddenly we slipped off the reef! I unwound the rope from the winch and pulled it through its series of blocks and pulleys, still panting, rivers of sweat pouring off me. The chain hung straight down over the stern and with the last little strength I had in my arms, I pulled the sixty pound anchor and its chain aboard and left it in a heap on the aft deck. Now we floated free and had about an hour of daylight left.

"I'm going over the side and see what damage has been done," I told Lyndy.

Quickly donning mask, snorkel and flippers, I jumped over and swam directly under the boat, not knowing what I'd find. This was a well-built trimaran and aside from the gouges and some missing patches of antifouling paint, it all looked solid. But as I swam under the mini keel, I could see about an inch of soft wood had been ground off by the reef. The most alarming sight was a big chunk of coral which had broken off the reef and wedged itself in the centerboard slot! There was no way I could lower the board, but we weren't holed, no water was flooding the interior and Imagine would sail another day...

I am very conscious of the environment and as a sailor, dedicated to preserving the natural wonders of the ocean. I'm careful not to anchor near coral and when we snorkel, we don't put our feet on the reef. It has always bothered me that I damaged a small part of that far-off reef, but I know it will eventually grow back. It is interesting to note that although coral reefs take thousands of years to proliferate, individual sections of reefs can restore themselves over just a few years.

WHERE'S THE BOAT?

Joell and I arrived in Marina del Rey, just south of Los Angeles in August, 1999 after spending nearly a year sailing JoJo, our 32' Fisher catamaran down from San Francisco. Now that's a very long time, considering it's only four hundred miles! But we had worked for a month helping friends with their cinnamon roll concession at the Bakersfield County Fair, then a few months living in Ventura when I was a Vessel Assist captain. We had sailed to San Diego where I landed a job in yacht sales but the broker turned out to have questionable ethics and I quit after a month.

I had met the owner of a large yacht dealership that represented eight boat lines, one of which was Hunter, the best selling sailboat in America. He said he had an opening for a qualified sales associate, if we would be willing to live in Marina del Rey. He also said they had slips available and we could live aboard there. Most of the boats they sold, both new and brokerage, were power boats, but they were all high quality, reputable marques. They needed a sailboat person and so a meeting was arranged with the general manager and we took a ride up there in the Bugatti.

I had first sold boats in Marina del Rey in 1978 and got to know a few of the guys in that business – there weren't a lot of us back then. So when I walked into the brokerage for my meeting I was thrilled that the manager was Steve, a man I had known when we were both selling sailboats twenty years earlier! We chatted for a while, catching up on sailing stories and old friends then he immediately offered me a job. I introduced him to Joell, who was waiting outside looking at sailboats and we walked out back, where he showed me the work yard and a clean, comfortable dock we could tie up at and live aboard. This was perfect and we told him we'd be there in a week (I didn't know what it was called back then, but this was definitely the law of attraction at work...).

We sailed the boat up and I took a train back to San Diego and picked up the Bugatti. Joell found a job at a health food store within walking distance and we settled in, looking forward to building a cruising kitty so we could eventually sail to Florida. I met the other five brokers, (including a pompous Englishman who wore a monocle!) and got to work calling prospects who had enquired about boats but had never been followed up on. I also started selling boats to walk-ins and was very good at it.

Having a lot of sailing experience and knowledge, I never sold a boat to someone that wasn't right for them. I always asked lots of questions and listened, discovering their main reasons for buying a boat and offering suggestions as to what would be best for them. Did they want a boat just for day sailing, or an occasional over-nighter? Were they planning on living aboard? Did they have dreams of sailing south to Mexico, or further afield across the Pacific or even around the world? Different boats for different reasons. I also followed up diligently, sent thank you cards and was pleasantly persistent. This resulted in my selling an average of one boat a week, a very good record which soon made me top salesman. Some of the others resented this, but none of them worked as hard as me, for I had a goal, a dream and all I needed was some money to achieve it...

We really enjoyed living in Marina del Rey and in the evenings would drive the Bugatti up the coast to Malibu, or walk around downtown Santa Monica, which now had pedestrian-only streets. We had fun sailing around the docks in my little sailing dinghy looking at the almost seven thousand boats of all sizes docked in this giant, man-made marina. With the commissions coming in, we were starting to save some money and Joell quit her job. Life was good and we thought we could be happy there for a couple of years.

266

The middle of October was the 32nd Long Beach Boat Show and Victory Yachts had a large presence there this year. There was a lot of activity the week before as a dozen boats were sailed down to the venue and set up for four days of visitors. We were showing five Hunters ranging from 31-45 feet. These were not the best-built boats in the world, but they were definitely the best-designed for their purpose. Because I had proven in a short time that I was one of the top brokers in the company, I was given the flagship of the fleet, the large and beautifully appointed 45-footer to work in. There was grumbling from the others, but all I needed was to sell one of these and the commission would keep us cruising for a year!

I had never worked a boat show before and it was both quite exhausting and lots of fun. I met so many people, was pleasant to all, but focused on those who sounded like they may be potential buyers, if not for the big one, then maybe for one of the smaller sizes or even a brokerage boat. I got names, addresses and phone numbers and the next week was spent sending thank you cards and making phone calls. Once again, there was some resentment amongst my fellow brokers, who on the whole were pretty lazy. That happens when you're not focused on a goal...

I set appointments and showed boats and quickly sold three new yachts in the 30-40 foot range from my contacts at the show. Two weeks later I received a phone call from a gentleman named Pete who said we had talked briefly at the show and could he set an appointment to see the Hunter 45?

"Yes sir. Certainly. When is convenient for you?"

He asked if it was possible this Sunday and although we were closed, I told him I'd be delighted to open the showroom for him. He was a dapper man in his fifties and we immediately hit it off. Pete was a very successful lawyer, something to do with the government and he often flew from Washington to L.A. for

267

business. The fact that I had attended law school years earlier, provided some common ground. He didn't know much about sailing, but hoped to head to the Pacific Islands when he retired in a few years. Rather than buy a condo in L.A., he wanted a comfortable live aboard that he could learn to sail on. And it had to be nice enough for his wife who would occasionally join him.

We went aboard one of the two 45's we had in stock, without being jammed in by dozens of people continually climbing aboard and leaving, as it was at the boat show. This yacht was lovely, with beige leather, a large galley, queen size bed and even a small bathtub! The other one, which was almost identical, had already been equipped with a full array of electronic navigational gear.

He asked me if I would teach him how to sail the boat and was delighted when I told him I had been a sailing instructor the previous year in San Francisco. Of course, I agreed and then we talked price. He said he had been researching navigation electronics and wanted to have specific models installed, so we settled on the boat that was still unequipped. This turned out to be an important factor as events unfolded over the next few weeks...

He took me to lunch and we talked about his dream of sailing to the Pacific Islands. It usually takes weeks for someone to make a decision to spend a quarter of a million dollars, but Pete wasn't just 'someone'. We drove back to my office and I couldn't believe it when he pulled out his checkbook and wrote a deposit for ten percent! He left an hour later with a contract and an arrangement to talk during the week about the commissioning process. He wanted the boat fully equipped and in the water by December 1st - less than four weeks away!

"No problem, Pete. I'll stay on top of it," as I shook his hand next to his red Ferrari.

I walked down the dock to JoJo floating on air - the commission would be huge! Joell was over the moon and we drove into Santa Monica that evening for a fabulous meal at our favourite little restaurant. The next morning at the sales meeting when Steve asked us if anything had happened on Saturday, I answered "No, but I sold a 45 footer at full retail on Sunday" - it felt great! But it did anger some of the other brokers who thought they should have been on the 45 at the show. By this time I was getting fed up with their resentment and jealousy and dreamed of heading south on JoJo.

There were a few live-aboards at the docks and we became friendly with a young couple who were living on a tired old 40 footer. They were from Croatia and had escaped the horrible fighting going on there. Their dream was to fix up their boat and sail to Tahiti, but I didn't think the boat they had was capable. They peppered us with questions about the cruising lifestyle. Fedor was also very curious about the Hunters we sold, especially the 45. He asked if he could go aboard and one evening I showed him Pete's boat and told him it was going to have state-of-the-art navigation equipment installed soon. He said he had a friend in Europe who was interested in buying a 45 and could I give him all the brochures about the boat and the equipment.

Work started on Pete's boat, $20,000 of top electronic equipment was ordered and we purchased everything he would need to equip the boat – dinghy, outboard, anchors, ropes, fenders – thousands of dollars more (and I made a small commission on all of it!). The bottom was painted with antifouling and the boat launched. I sailed the boat several times around the marina to test the equipment. One afternoon, a week before Pete was to take delivery, I brought the boat back to its slip and secured it. The autopilot had not been calibrated correctly and I left a note for the yard manager.

Joell and I had decided that when I received the commission cheque for Pete's boat, I would hand in my resignation and we would prepare to head south. We were excited and had fun buying charts and cruising guides to take us down the coast of Mexico, Central America, through the Panama Canal and up into the Caribbean.

The next morning the yard manager came to my office with my note in his hand and asked where Pete's boat was?

'What do you mean?" I said. "It's in its slip."

"No, it's not."

"Well, I left it there yesterday evening when I brought it back from its final test sail."

"I'm telling you, it's not there and no one in the yard has moved it."

I hurried down to the dock with him, expecting this to be a joke and find the boat bobbing quietly in its slip. But no, the slip was empty and she hadn't sunk at the dock! Where was she?

"Are you sure one of the sub-contractors or one of your guys hasn't moved her to another slip?" I asked, quickly scanning the slips nearby.

"No Jon, I've talked to everyone and walked the docks here. She's missing..."

I felt a knot in the pit of my stomach as I walked quickly back to the office. Steve had arrived while I was on the docks and had been told about the missing boat. Everyone was looking at me, as if I had some secret knowledge about the whereabouts of a large, brand new yacht that was nowhere to be found.

"What's going on, Jon?" Steve asked.

"Damned if I know. I brought the boat back to its slip around 6:00 last night and tied it up securely. I made sure the fenders were down and she was locked up. I have a big commission coming here, Steve..."

"Well, apparently she's been stolen. I'm going to call the police and let everyone in the marina know. It's kind of embarrassing..."

I couldn't care less about embarrassing. I saw a five figure commission disappearing and along with it our cruising plans.

"I'd like to call Pete. He'll be here to close on the deal in five days."

"No. Let's wait and see what happens today and then we'll make a decision on that."

I left the office and walked slowly down the dock to break the news to Joell. As I approached JoJo, she came out of the cabin, a big smile on her face. But that was gone in a second when she saw the look of consternation on mine.

"Are you OK?"

"No, I feel hollow inside, Joie. Pete's boat is missing – it looks like it's been stolen."

She climbed onto the dock, a distraught look on her face and hugged me. I admit I started crying and so did she.

"What happened? Oh my God. He was so looking forward to getting the boat and having you teach him how to sail."

"Yes, I worked so hard on this deal and it was going to get us cruising. We'll have to stay and keep working..."

I was getting so tired of the backbiting and office politics the past four months, I just wanted to quit and sail away from there.

"Don't worry, Jon. Focus on whatever deals you have going and this will all work out. That boat was meant for Pete and he'll get it!"

My positive wife who always looks on the bright side of life...

That day was a bit of a blur. Interviewed by the police and the sheriff. Four Coast Guard men looking around, asking everyone, especially me, lots of questions. The owner of the dealership showed up and wasn't very happy. I suppose because it was my deal and I was the last one to have seen the yacht they focused their suspicions on me. After ten minutes of not so subtle insinuations that this was an 'inside job' and I was the bloke 'inside', I blew up at them.

"Look, I've worked bloody hard here the past few months and have made you a lot of money. I've treated everyone, those I work with and my customers with the highest integrity. I've got a big commission coming from Pete's boat and I feel sick inside. I like Pete and he likes me. I don't bloody know what happened to the boat and I don't know how I'm going to break this to him. Now back off and let's find the boat. And I think he should be informed immediately – he's got a twenty-five grand deposit on it. This guy's a really powerful and well-connected attorney and you don't want to piss him off..."

I walked out and went down to JoJo where Joell was waiting. She knew it hadn't been an easy day and a strong rum and coke was waiting...

The next morning there was a buzz at work. There were two men in the conference room and I was called in and told to shut the door. They introduced themselves as being from the CIA and told me to sit down. Then they started asking questions about our Croatian friends! This was in 1999, and the civil war in Croatia had only recently ended. That whole area of Europe was in upheaval and acts of terrorism were still being committed.

How long had I known them? Had we discussed politics? What were their plans? How much sailing experience did they have? What did I know about the situation in Croatia? What were my political leanings?

This was like something out of a movie and I felt pretty intimidated and uncomfortable. I told them we were just acquaintances, that Joell and I didn't have a television and I don't read the negative newspapers. That I wasn't really aware of what was going on in Europe and that, although I sympathize with anyone who is being oppressed, I couldn't tell them who was oppressing who over there!

"So, why is the CIA here and why are you asking me these questions about Croatia?"

"Well, Mr. White," answered the senior officer, a caricature of every CIA officer in the movies - crew cut, unsmiling, bulge under his jacket, shiny shoes. "Early this morning the United States Coast Guard discovered a 40 foot sailboat registered to this Croatian couple drifting about half a mile offshore. All the thru-hull fittings had been opened in an attempt to sink her, but it hadn't worked. They have just towed the boat to their docks and are pumping out the bilges right now."

"OK, so where are Fedor and Cassandra? Oh, wait a minute, you think *they* took Pete's boat?"

"Yes, we know they did. We found a live-aboard boater in the marina who saw a large sailboat going toward the breakwater around nine o'clock two nights ago towing another sailboat. He thought it was strange, especially as they had no running lights on, but so many weird things happen here, he didn't pay any attention to it. We believe one of them broke into the new yacht

273

and took it out into the fairway. Then the other one probably met up with their old boat and they towed it out through the breakwater. They probably had food and water on their boat and transferred it to the new boat. Then we think they tried to scuttle their old boat, but it didn't work. They're somewhere out in the Pacific Ocean on the new yacht, but we don't know where they're heading. And we don't know if they are terrorists, but we can't take any chances."

OK, now I'm definitely in a movie! 'Croatian Terrorists Steal Yacht. Possible Plan to Invade Santa Barbara!'

I told the CIA that they had planned to sail to Tahiti, but obviously they had decided to do it in comfort – on Pete's new boat...

"OK, thank you for your help, Mr. White," they said as they motioned me out of the room. Steve called me into his office.

"So what did they ask you?"

I told him the gist of our conversation and what they had surmised.

"Right. So we know who has the boat and we know the general direction they're heading. The Coast Guard are sending out a reconnaissance plane to look for them. They can't be too far away. How much fuel was in the tank?"

"I think about fifty gallons, so let's see, say they're going flat out under sail and with engine at full revs. They could maintain seven or eight knots. So they couldn't be more than about three hundred miles away."

"Yes, but in which direction?"

"We'll have to leave that up to the Coasties. I'd like to call Pete."

"No, we'll wait another twenty-four hours. I'm going to call every marina up and down the coast, maybe they've pulled in somewhere and are waiting to make their next move..."

I didn't think that likely. If I were them I'd be heading out into the vast expanse of the Pacific! I went back to JoJo and told Joell what was happening – she was amazed that our 'friends' had done this, but relieved that we knew what had happened. Like me, she expected the Coast Guard to find them quickly and send out a cutter to overtake them and bring the boat back.

All day we waited for the phone call that would tell us that they'd found the yacht. But it didn't come. Word had quickly spread through the boating community and there was a constant stream of curious boat brokers and mechanics and anyone with nothing better to do, who all wanted more details on this unfolding story. The press arrived, but I was told not to tell them anything as the CIA considered this a potentially dangerous situation!

There was still no sighting of them by the evening. It was now forty-eight hours since they'd stolen the boat and their possible location became more difficult to pinpoint with each hour that went by. Calls were made to the French authorities alerting them to the possible arrival of the stolen boat in their territorial waters in about a month, the average time it takes to sail across the Pacific to Tahiti.

I was trying to figure out how I was going to break the news to Pete. Steve had told me to wait one more day before calling him. I didn't sleep well that night, anxious that the boat hadn't been spotted, concerned over Pete's reaction and upset about the probable loss of my large commission. Ever-positive Joell assured me that it would all work out, that we'd be able to leave in a few weeks as planned and go cruising. I wasn't so sure...

And then, at ten o'clock the next morning, Steve got a phone call and excitedly came into my office a few minutes later.

"They've found the boat and the thieves," he said.

"Are they towing them in?" I asked.

"No. You won't believe this. They motored into Ensenada last night. I just got a phone call from Manuel at the marina there, asking if we're missing a Hunter 45! He described it and the couple on board and it's definitely them. I've got to call those guys from the CIA."

In California, if you buy a new boat and complete the paperwork outside the three-mile limit and keep it out of the state for at least six months, you can avoid paying sales tax. On a large yacht, that can save a purchaser a lot of money and we had developed a relationship with the Marina Coral in Ensenada, Mexico, about two hundred miles south. A number of our buyers left their boats in the marina for the requisite six months. Manuel, the manager there, was suspicious when this couple checked in with no boat papers and a name spray painted on the side with paint runs down it! That's when he called Steve, as he knew we were the nearest Hunter dealer...

The two CIA guys arrived fifteen minutes later, dramatically screeching to a stop, jumping out and slamming their doors. They walked quickly to the conference room, calling to Steve and I brusquely to follow them.

"OK, does this Manuel speak English?" one of them asked.

"Er, yes – fluently," answered Steve.

"Get him on the phone, now!"

With Manuel on speaker phone, they peppered him with questions:

When did they arrive? How were they acting? Did they have any weapons? Did they have any money? Did he think they knew that he knew the boat was stolen?

Manuel was pretty laid back and amused by their intensity.

"Oh no, Senor. Zey are acting calm. I doan sink zey know zat I know ze boat is stole. Zey paint a name on ze side – 'Sandra'- but it was done wit a spray can an' it look terrible! Zey want a 'lectronic mechanic to fix de autopilot, rapido. What I should tell dem, senor?"

"Tell them you're arranging to have a mechanic arrive in a couple of hours and they should stay on the boat and wait for him. Don't act suspicious. Just tell them that and leave, OK?"

"Si senor, no problem".

Then the CIA guys started making phone calls and we were dismissed as they went to work contacting the police in Ensenada. I rushed down to Joell and excitedly told her the news. I thought we could send a delivery captain down and we'd have the boat back in a couple of days. It could be fixed and Pete could have his boat, albeit a few days late. But that wasn't going to happen...

Steve immediately sent our service manager down to Ensenada to survey the boat and take control of it, as the insurance company had ordered. Later that day we found out what had happened on the docks at Marina Coral around noon. The Ensenada police had sent their equivalent of a SWAT team to the docks and they rushed the boat and captured the thieves. In the process, they clumsily damaged the decks and broke some of the expensive navigation equipment in the cockpit after Fedor stupidly tried to resist.

The Mexican police don't take kindly to that and apparently they beat the crap out of him and there were blood stains all over the teak grating in the cockpit. They had dragged Fedor and Cassandra off the boat, thrown them into a car and whisked them off. The boat had been cordoned with yellow police tape and was now a crime scene.

The two CIA men had flown down to Ensenada to question the 'terrorists' and the local press were having a field day! Stolen yacht, suspected terrorists, CIA – what a great story!

"Well Steve, what do I do now? Apparently they're not going to release the boat, right?"

"No, they're not. We're dealing with an international situation now and it's going to involve the insurance company, the Mexicans, the CIA...I think we can forget about seeing Pete's boat for quite a while, mate."

"Well, we're supposed to close on the deal in three days, Steve. Can I tell Pete now?"

"Yes. Tell him what's happened and we'll work it out with the other 45-footer we have. I don't want to lose this deal and I know you don't want to either."

Just at that moment I got a call over the loudspeaker that I was wanted in the showroom. As I walked from Steve's office, a smiling Pete was walking toward me, hand outstretched. He had come a couple of days early and was anxious to see his new boat! My stomach sank...

"Hey Pete, how are you.? Come on into my office..."

Everyone was looking at us and there was a definite tense atmosphere. I closed the door and motioned Pete to a seat. He noticed I was a bit subdued and could feel the obvious tension in the place. I looked through my window to the showroom floor and some of the other brokers were smirking in my direction.

"So what's going on here? Everyone seems a bit uptight..."

"Pete, do you want the good news or the bad news first?"

"What? What's going on? Has something happened to my boat?"

"Yes. Here's the bad news." I looked him right in the eye. There was no point in trying to sugar coat this to an astute attorney. "Three days ago your boat was stolen by a Croatian couple living on an old boat here. They were planning on sailing it to Tahiti, but the autopilot hadn't been calibrated correctly. Obviously they couldn't continue until it was fixed. They sailed the boat to Ensenada, to the Marina Coral who called us this morning. They are now in custody in a Mexican jail and your boat has been impounded. The CIA are involved as they thought this might have been some kind of terrorist plot."

Pete looked at me piercingly for thirty seconds.

"Why wasn't I told about this immediately you knew it was stolen?"

Over the past few weeks, Pete and I had developed a solid relationship, built on trust and integrity. He was comfortable working with me and relied on me to provide him with all the information needed to properly equip his boat. We had gone sailing a couple of times on her and Pete was getting proficient with docking and maneuvering the boat in tight spaces.

"I wanted to, believe me. But apparently our insurance company had instructed the owners of Victory Yachts not to divulge any information and my hands were tied. I've been agonizing over this the past couple of days."

He was quiet for a full two minutes. I had no doubt he would

279

want his $25,000 deposit back and I would never see him again. But I had misjudged the man.

He steepled his fingers together and looking over them, piercing me with his eyes, told me this:

"I am upset that I wasn't in the loop, but I understand that was not your decision. I will talk directly with the owners about that. I do like the yacht and so does my wife, but I will not accept a new boat that has been abused. I'm sure you can understand that. I do have certain legal rights here and will look into them further at my office. I know there is a sister ship here and if you can equip it like the other one for the same price and do it within seven days we will close on the deal. You have been upfront and professional with me from the start, Jon and I certainly don't hold you responsible."

Inwardly I breathed a huge sigh of relief. We can still make this happen. Pete can get his dream boat and I can get our cruising money. We shook hands firmly and I escorted him to Steve's office, where the owners were nervously waiting. I closed the door behind them and walked briskly to JoJo.

"OK. It's up to the owners, but we can still pull this together, Joie. Pete's a hell of a man and he still wants a 45. And we can probably still take off in a couple of weeks!"

Apparently the owners agreed with Pete's demands and I think they were pleased they weren't getting sued. All the stops were pulled out and there was a beehive of activity around the other 45-footer to get her commissioned and equipped in only a week. I was constantly on top of it, bothering everyone, until I was told to bugger off and let them get on with it!

We never saw the CIA agents again. I think they realized that this was no political plot by would-be terrorists, but just a broke couple who saw an opportunity and took it. I now understood why Fedor had been asking all those questions about Pete's boat. He didn't have a friend interested in buying one. He wanted to learn all he could before stealing it! He had watched and waited until the electronics were installed but didn't know that the autopilot wasn't working correctly. If he had waited one more day, it would have been adjusted and they could have sailed to Tahiti. But there's no doubt they would have been captured there - Interpol had already been alerted.

We later learned that because Mexico had no extradition treaty with Croatia, Fedor and Cassandra were released from jail after a week and just let go. From photos of them in the Mexican press, which were later published in L.A. papers, it was obvious they'd both been roughly treated in jail.

Pete got his new boat, fully equipped the way he wanted it and I spent three days sailing with him and teaching him the basics. He was a happy man.

A week later I received my large commission check, immediately cashed it, went back to Victory and quit. We moved JoJo to a temporary slip on the other side of the marina. Joell flew up to San Francisco to see her family and two days later I took a chilly but glorious ride up highway 101 in the Bugatti. It was to stay with my brother Grant indefinitely. He loved to drive it, so it was a perfect situation.

Joell and I rented a one-way car, loaded it with personal items and excitedly drove back to L.A. The next day we bought huge amounts of cruising provisions and packed them into JoJo.

On December 24th, 1999, we cast off the dock lines and headed south, adventure before us. Our first stop, after two days was Marina Coral in Ensenada. We met Manuel, a charming man and he took us to Pete's original boat. Forlornly sitting in a slip, its poorly furled mainsail was flapping in the breeze. It was cordoned off with drooping yellow tape, but we went aboard anyway. There were still crusty bloodstains in the cockpit from where Fedor had tried to resist the SWAT team. There were some clothes strewn around below and the bed was unmade with crumpled sheets on the floor. A few dirty dishes attracted buzzing flies in the galley.

As we stepped off the boat we noticed on the side the crudely sprayed-on name in blue paint 'Sandra', with paint runs down to the waterline. We turned away, closing that chapter of our lives, a new one full of adventure ahead...

RAISON D'ETRE

What started out as a collection of a few stories for friends and family has grown into a trilogy with dozens of tales encompassing some hair-raising adventures, many exotic countries, and a multitude of diverse characters. At sixty-three years old when this book was published, I can look back on my life with few regrets and still look ahead with eager anticipation. Joell and I plan to spend a year or two living aboard our motor home on the coast, south of San Francisco. We have a gorgeous view of the Pacific out our front window, long and winding trails on the cliffs, a spectacular dog friendly beach. I'm writing and pitching my books to some movie executives; there has been some interest in making a TV mini-series! Joell is experimenting with pastels and playing her violin and has become a brand partner with a cutting edge DNA-based vitamin and supplement company. It's good to stop for a while, but we're not finished adventuring...

Often I reminisce about all the beautiful places I've been, the experiences I've had, the people who've added spice to my life. When I was in my mid-thirties, I asked myself what my purpose in life was, what is my 'raison d'etre', why was I here on this planet at this time? I had already made an impact on some people I had met, as I discovered when we crossed paths again; many told me I had been a catalyst for positive change in their lives. I have always believed that anyone can realize their dreams if they focus and commit; if they walk through their wall of fear and uncertainty and just do it.

How could I hitchhike to India, sail off over the horizon, risk everything on a wild business idea, I've been asked. It's variety and change and risk that have spurred me on; for me the fear is being stuck in a rut. I didn't want to live my life 'hanging on in quiet desperation', the 'English way', according to Pink Floyd!

For others it's the opposite; maybe their dream is a comfortable home, college for their kids, a secure retirement. Whatever their desire, I've always encouraged people to 'go for it', to live their dreams, to listen to their heart...apparently it has resonated with some.

An unanticipated result of my books is that I have continued to be a catalyst for some of my readers, people from all over the world who I'll never meet, as witnessed by remarks in the Amazon reviews; and I've received many personal emails with similar sentiments. One man wrote that after reading my books he was inspired to buy a 46-foot sailboat and was going to follow his dream and sail around the world! Whether he'll complete the voyage or not is irrelevant – what's important is that he reached for his dream...

An elderly cousin who used to read out loud to her sister and hadn't picked up a book in the five years since she had died, pulled me aside at my mothers funeral and told me that after reading my book, she now reads again. I have transported my fans to places some never knew existed and introduced them to people all over the world, expanding their horizons through my words. If I have ignited a spark in one person, if I have added a little push through their wall of fear, if because of something I've said or written they've shifted their focus, reached for their dreams, then my raison d'etre has been accomplished...

Will there be more books? Not in this series, but I'm thinking of writing a novel and there are still adventures in our future. Perhaps there's a book in them eventually…

Thank you all for sharing in my adventures...

Please write a review on Amazon – it helps others decide if my tales are something they might be interested in reading…

Made in the USA
San Bernardino, CA
19 January 2016